777

AND OTHER QABALISTIC WRITINGS OF ALEISTER CROWLEY

777

AND OTHER QABALISTIC WRITINGS OF ALEISTER CROWLEY

Including

GEMATRIA & SEPHER SEPHIROTH

Edited with an Introduction by

ISRAEL REGARDIE

SAMUEL WEISER, INC.

York Beach, Maine

This collection first published in 1973 as
The Qabalah of Aleister Crowley by
Samuel Weiser, Inc.
P.O. Box 612
York Beach, Maine 03910-0612

Retitled in 1977
First paper edition, 1986

This printing, 1998

Library of Congress Catalog Number: 83-160567

ISBN 0-87728-670-1
EB

Printed in the United States of America

The paper used in this publication meets the minimum requirements of the American National Standard for Permanence of Paper for Printed Library Materials Z39.48-1984.

CONTENTS

INTRODUCTION

This is a unique collection of Qabalistic texts without parallel in the entire history of this vast mystical literature. All of them belong to the very early professional career of Aleister Crowley; that is they were written before he had reached the age of 40 years. As every student of the Crowley corpus of writings should know, however, they were used constantly and continuously by him throughout his lifetime.

In the obscure footnotes to *The Vision and The Voice* (Sangreal Foundation, Dallas, 1972) which I recently edited, it soon became evident that few of those explanatory notes of his would make rhyme or reason to the average student unless he were exceedingly well-grounded in the material and methods delineated in those three books. All three need to be studied assiduously over a long period of time before those footnotes become intelligible to any degree. Or until the intrinsic value of the texts themselves is perceived as being of the purest gold.

The first of these three texts is actually one of the installments from the *Equinox,* the fifth, containing a biographical serial entitled *The Temple of King Solomon.* This serial strove to present a more or less dynamic picture of the personality of Aleister Crowley or Frater Perdurabo, to use his Order name, in the course of his progress along the mystical and magical path. The first few installments were written by one of his major disciples of the first decade of this century, Captain (later General) J. F. C. Fuller. After a while, these two men separated, as narrated in *The Confessions of Aleister Crowley* (Hill & Wang, New York 1970). The result was that Crowley being left in the lurch, as it were, wrote the fifth installment as a kind of filler, enabling him to find time to resume the narrative of his attainment interrupted by Fuller's departure.

The "filler" has nothing to do, in reality, with the biographical narrative. It consisted of a set of Qabalistic and pragmatic notes on Number that Crowley had accumulated over the years, and which he now tied together for this purpose.

It consisted of a study of one phase of the Qabalistic process which is held in rather poor esteem today, mostly—so I believe—because the majority of modern writers have not been able to penetrate its mystery. They cannot cope with it in any way. They regard it, unfortunately, on a par with the common practice of numerology and fortune telling, thus missing the boat entirely.

Gematria, as this process is named, is pronounced as *g'mut'ree'ah.* As a method it reminds me somewhat of the mysteries surrounding the usage of the koan in the Rinzai sect of Zen. It seems at first sight nothing but perfect nonsense, this taking liberties with names and letters and numbers. But in point of fact, just as the koan is a meaningful but not necessarily rational statement made from a mystical level of consciousness, so also it may be used to induce a similar type of illumination in the determined student who uses it. Depending on the spiritual state of the reader, Gematria will be perceived either as nonsense of the most grotesque description, or it will awaken some simulacrum of the mystical state originally experienced by its writer.

If you study Crowley's exposition of the number 418, in this second book *Gematria,* for example, something of this high point of view may be perceived. It was not arbitrarily chosen as an important or significant number for him, or for that matter for anyone else. And so with many other numbers. The method does have a definite sphere of usefulness and a vital place in Qabalistic exegetical process, but it does require to be understood.

Never for one moment suspect Crowley of gullibility or naiveté. It may seem at first sight as if he were. But read the first few pages of the essay on Gematria where you will notice his satire, his ridicule, his humor. This should never be ignored or minimized. He never had difficulty poking fun at himself or the methods he used for different purposes. It saved him from gullibility and credulity, the curse of the average occult student. Some of his conclusions on his numerical manipulations therefore are entitled, at the very least, to some scrutiny and examination, and this in turn may lead to respect.

For example, I have always been profoundly impressed by his handling of the number 913 (Equinox I, No. V, p. 107). It is the gematria of *Berashith,* a Hebrew word meaning "the beginning", the first word of the Book of Genesis. He starts with a discussion of the number nine, and reduces it by several brilliant permutations and attributions to one, stating that "the many being but veils of the One; and the course of argument leads one to knowledge and worship of each number in turn." In concluding the lengthy analysis, he does state explicitly that "9 is not equal to 1 for the neophyte. These equivalences are dogmatic, and only true by favour of Him in whom All is Truth."

Any man who can write thus of a subject which is taboo because capable of infinite abuse, and which has earned the contempt of several reasonable students of the mysteries, is worthy of respect and consideration.

Right to the end of his days, Crowley felt that gematria was a most useful tool, and tested many of his theoretical and intuitive findings relative to *The Book of the Law* against the manipulations and inspirations of gematria. I must say that I am in complete accord with him in this respect, as testified to by my earliest piece of writing *A Garden of Pomegranates,* in which there is a chapter on gematria.

The second of these, *Liber 777* has been reprinted several times in recent years. All of the new editions improved on the first one, which is rare nowadays and most expensive, by the inclusion of many short essays and commentaries written at various times of Crowley, and added skillfully by the editor after Crowley's demise in 1947.

This book was first started in 1907 shortly after his return from the China expedition. It is humorously referred to in the second essay in *Konx Om Pax* where there are references to the Table of Correspondences in preparation. In point of fact, these tables of correspondences which comprise *Liber 777* and which were not published until 1909, consist of basic information provided originally, piecemeal, in the knowledge lectures of the Hermetic Order of the Golden Dawn. Predicated on his own further studies and experiences, they were enormously expanded by Crowley so that, at first sight, they bear little resemblance to the fragmented tables in the Golden Dawn.

There is a wealth of valuable material here just waiting to be used. Many writers have done so without due acknowledgment.

The book provides a basic system or method of filing new information on any topic and subject. The filing system is predicated on a mere thirty two categories, the Ten Sephiroth of the Tree of Life, and the twenty two letters of the Hebrew Alphabet. Once this schema is understood, any new set of data of any kind can be referred to it, thus undergoing immediate and spontaneous organization and synthesis within the psyche. True, most of the material relates to comparative religion and mythology, including precious stones, herbs and plants, and a multitude of other matters. Because these comprise the basic notions currently employed, one should not feel limited only to these topics. At one time, I experimented allocating the elements on the atomic scale to this Tree, with some modicum of success. Somewhere along the line, in the course of my travels, this set of attributions has got lost, and I never made another attempt to duplicate it. It is mentioned here, though, in the hope that enterprising students will realize the enormous potentialities which lie ahead when using the Tree of Life in this way.

Liber 777 created a new type of literature when it first appeared. It was the first of its kind, and Crowley deserves credit for that, even if some of the material itself is not original. The concept is, and that is all that matters.

In order to get some theoretical idea of the Qabalah as a philosophical schema, there are some modern books outside the Crowley corpus which could be consulted to considerable advantage.

First of all, there is Dion Fortune's masterpiece *The Mystical Qabalah,* which is similarly based on Golden Dawn material. Its value lies in the manner in which she has considered each item and each detail with an exposition which ties them all together intelligibly.

Parallel to this is William Gray's *Ladder of Lights,* which is another elucidation of the Tree from a different viewpoint but equally illuminating. Both of these books are limited however merely to a study of the Ten Sephiroth, the main categories of the Tree. Supplementing these is Gareth Knight's *Practical Course in Qabalistic Symbolism* which extends the scope of the previous two books. By studying these three books, good background material should be provided from which to learn to appreciate the enormously valuable task performed by Crowley in *Liber 777* several decades ago. The student can accept as much or as little of the philosophy described in the above-named books as he wishes. It does not matter, so long as the basic schema is understood and applied to *Liber 777*. I foresee but little difficulty in this task.

The third volume included here is *Sepher Sephiroth,* which means simply the Book of Numbers. It is extrapolated from

Equinox I, No. 8. Originally, the book was started by Allan Bennett, one of the Golden Dawn adepts who took Crowley under his wing to ground him in the fundamental processes of Magic, Qabalah, and meditation. He must have been a most extraordinary man, for his mark on Crowley proved to be indelible—and there are few for whom this may be said.

Allan left one or two other pieces of writing which Crowley reproduced in one or other of the several volumes of the *Equinox*; they are worthy of being referred to. *A Note on Genesis* is a brilliant piece of exposition of Qabalistic principles demonstrating the whole gamut of Golden Dawn teachings, including some of the Qabalistic methods described here. For this reason alone it should be studied. The other was written after he had abandoned the Order to become a Buddhist monk with the sacramental name of the Bhikkhu Ananda Metteya. It is entitled *The Training of the Mind,* a study of how to acquire skill in meditation, one of the fundamentals of the Buddhist way of life. Both essays show the fine calibre of his mind, demonstrating why Crowley was so profoundly impressed by him. Anyway—this book is due in large measure to his efforts which Crowley continued.

Sepher Sephiroth consists of hundreds of Hebrew words selected from several sources that are listed in the front of the text. Most of the words are from the Old Testament and a couple of non-Zoharic texts translated by McGregor Mathers under the title of *The Kaballah Unveiled,* from the Latin edition of Knorr von Rosenroth. These words were arranged according to their numerical value by Bennett. The process and additional words were continued by Crowley after he had inherited the book from his mentor.

There are some strange gematria combinations to be found there, but it is traditionally assumed that if two words have the same number value, a connection of some kind may be said to exist between them. At first sight, in some instances, no such relationship may be perceived, but if the student persists in his study and meditation, he may come to realize something of the profundities of these subtle connections and associations that are not immediately perceived.

I have taken the liberty of deleting a *Table of Factor* (*Equinox* I, No. 8, p. viii-xv), which in reality has nothing whatsoever to do with *Sepher Sephiroth.** In my opinion it is

*This table is included by the publisher in the third edition, 1975

one of the occasional examples of Crowley's exhibitionism. Sometimes he just *had* to demonstrate his erudition. Much the same is true of many numbers in the last few pages of the text, (*Equinox* I, No. 8, p. 68-101) save for a few with their corresponding Hebrew words that could be condensed and brought closer together. These pages are omitted because there are no corresponding Hebrew words listed; for the time being they are just a waste of space and paper.

While it is true that the serious student might study other Qabalistic texts and in the future discover new Hebrew words having a numerical value that corresponds to those that I have just now deleted, nevertheless he could make his own additions to *Sepher Sephiroth,* insert a new string of numbers to make a place for his newly found words. And that is as it should be. There should be nothing fixed or rigid about any of these three books. They can be supplemented and expanded by the explorations of each student, depending on his own judgment and ingenuity. But he must not fall into the pitfall of some modern writers who, having no sympathy or understanding of the process, decry it and declare it of little value in the Qabalistic scheme of things.

I am also omitting Crowley's Preface to the book. It is a nasty malicious piece of writing, and does not do justice to the system with which he is dealing. Every so often, Crowley falls from the heights which he has seen, and swallows someone else's folly—someone whom he has had occasion to admire. In this case, Sir Richard Burton, not always a wholly reliable authority—outside of *The Arabian Nights.*

The essay on *Gematria* and *Sepher Sephiroth* should be studied together. Some of the profundities of the first will never be perceived until one has meditated long and often on some of the words analyzed in that essay.

I must confess that every now and again during the course of my life I have experienced a thoroughgoing revulsion to Crowley as a person, resulting in the total rejection and neglect of what he has written.

Days, weeks, months or years may elapse. Then "accidentally" I stumble across something he wrote—such as *Gematria* and become so engrossed and enamored of his ingenuity and inspiration that my revulsion becomes almost immediately transcended. This is probably more true of *Gematria* than either of the other two here included. (I am not making reference to his other later writings or poetry or holy books at this moment. They belong in a class by themselves.) The student who has missed the excitement and inner elevation experienced by Gematria—whether of his own making or merely reading Crowley—has missed a very great deal.

One scholar recently suggested to me in a letter that Crowley's knowledge of Hebrew was most limited. He made a very impressive "showing" only. In some ways, I am inclined to agree. But on the other hand, what little he did know he has used extremely effectively and creatively.

Anyway, he was not a dull bluffer like Arthur Edward Waite who pretended to all sorts of linguistic and scholastic skills he in fact never had. Take for example his book *The Secret Doctrine in Israel,* which is a lengthy analysis of the Zohar. That book was not written until after a French translation of the Zohar had been made—and of course long before the English one had appeared. The footnotes bear ample testimony to this conclusion. Yet he pretended years prior to that book that his Latin and Hebrew were more than adequate to the task—though they were not. Even his Latin translations of many alchemical texts were merely good editing jobs, the translators having been, amongst others, some elderly Anglican priests, preferring to remain if not anonymous then in obscurity, who had got mixed up with the Golden Dawn and the occult arts in general. They did the "donkey work" of translating difficult material, but Waite got the glory and the swollen head. Whatever may be said of Aleister Crowley's inflated ego—and I have often said perhaps too much about this—he never stooped quite that low.

All of this makes this book *The Qabalah of Aleister Crowley* of greater interest to the average good student whose Hebrew may be no better or no worse than that of Crowley. It may give him heart to pursue his own personal addenda to those books and become as good a Qabalist as was Crowley.

Finally, let me add that the student should own a good Hebrew-English lexicon. Perhaps one of the best ways of using this is to browse through it at random—casually as it were, and then as his interest and excitement mount, look for certain words deliberately and methodically.

For example. Open the lexicon at random, and on that particular page point carelessly to the first word noticed.

Transfer the word and its translation to a sheet of paper, and then work out its gematria. Then turn to *Sepher Sephiroth* to see if that number and word are represented. If not, add them, using page inserts if necessary. Make special entries of such words. As time proceeds, certain other words will evoke special interest and should be treated in the same manner. Try to follow Crowley's analysis of *Berashith* in the essay *Gematria* as a model for the management of these words, and as the basis for meditation to lead to the highest.

Here are a couple of examples. I opened the lexicon at random and selected two words. A variety of Qabalistic methods may be used to elaborate on them. Practice will produce skill and insight.

The first word selected was one meaning "empty." In Hebrew, it is spelled Nun, Ayin, Vav, Resh. Thus its gematria is: 50, 70, 6, 200 = 326. This is a number that is listed in *Sepher Sephiroth,* and surprisingly is that of *Yeheshuah,* the Redeemer. The word for "vision" also comes within the purview of this number. Our lexicon word "empty" may seem a far cry from any of these words just mentioned, but . . . See what a little meditation can do, after having followed a similar procedure to that used by Crowley relative to *Berashith.*

Another word selected at random is "defect, or want." In Hebrew this is spelled Cheth, Samekh, Resh, Vav, final Nun. Its gematria comes to 324 (counting the Nun as 50). This, too, is another number already in *Sepher Sephiroth.* But it is worth comparing with the words already given there. "Redness", "darkness", "roaring", etc. All three of these Qabalistic texts must be consulted to make sense of these apparently unrelated words and numbers. The process thus becomes a test for one's Qabalistic knowledge and skill, but more importantly the process becomes a stimulus for the surrender of the mind to the mystical experience in which the One is seen to be All, and vice versa.

There are simply no limits to be set to the applications of these numerical processes. It will take only a little practice and experience for the sincere and ingenious student to become aware of the possibilities inherent in gematria. And he will conclude by developing a fine appreciation for the value—individually and collectively—of these three books assembled for the first time as *The Qabalah of Aleister Crowley.*

ISRAEL REGARDIE

GEMATRIA

GEMATRIA

This is taken verbatim
from Aleister Crowley's
Equinox, Vol. 1, No. 5.

It must first here be spoken of the Exoteric Qabalah to be found in books, a shell of that perfect fruit of the Tree of Life. Next we will deal with the esoteric teachings of it, as Frater P. was able to understand them. And of these we shall give examples, showing the falsity and absurdity of the uninitiated path, the pure truth and reasonableness of the hidden Way.

For the student unacquainted with the rudiments of the Qabalah we recommend the study of S. L. Mathers' "Introduction" to his translation of the three principal books of the Zohar, and Westcott's "Introduction to the Study of the Qabalah." We venture to append a few quotations from the former document, which will show the elementary principles of calculation. Dr Westcott's little book is principally valuable for its able defence of the Qabalah as against exotericism and literalism.

The literal Qabalah . . . is divided into three parts: GMTRIA, Gematria; NVTRIQVN, Notariqon; and ThMVRH, Temura.

Gematria is a metathesis of the Greek word *γραμματεια*. It is based on the relative numerical values of words. Words of similar numerical values are considered to be explanatory of each other, and this theory is extended to phrases. Thus the letter Shin, Sh, is 300, and is equivalent to the number obtained by adding up the numerical values of the letters of the words RVCh ALHIM, Ruach Elohim, the spirit of Elohim; and it is therefore a symbol of the spirit of Elohim. For R=200, V=6, Ch=8, A=1, L=30, H=5, I=10, M=40; total=300. Similarly, the words AChD, Achad, Unity, One, and AHBH, Ahebah, love, each=13; for A=1, Ch=8, D=4, total=13; and A=1, H=5, B=2, H=5, total=13. Again, the name of the angel MTTRVN, Metatron or Methraton, and the name of the Deity, ShDI, Shaddai, each make 314; so the one is taken as symbolical of the other. The angel Metatron is said to have been the conductor of the children of Israel through the wilderness, of whom God says, "My name is in him." With regard to Gematria of phrases (Gen. xlix. 10), IBA ShILH, Yeba Shiloh, "Shiloh shall come"=358, which is the numeration of the word MShICh, Messiah. Thus also the passage, Gen. xviii. 2, VHNH ShLShH, Vehenna Shalisha, "And lo, three men," equals in numerical value ALV MIKAL GBRIAL VRPAL, Elo Mikhael Gabriel Ve-Raphael, "These are Mikhael, Gabriel and Raphael"; for each phrase=701. I think these instances will suffice to make clear the nature of Gematria.

Notariqon is derived from the Latin word notarius, a shorthand writer. Of Notariqon there are two forms. In the first every letter of a word is taken from the initial or abbreviation of another word, so that from the letters of a word a sentence may be formed. Thus every letter of the word BRAShITH, Berashith, the first word in Genesis, is made the initial of a word, and we obtain BRAShITh RAH ALHIM ShIQBLV IShRAL ThVRH, Berashith Rahi Elohim Sheyequebelo Israel Torah; "In the beginning Elohim saw that Israel would accept the law." In this connection I may give six very interesting specimens of Notariqon formed from this same word BRAShITh by Solomon Meir Ben Moses, a Jewish Qabalist, who embraced the Christian faith in 1665, and took the name of Prosper Rugere. These have all a Christian tendency, and by their means Prosper converted another Jew, who had previously been bitterly opposed to Christianity. The first is, BN RVCh AB ShLVShThM IChD ThMIM, Ben, Ruach, Ab, Shaloshethem Yechad Thaubodo: "The Son, the Spirit, the Father, ye shall equally worship Their Trinity." The third is BKVRI RAShVNI AShR ShMV IShVO ThOBVDV, Bekori Rashuni Asher Shamo Yeshuah Thaubodo: "Ye shall worship My first-born, My first, Whose name is Jesus." The fourth is, BBVA RBN AShR ShMV IShVo ThOBVDV, Beboa Rabban Asher Shamo Yeshuah Thaubodo: "When the Master shall come Whose Name is Jesus ye shall worship." The fifth is, BThVLH RAVIH ABChR ShThLD ISh VO ThAShRVH, Bethulh Raviah Abachar Shethaled Yeshuah Thashroah: "I will choose a virgin worthy to bring forth Jesus, and ye shall call her blessed." The sixth is, BOVGTh RTzPIM ASThThR ShGVPI IShVO ThAKLV, Beaugoth Ratzephim Asattar Shegopi Yeshuah Thakelo: "I will hide myself in cake (baked with) coals, for ye shall eat Jesus, My Body."

The Qabalistical importance of these sentences as bearing upon the doctrines of Christianity can hardly be overrated.

The second form of the Notariqon is the exact reverse of the first. By this the initials or finals, or both, or the medials, of a sentence, are taken to form a word or words. Thus the Qabalah is called ChKMH NSThRH, Chokhmah Nesethrah, "the secret wisdom"; and if we take the initials of these two words Ch and N, we form by the second kind of Notariqon the word ChN, Chen, "grace." Similarly, from the initials and finals of the words MI IOLH LNV HShMIMH, Mi Iaulah Leno Ha-Shamayimah, "Who shall go up for us to heaven?" (Deut. xxx. 12), are formed MILH, Milah, "circumcision," and IHVH, the Tetragrammaton, implying that God hath ordained circumcision as the way to heaven.

Temura is permutation. According to certain rules, one letter is substituted for another letter preceding or following it in the alphabet, and thus from one word another word of totally different orthography may be formed. Thus the alphabet is bent exactly in half, in the middle, and one half is put over the other; and then by changing alternately the first letter or the first two letters at the beginning of the second line, twenty-two commutations are produced. These are called the "Table of the Combinations of TzIRVP," Tziruph. For example's sake, I will give the method called ALBTh, Albath, thus:—

11	10	9	8	7	6	5	4	3	2	1
K	I	T	Ch	Z	V	H	D	G	B	A
M	N	S	O	P	Tz	Q	R	Sh	Th	L

Each method takes its name from the first two pairs composing it, the system of pairs of letters being the groundwork of the whole, as either letter in a pair is substituted for the other letter. Thus, by Albath, from RVCh, Ruach, is formed DTzO, Detzau. The names of the other twenty-one methods are: ABGTh, AGDTh, ADBG, AHBD, AVBH, AZBV, AChBZ, ATBCh, AIBT, AKBI, ALBK, AMBL, ANBM, ASBN, AOBS, APBO, ATzBP, AQSTz, ARBQ, AShBR, and AThBSh. To these must be added the modes ABGD and ALBM. Then comes the "Rational Table of Tziruph," another set of twenty-two combinations. There are also three "Tables of the Commutations," known respectively as the Right, the Averse, and the Irregular. To make any of these, a square, containing 484 squares, should be made, and the letters written in. For the "Right Table" write the alphabet across from right to left; in the second row of squares do the same, but begin with B and end with A; in the third begin with G and end with B; and so on. For the "Averse Table" write the alphabet from right to left backwards, beginning with Th and ending with A; in the second row begin with Sh and end with Th, &c. The "Irregular Table" would take too long to describe. Besides all these, there is the method called ThShRQ, Thashraq, which is simply writing a word backwards. There is one more very important form called the "Qabalah of the Nine Chambers" or AIQ BKR, Aiq Bekar. It is thus formed:

300 Sh	30 L	3 G	200 R	20 K	2 B	100 Q	10 I	1 A
600 M final	60 S	6 V	500 K final	50 N	5 H	400 Th	40 M	4 D
900 Tz final	90 Tz	9 T	800 P final	80 P	8 Ch	700 N final	70 O	7 Z

I have put the numeration of each letter above to show the affinity between the letters in each chamber. Sometimes this is used as a cipher, by taking the portions of the figure to show the letters they contain, putting one point for the first letter, two for the second, &c. Thus the right angle, containing AIQ, will answer for the letter Q if it have three dots or points within it. Again a square will answer for H, N, or K final, according to whether it has one, two, or three points respectively placed within it. So also with regard to the other letters. But there are many other ways of employing the Qabalah of the Nine Chambers, which I have not space to describe. I will merely mention as an example, that by the mode of Temura called

AThBSh, Athbash, it is found that in Jeremiah xxv. 26, the word ShShK, Sheshakh, symbolises BBL, Babel.

Besides all these rules, there are certain meanings hidden in the shape of the letters of the Hebrew alphabet; in the form of a particular letter at the end of a word being different from that which it generally bears when it is a final letter, or in a letter being written in the middle of a word in a character generally used only at the end; in any letters or letter being written in a size smaller or larger than the rest of the manuscript, or in a letter being written upside down; in the variations found in the spelling of certain words, which have a letter more in some places than they have in others; in peculiarities observed in the position of any of the points or accents, and in certain expressions supposed to be elliptic or redundant.

For example the shape of the Hebrew letter Aleph, A, is said to symbolise a Vau, V, between a Yod, I, and a Daleth, D; and thus the letter itself represents the word IVD, Yod. Similarly the shape of the letter He, H, represents a Daleth, D, with a Yod, I, written at the lower left-hand corner, &c.

In Isaiah ix. 6, 7, the word LMRBH, Lemarbah, "for multiplying," is written with the character for M final in the middle of the word, instead of with the ordinary initial and medial M. The consequence of this is that the total numerical value of the word, instead of being 30+40+200+2+5=277, is 30+600+200+2+5=837=by Gematria ThTh ZL, Tet Zal, the profuse Giver. Thus by writing the M final instead of the ordinary character, the word is made to bear a different qabalistical meaning.

. . . .

It is to be further noted with regard to the first word in the Bible, BRAShITH, that the first three letters, BRA, are the initial letters of the names of the three persons of the Trinity: BN, Ben the Son; RVCH, Ruach, the Spirit; and AB, Ab the Father. Furthermore the first letter of the Bible is B, which is the initial letter of BRKH, Berakhah, blessing; and not A, which is that of ARR, Arar, cursing. Again, the letters of Berashith, taking their numerical powers, express the number of the years between the Creation and the birth of Christ, thus: B=2,000, R=200, A=1,000, Sh=300, I=10, and Th=400; total=3910 years, being the time in round numbers. Picus de Mirandola gives the following working out of BRAShITh, Berashith:—By joining the third letter, A, to the first, B, AB, Ab=Father, is obtained. If to the first letter B, doubled, the second letter, R, be added, it makes BBR, Bebar=in or through the Son. If all the letters be read except the first, it makes RAShITh, Rashith=the beginning. If the fourth letter, Sh, the first B and the last Th be connected, it makes ShBTh, Shebeth=the end or rest.

If the first three letters be taken, they make BRA, Bera = created. If, omitting the first, the three following be taken, they make RASh, Rash = head. If, omitting the two first, the next two be taken, they give ASh, Ash = fire. If the fourth and the last be joined, they give ShTh, Sheth = foundation. Again if the second letter be put before the first, it makes RB, Rab = great. If after the third be placed the fifth and the fourth, it gives AISh, Aish = man. If to the two first be joined the two last, they give BRITh, Berith = covenant. And if the first be added to the last, it gives ThB, Theb, which is sometimes used for TVB, Thob = good.

. . . .

There are three qabalistical veils of the negative existence, and in themselves they formulate the hidden ideas of the Sephiroth not yet called into being, and they are concentrated in Kether, which in this sense is the Malkuth of the hidden ideas of the Sephiroth. I will explain this. The first veil of the negative existence is the AIN, Ain, Negativity. This word consists of three letters, which thus shadow forth the first three Sephiroth or numbers. The second veil is the AIN SVP, the limitless. This title consists of six letters, and shadows forth the idea of the first six Sephiroth or numbers. The third veil is the AIN SVP AVR, Ain Soph Aur, the Limitless Light. This again consists of nine letters, and symbolises the first nine Sephiroth, but of course in their hidden idea only. But when we reach the number nine we cannot progress farther without returning to the unity, or the number one, for the number ten is but a repetition of unity freshly derived from the negative, as is evident from a glance at its ordinary representation in Arabic numerals, where the circle O represents the Negative and the I the Unity. Thus, then, the limitless ocean of negative light does not proceed from a centre, for it is centreless, but it concentrates a centre, which is the number one of the Sephiroth, Kether, the Crown, the First Sephira; which therefore may be said to be the Malkuth or the number ten of the hidden Sephiroth. Thus, "Kether is in Malkuth and Malkuth is in Kether." Or as an alchemical author of great repute (Thomas Vaughan, better known as Eugenius Philalethes) says, apparently quoting from Proclus; "That the heaven is in the earth, but after an earthly manner; and that the earth is in the heaven, but after a heavenly manner." But inasmuch as negative existence is the subject incapable of definition, as I have before shown, it is rather considered by the Qabalists as depending back from the number of unity than as a separate consideration therefrom; therefore they frequently apply the same terms and epithets indiscriminately to either. Such epithets are "The concealed of the Concealed," "The Ancient of the Ancient Ones," the "Most Holy Ancient One," etc.

I must now explain the real meaning of the terms Sephira and Sephiroth. The first is singular, the second is plural. The best rendering of the word is "numerical emanation." There are ten Sephiroth, which are the most abstract forms of the ten numbers of the decimal scale—*i.e.*, the numbers 1, 2, 3, 4, 5, 6, 7, 8, 9, 10. Therefore, as in the higher mathematics we reason of numbers in their abstract sense, so in the Qabalah we reason of the Deity by the abstract forms of the numbers in other words, by the SPIRVTh, Sephiroth. It was from this ancient Oriental theory that Pythagoras derived his numerical symbolic ideas.

Among the Sephiroth, jointly and severally, we find the development of the persons and attributes of God. Of these some are male and some female. Now, for some reason or other best known to themselves, the translators of the Bible have carefully crowded out of existence and smothered up every reference to the fact that the Deity is both masculine and feminine. They have translated a feminine plural by a masculine singular in the case of the word Elohim. They have, however, left an inadvertent admission of their knowledge that it was plural in Genesis iv. 26: "And Elohim said: Let Us make man." Again (v. 27), how could Adam be made in the image of Elohim, male and female, unless the Elohim were male and female also? The word Elohim is a plural formed from the feminine singular ALH, Eloh, by adding IM to the word. But inasmuch as IM is usually a termination of the masculine plural and is here added to a feminine noun, it gives to the word Elohim the sense of a female potency united to a masculine idea, and thereby capable of producing an offspring. Now, we hear much of the Father and the Son, but we hear nothing of the Mother in the ordinary religions of the day. But in the Qabalah we find that the Ancient of Days conforms Himself simultaneously into the Father and the Mother, and thus begets the Son. Now, this Mother is Elohim. Again, we are usually told that the Holy Spirit is masculine. But the word RVCh, Ruach, Spirit, is feminine, as appears from the following passage of the Sepher Yetzirah: "AChTh RVCh ALHIM ChIIM, Achath (feminine, not Achad, masculine) Ruach Elohim Chiim: One is She the Spirit of the Elohim of Life."

Now, we find that before the Deity conformed Himself thus—*i.e.*, as male and female—that the worlds of the universe could not subsist, or, in the words of Genesis, "The earth was formless and void." These prior worlds are considered to be symbolised by the "kings who reigned in Edom before there reigned a king in Israel," and they are therefore spoken of in the Qabalah as the "Edomite kings." This will be found fully explained in various parts of this work.

We now come to the consideration of the first Sephira, or the Number One, the Monad of Pythagoras. In this number are the other nine hidden. It is indivisible, it is also incapable of multiplication; divide 1 by itself and it still remains 1, multiply 1 by itself and it is still 1 and unchanged. Thus it is a fitting representative of the unchangeable Father of all. Now this number of unity has a twofold nature, and thus forms, as it were, the link between the negative and the positive. In its unchangeable one-ness it is scarcely a number; but in its property of capability of addition it may be called the first number of a numerical series. Now, the zero, 0, is incapable even of addition, just as also is negative existence. How, then, if 1 can neither be multiplied nor divided, is another 1 to be obtained to add to it; in other words how is the number 2 to be found? By reflection of itself. For though 0 be incapable of definition, 1 is definable. And the effect of a definition is to form an Eidolon, duplicate, or image, of the thing defined. Thus, then, we obtain a duad composed of 1 and its reflection. Now also we have the commencement of a vibration established, for the number 1 vibrates alternately from changelessness to definition, and back to changelessness again. Thus, then, it is the father of all numbers, and a fitting type of the Father of all things.

The name of the first Sephira is KThR, Kether, the Crown. The Divine Name attributed to it is the Name of the Father given in Exod. iii. 4: AHIH, Eheieh, I am. It signifies Existence.

. . . .

The first Sephira contains nine, and produces them in succession thus:—

The number 2 or the Duad. The name of the second Sephira is ChKMH, Chokmah, Wisdom, a masculine active potency reflected from Kether, as I have before explained. This Sephira is the active and evident Father, to whom the Mother is united, who is the number 3. This second Sephira is represented by the Divine Names, IH, Yah, and IHVH; and the angelic hosts by AVPNIM, Auphanim, the Wheels (Ezek. i.). It is also called AB, Ab, the Father.

The third Sephira, or triad, is a feminine passive potency, called BINH, Binah, the Understanding, who is co-equal with Chokmah. For Chokmah, the number 2, is like two straight lines which can never enclose a space, and therefore it is powerless till the number 3 forms a triangle. Thus this Sephira completes and makes evident the supernal Trinity. It is also called AMA, Ama, Mother, and AIMA, Aima, the great productive Mother, who is eternally conjoined with AB, the Father, for the maintenance of the universe in order. Therefore is she the most evident form in whom we can know the Father, and therefore is she worthy of all honour. She is the supernal Mother, co-equal with Chokmah, and the great feminine form of God, the Elohim, in whose image man and woman are created, according to the teaching of the Qabalah, equal before God. Woman is equal with man, and certainly not inferior to him, as it has been the persistent endeavour of so-called Christians to make her. Aima is the woman described in the Apocalypse (chap. xii.). This third Sephira is also sometimes called the Great Sea. To her are attributed the Divine names, ALHIM, Elohim, and IHVH ALHIM; and the angelic order, ARALIM, Aralim, The Thrones. She is the Supernal Mother as distinguished from Malkuth, the inferior Mother, Bride, and Queen.

The number 4. This union of the second and third Sephiroth produced ChSD, Chesed, Mercy or Love, also called GDVLH, Gedulah, Greatness or Magnificence; a masculine potency represented by the Divine Name AL, El, the Mighty One, and the angelic name, ChShMLIM, Chashmalim, Scintillating Flames (Ezek. iv. 4).

The number 5. From this emanated the feminine passive potency GBVRH, Geburah, strength or fortitude; or DIN, Deen, Justice; represented by the Divine Names, ALHIM GBVR, and ALH, Eloh, and the angelic name ShRPIM, Seraphim (Isa. vi. 6). This Sephira is also called PChD, Pachad, Fear.

The number 6. And from these two issued the uniting Sephira, ThPARTh, Tiphereth, Beauty or Mildness, represented by the Divine Name ALVH VDOTh, Eloah Va-Daath, and the angelic names, Shinanim, ShNANIM (Ps. lxviii. 18), or MLKIM, Melakim, kings. Thus by the union of justice and mercy we obtain beauty or clemency, and the second trinity of the Sephiroth is complete. This Sephira, or "Path," or "Numeration"—for by these latter appellations the emanations are sometimes called—together with the fourth, fifth, seventh, eighth, and ninth Sephiroth, is spoken of as ZOIR ANPIN, Zaur Anpin, the Lesser Countenance, Microprosopus, by way of antithesis to Macroprosopus, or the Vast Countenance, which is one of the names of Kether, the first Sephira. The six Sephiroth of which Zauir Anpin is composed, are then called His six members. He is also called MLK, Melekh the King.

The number 7. The seventh Sephira is NTzCh, Netzach, or Firmness and Victory, corresponding to the Divine Name Jehovah Tzabaoth, IHVH TzBAVTh, the Lord of Armies, and the angelic names ALHIM, Elohim, gods, and ThRShIShIM, Tharshishim, the brilliant ones (Dan. x. 6).

The number 8. Thence proceeded the feminine passive potency HVD, Hod, Splendour, answering to the Divine Name ALHIM TzBAVTh, Elohim Tzabaoth, the God of Armies, and among the angels to BNI ALHIM, Beni Elohim, the sons of the Gods (Gen. vi. 4).

The number 9. These two produced ISVD, Yesod, the Foundation or Basis, represented by AL ChI, El Chai, the Mighty Living One, and ShDI, Shaddai; and among the angels by AShIM, Aishim, the Flames (Ps. civ. 4), yielding the third Trinity of the Sephiroth.

The number 10. From this ninth Sephira came the tenth and last, thus completing the decad of the numbers. It is called MLVTh, Malkuth, the Kingdom, and also the Queen, Matrona, the inferior Mother, the Bride of Microprosopus; and ShKINH, Shekinah, represented by the Divine Name Adonai, ADNI, and among the angel hosts by the kerubim, KRVBIM. Now, each of these Sephiroth will be in a certain degree androgynous, for it will be feminine or receptive with regard to the Sephira which immediately precedes it in the sephirotic scale, and masculine or transmissive with regard to the Sephira which immediately follows it. But there is no Sephira anterior to Kether, nor is there a Sephira which succeeds Malkuth. By these remarks it will be understood how Chokmah is a feminine noun, though marking a masculine Sephira. The connecting-link of the Sephiroth is the Ruach, spirit, Mezla, the hidden influence.

I will now add a few more remarks on the qabalistical meaning of the term MThQLA, Metheqla, balance. In each of the three trinities or triads of the Sephiroth is a duad of opposite sexes, and a uniting intelligence which is the result. In this, the masculine and feminine potencies are regarded as the two scales of the balance, and the uniting Sephira as the beam that joins them. Thus, then, the term balance may be said to symbolise the Triune, Trinity in Unity, and the Unity represented by the central point of the beam. But, again, in the Sephiroth there is a triple Trinity, the upper, lower, and middle. Now, these three are represented thus: the supernal, or highest, by the Crown, Kether; the middle by the King, and the inferior by the Queen; which will be the greatest trinity. And the earthly correlatives of these will be the primum mobile, the sun and the moon. Here we at once find alchemical symbolism.

. . . .

The Sephiroth are futher divided into three pillars—the right-hand Pillar of Mercy, consisting of the second, fourth, and seventh emanations; the left-hand Pillar of Judgment, consisting of the third, fifth, and eighth; and the middle Pillar of Mildness, consisting of the first, sixth, ninth, and tenth emanations.

In their totality and unity the ten Sephiroth represent the archetypal man, ADM QDMVN, Adam Qadmon, the Protogonos. In looking at the Sephiroth constituting the first triad, it is evident that they represent the intellect; and hence this triad is called the intellectual world, OVLM MVShKL, Olahm Mevshekal. The second triad corresponds to the moral world, OVLM MVRGSh, Olahm Morgash. The third represents power and stability, and is therefore called the material world, OLVM HMVTHBO, Olahm Ha-Mevethau. These three aspects are called the faces, ANPIN, Anpin. Thus is the tree of life, OTz ChIIM, Otz Chaiim, formed; the first triad being placed above, the second and third below, in such a manner that the three masculine Sephiroth are on the right, the three feminine on the left, whilst the four uniting Sephiroth occupy the centre. This is the qabalistical "tree of life," on which all things depend. There is considerable analogy between this and the tree Yggdrasil of the Scandinavians. I have already remarked that there is one trinity which comprises all the Sephiroth, and that it consists of the crown, the king, and the queen. (In some senses this is the Christian Trinity of Father, Son, and Holy Spirit, which in their highest Divine nature are symbolised by the first three Sephiroth, Kether, Chokmah, and Binah.) It is the Trinity which created the world; or, in qabalistical language, the universe was born from the union of the crowned king and queen. But according to the Qabalah, before the complete form of the heavenly man (the ten Sephiroth) was produced, there were certain primordial worlds created, but these could not subsist, as the equilibrium of balance was not yet perfect, and they were convulsed by the unbalanced force and destroyed. These primordial worlds are called the "kings of ancient time" and the "kings of Edom who reigned before the monarchs of Israel." In this sense, Edom is the world of unbalanced force, and Israel is the balanced Sephiroth (Gen. xxxvi. 31). This important fact, that worlds were created and destroyed prior to the present creation, is again and again reiterated in the Zohar.

Now the Sephiroth are also called the World of Emanations, or the Atziluthic World, or the archetypal world, OVLM ATzILVTh, Olahm Atziloth; and this world gave birth to three other worlds each containing a repetition of the Sephiroth, but in a descending scale of brightness.

The second world is the Briatic world, OVLM HBRIAH, Olahm Ha-Briah, the world of creation, also called KVRSIA, Khorsia, the throne. It is an immediate emanation from the world of Atziloth, whose ten Sephiroth are reflected herein, and are consequently more limited, though they are still of the purest nature, and without any admixture of matter.

The third is the Jetziratic world, OVLM HITzIRH, Olahm Ha-Yetzirah, or world of formation and of angels, which proceeds from Briah, and, though less refined in substance, is still without matter. It is in this angelic world that reside those intelligent and incorporeal beings who are wrapped in a luminous garment, and who assume a form when they appear unto man.

The fourth is the Asiatic world, OVLM HOShIH, Olahm Ha-Asiah, the world of action, called also the world of shells, OVLM HQLIPVTh, Olahm Ha-Qliphoth, which is this world of matter, made up of the grosser elements of the other three. In it is also the abode of the evil spirits, which are called "the shells" by the Qabalah, QLIPVTH, Qliphoth, material shells. The devils are also divided into ten classes, and have suitable habitations. (See Tables in 777.)

The demons are the grossest and most deficient of all forms. Their ten degrees answer to the decad of the Sephiroth, but in inverse ratio, as darkness and impurity increase with the descent of each degree. The two first are nothing but absence of visible form and organisation. The third is the abode of darkness. Next follow seven Hells occupied by those demons which represent incarnate human vices, and those who have given themselves up to such vices in earth-life. Their prince is Samael, SMAL, the angel of poison and death. His wife is the harlot, or woman of whoredom, AShTh ZNVNIM, Isheth Zenunim ; and united they are called the beast, CHIVA, Chioa. Thus the infernal trinity is completed which is, so to speak, the averse and caricature of the supernal Creative One. Samael is considered to be identical with Satan.

The name of the Deity, which we call Jehovah, is in Hebrew a name of four letters, IHVH ; and the true pronunciation of it is known to very few. I myself know some score of different mystical pronunciations of it. The true pronunciation of it is a most secret arcanum, and is a secret of secrets. "He who can rightly pronounce it, causeth heaven and earth to tremble, for it is the name which rusheth through the universe." Therefore when a devout Jew comes upon it in reading the Scripture, he either does not attempt to pronounce it, but instead makes a short pause, or else he substitutes for it the name Adonai, ADNI, Lord. The radical meaning of the word is "to be," and it is thus, like AHIH, Eheieh, a glyph of existence. It is capable of twelve transpositions, which all convey the meaning of "to be" ; it is the only word that will bear so many transpositions without its meaning being altered. They are called the "twelve banners of the mighty name," and are said by some to rule the twelve signs of the Zodiac. These are the twelve banners:—IHVH, IHHV, IVHH, HVHI, HVIH, HHIV, VHHI, VIHH, VHIH, HIHV, HIVH, HHVI. There are three other tetragrammatic names, which are AHIH, Eheieh, existence ; ADNI, Adonai, Lord ; and AGLA. This last is not, properly speaking, a word, but is a notariqon of the sentence, AThH GBVR LOVLM ADNI, Ateh Gebor Le-Olahm Adonai : "Thou art mighty, for ever, O Lord!" A brief explanation of Agla is this ; A, the one first ; A, the one last ; G, the Trinity in Unity ; L, the completion of the great work.

. . . .

But IHVH, the Tetragrammaton, as we shall presently see, contains all the Sephiroth with the exception of Kether, and specially signifies the Lesser Countenance, Microprosopus, the King of the qabalistical Sephirotic greatest Trinity, and the Son in His human incarnation, in the Christian acceptation of the Trinity. Therefore, as the Son reveals the Father, so does IHVH, Jehovah, reveal AHIH, Eheieh. And ADNI is the Queen, by whom alone Tetragrammaton can be grasped, whose exaltation into Binah is found in the Christian assumption of the Virgin.

The Tetragrammaton IHVH is referred to the Sephiroth, thus: the uppermost point of the letter Yod, I, is said to refer to Kether; the letter I itself to Chokmah, the father of Microprosopus; the letter H, or "the supernal He," to Binah, the supernal Mother; the letter V to the next six Sephiroth, which are called the six members of Microprosopus (and six is the numerical value of V, the Hebrew Vau); lastly, the letter H, the "inferior He," to Malkuth, the tenth Sephira, the bride of Microprosopus.

Advanced students should then go to the fountain head, Knorr von Rosenroth's "Kabbala denudata," and study for themselves. It should not prove easy; Frater P., after years of study, confessed: "I cannot get much out of Rosenroth"; and we may add that only the best minds are likely to obtain more than an academic knowledge of a system which we suspect von Rosenroth himself never understood in any deeper sense. As a book of reference to the hierarchical correspondences of the Qabalah, of course 777 stands alone and unrivalled.

The graphic Qabalah has been already fully illustrated in this treatise. See Illustrations 2, 12, 16, 17, 18, 19, 21, 22, 24, 27, 28, 29, 33, 34, 35, 38, 39, 40, 41, 43, 45, 46, 47, 48, 50, 51, 61, 63, 64, 65, 66, 71, 72, 73, 74, 75, 76, 77, 78, 79, 82.

By far the best and most concise account of the method of the Qabalah is that by an unknown author, which Mr Aleister Crowley has printed at the end of the first volume of his Collected Works, and which we here reprint in full.

QABALISTIC DOGMA

The Evolution of Things is thus described by the Qabalists.

First is Nothing, or the Absence of Things, אין, which does not and cannot mean Negatively Existing (if such an Idea can be said to mean anything), as S. Liddell Macgregor Mathers, who misread the Text and stultified the

Commentary by the Light of his own Ignorance of Hebrew and Philosophy, pretends in his Translation of v. Rosenroth.

Second is Without Limit אין סוף, *i.e.*, Infinite Space.

This is the primal Dualism of Infinity; the infinitely small and the infinitely great. The Clash of these produces a finite positive Idea which happens (see בראשית, in "The Sword of Song," for a more careful study, though I must not be understood to indorse every Word in our Poet-Philosopher's Thesis) to be Light, אור. This word אור is most important. It symbolises the Universe immediately after Chaos, the Confusion or Clash of the infinite Opposites. א is the Egg of Matter; ו is ♉, the Bull, or Energy-Motion; and ר is the Sun, or organised and moving System of Orbs. The three Letters of אור thus repeat the three Ideas. The Nature of אור is thus analysed, under the figure of the ten Numbers and the 22 Letters which together compose what the Rosicrucians have diagrammatised under the name of Minutum Mundum. It will be noticed that every Number and Letter has its "Correspondence" in Ideas of every Sort; so that any given Object can be analysed in Terms of the 32. If I see a blue Star, I should regard it as a Manifestation of Chesed, Water, the Moon, Salt the Alchemical Principle, Sagittarius or What not, in respect of its Blueness—one would have to decide which from other Data—and refer it to the XVIIth Key of the Taro in Respect of its Starriness.

The Use of these Attributions is lengthy and various: I cannot dwell upon it: but I will give one Example.

If I wish to visit the Sphere of Geburah, I use the Colours and Forces appropriate: I go there: if the Objects which then appear to my spiritual Vision are harmonious therewith, it is one Test of their Truth.

So also, to construct a Talisman, or to invoke a Spirit.

The methods of discovering Dogma from sacred Words are also numerous and important: I may mention:—

(*a*) The Doctrine of Sympathies: drawn from the total Numeration of a Word, when identical with, or a Multiple or Submultiple of, or a Metathesis of, that of another Word.

(*b*) The Method of finding the Least Number of a Word, by adding (and re-adding) the Digits of its total Number, and taking the corresponding Key of the Taro as a Key to the Meaning of the Word.

(*c*) The Method of Analogies drawn from the Shape of the Letters.

(*d*) The Method of Deductions drawn from the Meanings and Correspondences of the Letters.

(*e*) The Method of Acrostics drawn from the Letters. This Mode is only valid for Adepts of the highest Grades, and then under quite exceptional and rare Conditions.

(*f*) The Method of Transpositions and Transmutations of the Letters, which suggest Analogies, even when they fail to explain in direct Fashion.

All these and their Varieties and Combinations, with some other more abstruse or less important Methods, may be used to unlock the Secret of a Word.

Of course with Powers so wide it is easy for the Partisan to find his favourite Meaning in any Word. Even the formal Proof $0=1=2=3=4=5=\ldots\ldots\ldots=n$ is possible.

But the Adept who worked out this Theorem, with the very Intent to discredit the Qabalistic Mode of Research, was suddenly dumfounded by the Fact that he had actually stumbled upon the Qabalistic Proof of Pantheism or Monism.

What really happens is that the Adept sits down and performs many useless Tricks with the Figures, without Result.

Suddenly the Lux dawns, and the Problem is solved.

The Rationalist explains this by Inspiration, the superstitious Man by Mathematics.

I give an Example of the Way in which one works. Let us take IAO, one of the "Barbarous Names of Evocation," of which those who have wished to conceal their own Glory by adopting the Authority of Zarathustra have said that in the holy Ceremonies it has an ineffable Power.

But what Kind of Power? By the Qabalah we can find out the Force of the Name IAO.

We can spell it in Hebrew יאו or יאע. The Qabalah will even tell us which is the true Way. Let us however suppose that it is spelt יאו. This adds up to 17.

But first of all it strikes us that I, A, and O are the three Letters associated with the three Letters ה in the great Name of Six Letters, אהיהוה, which combines אהוה and יהוה, Macroprosopus and Microprosopus. Now these feminine Letters ה conceal the "Three Mothers" of the Alphabet, א, מ, and ש. Replace these, and we get אשימוא, which adds up to 358, the Number alike of נחש, the Serpent of Genesis, and the Messiah. We thus look for redeeming Power in IAO, and for the Masculine Aspect of that Power.

Now we will see how that Power works. We have a curious Dictionary, which was made by a very learned Man, in which the Numbers 1 to 10,000 fill the left hand Column, in Order, and opposite them are written all the sacred or important Words which add up to each Number.

We take this Book, and look at 17. We find that 17 is the number of Squares in the Swastika, which is the Whirling Disc or Thunderbolt. Also there is חוג, a Circle or Orbit; זור, to seethe or boil; and some other Words, which we will neglect in this Example, though we should not dare to do so if we were really trying to find out a Thing we none of us knew. To help our Deduction about Redemption, too, we find הדה, to brighten or make glad.

We also work in another Way. I is the Straight Line or Central Pillar of the Temple of Life ; also it stands for Unity, and for the Generative Force. A is the Pentagram, which means the Will of Man working Redemption. O is the Circle from which everything came, also Nothingness, and the Female, who absorbs the Male. The Progress of the Name shows then the Way from Life to Nirvana by means of the Will: and is a Hieroglyph of the Great Work.

Look at all our Meanings! Every one shows that the Name, if it has any Power at all, and that we must try, has the Power to redeem us from the Love of Life which is the Cause of Life, by its masculine Whirlings, and to gladden us and to bring us to the Bosom of the Great Mother, Death.

Before what is known as the Equinox of the Gods, a little While ago, there was an initiated Formula which expressed these Ideas to the Wise. As these Formulas are done with, it is of no Consequence if I reveal them. Truth is not eternal, any more than God ; and it would be but a poor God that could not and did not alter his Ways at his Pleasure.

This Formula was used to open the Vault of the Mystic Mountain of Abiegnus, within which lay (so the Ceremony of Initiation supposed) the Body of our Father Christian Rosen Creutz, to be discovered by the Brethren with the Postulant as said in the Book called Fama Fraternitatis.

There are three Officers, and they repeat the Analysis of the Word as follows:—

Chief. Let us analyse the Key Word—I.
2nd. N.
3rd. R.
All. I.
Chief. Yod. י
2nd. Nun. נ
3rd. Resh. ר
All. Yod. י
Chief. Virgo (♍) Isis, Mighty Mother.
2nd. Scorpio (♏) Apophis, Destroyer.
3rd. Sol (☉) Osiris, slain and risen.
All. Isis, Apophis, Osiris, IAO.

All spread Arms as if on a Cross, and say:—

The Sign of Osiris slain!

Chief bows his Head to the Left, raises his Right Arm, and lowers his Left keeping the Elbow at right Angles, thus forming the Letter L (also the Swastika).

The Sign of the Mourning of Isis.

2nd. With erect Head, raises his Arms to form a V (but really to form the triple Tongue of Flame, the Spirit), and says:—

The Sign of Apophis and Typhon.

3rd. Bows his Head and crosses his Arms on his Breast (to form the Pentagram).

The Sign of Osiris risen.

All give the Sign of the Cross, and say:—

L.V.X.

Then the Sign of Osiris risen, and say:—

Lux, the Light of the Cross.

This Formula, on which one may meditate for Years without exhausting its wonderful Harmonies, gives an excellent Idea of the Way in which Qabalistic Analysis is conducted.

First, the Letters have been written in Hebrew Characters.

Then the Attributions of them to the Zodiac and to Planets are substituted, and the Names of Egyptian Gods belonging to these are invoked.

The Christian Idea of I.N.R.I. is confirmed by these, while their Initials form the sacred Word of the Gnostics. That is, IAO. From the Character of the Deities and their Functions are deduced their Signs, and these are found to signal (as it were) the Word Lux (אור), which itself is contained in the Cross.

A careful Study of these Ideas, and of the Table of Correspondences, which one of our English Brethren is making, will enable him to discover a very great Deal of Matter for Thought in these Poems which an untutored Person would pass by.

To return to the general Dogma of the Qabalists.

The Figure of Minutum Mundum will show how they suppose one Quality to proceed from the last, first in the pure God-World Atziluth, then in the Angel-World Briah, and so on down to the Demon-Worlds, which are however not thus organised. They are rather Material that was shed off in the Course of Evolution, like the Sloughs of a Serpent, from which comes their Name of Shells, or Husks.

Apart from silly Questions as to whether the Order of the Emanations is confirmed by Palæontology, a Question it is quite impertinent to discuss, there is no Doubt that the Sephiroth are types of Evolution as opposed to Catastrophe and Creation.

The great Charge against this Philosophy is founded on its alleged Affinities with Scholastic Realism. But the Charge is not very true. No Doubt but they did suppose vast Storehouses of "Things of one Kind" from which, pure or mingled, all other Things did proceed.

Since ג, a Camel, refers to the Moon, they did say that a Camel and the Moon were sympathetic, and came, that Part of them, from a common Principle: and that a Camel being yellow brown, it partook of the Earth Nature, to which that Colour is given.

Thence they said that by taking all the Natures involved, and by blending them in the just Proportions, one might have a Camel.

But this is no more than is said by the Upholders of the Atomic Theory.

They have their Storehouses of Carbon, Oxygen, and such (not in one Place, but no more is Geburah in one Place), and what is Organic Chemistry but the Production of useful Compounds whose Nature is deduced absolutely from theoretical Considerations long before it is ever produced in the Laboratory?

The difference, you will say, is that the Qabalists maintain a Mind of each Kind behind each Class of Things of one Kind; but so did Berkeley, and his Argument in that Respect is, as the great Huxley showed, irrefragable. For by the Universe I mean the Sensible; any other is Not to be Known; and the Sensible is dependent upon Mind. Nay, though the Sensible is said to be an Argument of an Universe Insensible, the latter becomes sensible to Mind as soon as the Argument is accepted, and disappears with its Rejection.

Nor is the Qabalah dependent upon its Realism, and its Application to the Works magical—but I am defending a Philosophy which I was asked to describe, and this is not lawful.

A great Deal may be learned from the Translation of the Zohar by S. Liddell Macgregor Mathers, and his Introduction thereto, though for those who have Latin and some acquaintance with Hebrew it is better to study the Kabbala Denudata of Knorr von Rosenroth, in Despite of the heavy Price; for the Translator has distorted the Text and its Comment to suit his belief in a supreme Personal God, and in that degraded Form of the Doctrine of Feminism which is so popular with the Emasculate.

The Sephiroth are grouped in various Ways. There is a Superior Triad or Trinity; a Hexad; and Malkuth: the Crown, the Father, and the Mother; the Son or King; and the Bride.

Also, a Division into seven Palaces, seven Planes, three Pillars or Columns, and the like.

The Flashing Sword follows the Course of the Numbers; and the Serpent Nechushtan or of Wisdom crawls up the Paths which join them upon the Tree of Life, namely the Letters.

It is important to explain the Position of Daath or Knowledge upon the Tree. It is called the Child of Chokmah and Binah, but it hath no Place. But it is really the Apex of a Pyramid of which the three first Numbers form the Base.

Now the Tree, or Minutum Mundum, is a Figure in a Plane of a solid Universe. Daath, being above the Plane, is therefore a Figure of a Force in four Dimensions, and thus it is the Object of the Magnum Opus. The three Paths which connect it with the First Trinity are the three lost Letters or Fathers of the Hebrew Alphabet.

In Daath is said to be the Head of the great Serpent Nechesh or Leviathan, called Evil to conceal its Holiness. (נחש = 358 = משיח, the Messiah or Redeemer, and לויתן = 496 = מלכות, the Bride.) It is identical with the Kundalini of the Hindu Philosophy, the Kwan-se-on of the Mongolian Peoples, and means the magical Force in Man, which is the sexual Force applied to the Brain, Heart, and other Organs, and redeemeth him.

The gradual Disclosure of these magical Secrets to the Poet may be traced in these Volumes, which it has been my Privilege to be asked to explain. It has been impossible to do more than place in the Hands of any intelligent Person the Keys which will permit him to unlock the many Beautiful Chambers of Holiness in these Palaces and Gardens of Beauty and Pleasure.

Of the results of the method we possess one flawless gem, already printed in the EQUINOX (Vol. II. pp. 163-185), "A Note on Genesis" by V. H. Fra. I.A.

From this pleasant, orthodox, and-so-they-all-lived-happy-ever-after view let us turn for a moment to the critical aspect. Let us demolish in turn the qabalistic methods of exegesis; and then, if we can, discover a true basis upon which to erect an abiding Temple of Truth.

1. Gematria.

The number 777 affords a good example of the legitimate and illegitimate deductions to be drawn. It represents the sentence AChTh RVCh ALHIM ChIIM, "One is the Spirit of the Living God," and also OLAHM H-QLPVTh, "The world of the Shells (excrements—the demon-world)."

Now it is wrong to say that this idea of the unity of the divine spirit is identical with this idea of the muddle of chaos —unless in that exalted grade in which "The One is the Many." But the compiler of Liber 777 was a great Qabalist when he thus entitled his book; for he meant to imply, "One is the Spirit of the Living God," *i.e.* I have in this book unified all the diverse symbols of the world; and also, "the world of shells," *i.e.* this book is full of mere dead symbols; do not mistake them for the living Truth. Further, he had an academic reason for his choice of a number; for the tabulation of the book is from Kether to Malkuth, the course of the Flaming Sword; and if this sword be drawn upon the Tree of Life, the numeration of the Paths over which it passes (taking ג, 3, as the non-existent path from Binah to Chesed, since it connects Macroprosopus and Microprosopus) is 777. [See Diagrams 2 and 12.]

To take another example, it is no mere coincidence that 463, the Staff of Moses, is ת, ס, ג, the paths of the Middle Pillar; no mere coincidence that 26, יהוה, is 1+6+9+10, the Sephiroth of the Middle Pillar. But ought we not to have some supreme Name for 489, their sum, the Middle Pillar perfect? Yet the Sepher Sephiroth is silent. (We find only 489 = MShLM GMVL, the avenger. Ed.)

Again, 111 is Aleph, the Unity, but also APL, thick Darkness, and ASN, Sudden Death. This can only be interpreted as meaning the annihilation of the individual in the Unity, and the Darkness which is the Threshold of the Unity; in other words, one must be an expert in Samadhi before this simple Gematria has any proper meaning. How, then, can it serve the student in his research? The uninitiated would expect Life and Light in the One; only by experience can he know that to man the Godhead must be expressed by those things which most he fears.

We here purposely avoid dwelling on the mere silliness of many Gematria correspondences, *e.g.*, the equality of the Qliphoth of one sign with the Intelligence of another. Such misses are more frequent than such hits as AChD, Unity, 13 = AHBH, Love, 13.

The argument is an argument in a circle. "Only an adept can understand the Qabalah," just as (in Buddhism) Sakyamuni said, "Only an Arahat can understand the Dhamma."

In this light, indeed, the Qabalah seems little more than a convenient language for recording experience.

We may mention in passing that Frater P. never acquiesced in the obvious "cook" of arguing: $x = y + 1 \therefore x = y$, by assuming that x should add one to itself "for the concealed unity." Why shouldn't y have a little concealed unity of its own?

That this method should ever have been accepted by any Qabalist argues a bankruptcy of ingenuity beyond belief. In all conscience, it is easy enough to fake identities by less obviously card-sharping methods!

2. Notariqon.

The absurdity of this method needs little indication. The most unsophisticated can draw pity and amusement from Mr Mathers' Jew, converted by the Notariqons of "Berashith." True, F.I.A.T. is Flatus, Ignis, Aqua, Terra; showing the Creator as Tetragrammaton, the synthesis of the four elements;

showing the Eternal Fiat as the equilibrated powers of Nature. But what forbids Fecit Ignavus Animam Terrae, or any other convenient blasphemy, such as Buddha would applaud?

Why not take our converted Jew and restore him to the Ghetto with Be'n, Ruach, Ab, Sheol!—IHVH, Thora? Why not take the sacred 'Ιχθυς of the Christian who thought it meant 'Ιησους Χριστος Θεου 'Υιος Σωτηρ and make him a pagan with "'Ισιδος Χαρις Θησαυρος 'Υιων Σοφιας"?

Why not argue that Christ in cursing the fig, F.I.G., wished to attack Kant's dogmas of Freewill, Immortality, God?

3. Temurah.

Here again the multiplicity of our methods makes our method too pliable to be reliable. Should we argue that BBL = ShShK (620) by the method of Athbash, and that therefore BBL symbolises Kether (620)? Why, BBL is confusion, the very opposite of Kether.

Why Athbash? Why not Abshath? or Agrath? or any other of the possible combinations?

About the only useful Temurah is Aiq Bkr, given above. In this we do find a suggestive reasoning. For example, we find it in the attribution of ALHIM to the pentagram which gives π. [See EQUINOX, No. II. p. 184.] Here we write Elohim, the creative deities, round a pentagram, and read it reverse beginning with ל, ♎, the letter of equilibrium, and obtain an approximation to π 3.1415 (good enough for the benighted Hebrews), as if thereby the finite square of creation was assimilated to the infinite circle of the Creator.

Yes: but why should not Berashith 2, 2, 1, 3, 1, 4, give, say, *e*? The only answer is, that if you screw it round long enough, it perhaps will!

The Rational Table of Tziruph should, we agree with Fra. P., be left to the Rationalist Press Association, and we may present the Irregular Table of Commutations to Irregular Masons.

4. To the less important methods we may apply the same criticism.

We may glance in passing at the Yetziratic, Tarot, and significatory methods of investigating any word. But though Frater P. was expert enough in these methods they are hardly pertinent to the pure numerical Qabalah, and we therefore deal gently with them. The attributions are given in 777. Thus א in the Yetziratic world is "Air," by Tarot "the Fool," and by signification "an ox." Thus we have the famous I.N.R.I. = י. נ. ר. י = ♍, ♏, ☉, ♍; the Virgin, the Evil Serpent, the Sun, suggesting the story of Genesis ii. and of the Gospel. The initials of the Egyptian names Isis, Apophis, Osiris, which correspond, give in their turn the Ineffable Name IAO; thus we say that the Ineffable is concealed in and revealed by the Birth, Death, and Resurrection of Christ; and further the Signs of Mourning of the Mother, Triumph of the Destroyer, and Rising of the Son, give by shape the letters L.U.X., Lux, which letters are (again) concealed in and revealed by the Cross—L V X the Light of the Cross. Further examples will be found in "A Note on Genesis." One of the most famous is the Mene, Tekel, Upharsin of Daniel, the imaginary prophet who lived under Belshazzar the imaginary king.

MNA. The Hanged Man, Death, the Fool = "Sacrificed to Death by thy Folly."

ThKL. The Universe, the Wheel of Fortune, Justice = "Thy kingdom's fortune is in the Balance."

PRSh. The Blasted Tower, the Sun, the Last Judgment = "Ruined is thy glory, and finished."

But we cannot help thinking that this exegesis must have been very hard work.

We could more easily read

MNA. To sacrifice to death is folly.

ThKL. Thy kingdom shall be fortunate, for it is just.

PRSh. The Tower of thy glory shall endure until the Last Day.

There! that didn't take two minutes; and Belshazzar would have exalted us above Daniel.

Similarly AL, God, may be interpreted, "His folly is justice," as it is written: "The wisdom of this world is foolishness with God."

Or, by Yetzirah: "The air is His balance," as it is written: "God made the firmament, and divided the waters which were under the firmament from the waters which were above the firmament."

Or, by meaning: "The ox and the goad," *i.e.*, "He is both matter and motion."

We here append a sketch MS. by Frater P., giving his explanation by Tarot, etc., of the letters of the alphabet spelt in full.

Mystic Readings of the Letters of the Alphabet

(*See* Tarot Cards, *and meditate*)

ALP. Folly's Doom is Ruin.

BITh. The Juggler with the Secret of the Universe.

GML. The Holy Guardian Angel is attained by Self-Sacrifice and Equilibrium.

DLTh. The Gate of the Equilibrium of the Universe. (Note D, the highest reciprocal path.)
HH. The Mother is the Daughter; and the Daughter is the Mother.
VV. The Son is (but) the Son. (These two letters show the true doctrine of Initiation as given in Liber 418; opposed to Protestant Exotericism.)
ZIN. The answer of the Oracles is always Death.
ChITh. The Chariot of the Secret of the Universe.
TITh. She who rules the Secret Force of the Universe.
IVD. The Secret of the Gate of Initiation.
KP. In the Whirlings is War.
LMD. By Equilibrium and Self-Sacrifice, the Gate!
MIM. The Secret is hidden between the Waters that are above and the Waters that are beneath. (Symbol, the Ark containing the secret of Life borne upon the Bosom of the Deluge beneath the Clouds.)
NVN. Initiation is guarded on both sides by death.
SMK. Self-control and Self-sacrifice govern the Wheel.
OIN. The Secret of Generation is Death.
PH. The Fortress of the Most High. (Note P, the lowest reciprocal path).
TzDI. In the Star is the Gate of the Sanctuary.
QVP. Illusionary is the Initiation of Disorder.
RISh. In the Sun (Osiris) is the Secret of the Spirit.
ShIN. Resurrection is hidden in Death.
ThV. The Universe is the Hexagram.

(Other meanings suit other planes and other grades.)

Truly there is no end to this wondrous science; and when the sceptic sneers, "With all these methods one ought to be able to make everything out of nothing," the Qabalist smiles back the sublime retort, "With these methods One did make everything out of nothing."

Besides these, there is still one more method—a method of some little importance to students of the Siphra Dzenioutha, namely, the analogies drawn from the shapes of letters;

these are often interesting enough. א, for example, is a ו between י and י, making 26. Thus יהוה 26 = א, 1. Therefore Jehovah is One. But it would be as pertinent to continue 26 = 2 × 13, and 13 = Achad = 1, and therefore Jehovah is Two.

This then is an absurdity. Yes; but it is also an arcanum!

How wonderful is the Qabalah! How great is its security from the profane; how splendid its secrets to the initiate!

Verily and Amen! yet here we are at the old dilemma, that one must know Truth before one can rely upon the Qabalah to show Truth.

Like the immortal burglar:

> "Bill wouldn't hurt a baby—he's a pal as you can trust,
> He's all right when yer know 'im; but yer've got to know 'im fust."

So those who have committed themselves to academic study of its mysteries have found but a dry stick: those who have understood (favoured of God!) have found therein Aaron's rod that budded, the Staff of Life itself, yea, the venerable Lingam of Mahasiva!

It is for us to trace the researches of Frater P. in the Qabalah, to show how from this storehouse of child's puzzles, of contradictions and incongruities, of paradoxes and trivialities, he discovered the very canon of Truth, the authentic key of the Temple, the Word of that mighty Combination which unlocks the Treasure-Chamber of the King.

And this following is the Manuscript which he has left for our instruction.

AN ESSAY UPON NUMBER

(May the Holy One mitigate His severities toward His servant in respect of the haste wherewith this essay hath been composed !

When I travelled with the venerable Iehi Aour in search of Truth, we encountered a certain wise and holy man, Shri Parananda. Children ! said he, for two years must ye study with me before ye fully comprehend our Law.

"Venerable Sir !" answered Frater I.A., "the first verse of *Our* Law contains but seven words. For seven years did I study that verse by day and by night ; and at the end of that time did I presume—may the Dweller of Eternity pardon me !—to write a monograph upon the first word of those seven words."

"Venerable Sir !" quoth I : "that First Word of our law contains but six letters. For six years did I study that word by day and by night ; and at the end of that time did I not dare to utter the first letter of those six letters."

Thus humbling myself did I abash both the holy Yogi and my venerable Frater I. A. But alas ! Tetragrammaton ! Alas ! Adonai ! the hour of my silence is past. May the hour of my silence return ! Amen.)

PART I

THE UNIVERSE AS IT IS

Section I

0. The Negative—the Infinite—the Circle, or the Point.

1. The Unity—the Positive—the Finite—the Line, derived from 0 by extension. The divine Being.

2. The Dyad—the Superficies, derived from 1 by reflection $\frac{1}{1}$, or by revolution of the line around its end. The Demiurge. The divine Will.

3. The Triad, the Solid, derived from 1 and 2 by addition. Matter. The divine Intelligence.

4. The Quaternary, the solid existing in Time, matter as we know it. Derived from 2 by multiplication. The divine Repose.

5. The Quinary, Force or Motion. The interplay of the divine Will with matter. Derived from 2 and 3 by addition.

6. The Senary, Mind. Derived from 2 and 3 by multiplication.

7. The Septenary, Desire. Derived from 3 and 4 by addition. (There is

however a secondary attribution of 7, making it the holiest and most perfect of the numbers.)

8. The Ogdoad, Intellect (also Change in Stability). Derived from 2 and 3 by multiplication, $8=2^3$.

9. The Ennead, Stability in Change. Derived from 2 and 3 by multiplication, $9=3^2$.

(Note all numbers divisible by nine are still so divisible, however the order of the figures is shifted.)

10. The Decad, the divine End. Represents the 1 returning to the 0. Derived from $1+2+3+4$.

11. The Hendecad, the accursed shells, that only exist without the divine Tree. $1+1=2$, in its evil sense of not being 1.

Section II

0. The Cosmic Egg.
1. The Self of Deity, beyond Fatherhood and Motherhood.
2. The Father.
3. The Mother.
4. The Father made flesh—authoritative and paternal.
5. The Mother made flesh—fierce and active.
6. The Son—partaking of all these natures.
7. The Mother degraded to mere animal emotion.
8. The Father degraded to mere animal reason.
9. The Son degraded to mere animal life.
10. The Daughter, fallen and touching with her hands the shells.

It will be noticed that this order represents creation as progressive degeneration—which we are compelled to think of as evil. In the human organism the same arrangement will be noticed.

Section III

0. The Pleroma of which our individuality is the monad: the "All-Self."

1. The Self—the divine Ego of which man is rarely conscious.

2. The Ego; that which thinks "I"—a falsehood, because to think "I" is to deny "not-I" and thus to create the Dyad.

3. The Soul; since 3 reconciles 2 and 1, here are placed the aspirations to divinity. It is also the receptive as 2 is the assertive self.

4-9. The Intellectual Self, with its branches:

   4. Memory.

5. Will.
6. Imagination.
7. Desire.
8. Reason.
9. Animal being.

6. The Conscious Self of the Normal Man: thinking itself free, and really the toy of its surroundings.

9. The Unconscious Self of the Normal Man. Reflex actions, circulation, breathing, digestion, etc., all pertain here.

10. The illusory physical envelope; the scaffolding of the building.

SECTION IV

Having compared these attributions with those to be found in 777, studied them, assimilated them so thoroughly that it is natural and needs no effort to think "Binah, Mother, Great Sea, Throne, Saturn, Black, Myrrh, Sorrow, Intelligence, etc. etc. etc.," in a flash whenever the number 3 is mentioned or seen, we may profitably proceed to go through the most important of the higher numbers. For this purpose I have removed myself from books of reference; only those things which have become fixed in my mind (from their importance) deserve place in the simplicity of this essay.

12. HVA, "He," a title of Kether, identifying Kether with the Zodiac, the "home of 12 stars" and their correspondences. See 777.

13. AChD, Unity, and AHBH Love. A scale of unity; thus $13 \times 1 = 1$; $26 = 13 \times 2 = 2$; $91 = 13 \times 7 = 7$; so that we may find in 26 and 91 elaborations of the Dyad and the Septenary respectively.

14. An "elaboration" of 5 $(1+4=5)$, Force; a "concentration" of 86 $(8+6=14)$ Elohim, the 5 elements.

15. IH, Jah, one of the ineffable names; the Father and Mother united. Mystic number of Geburah : $1+2+3+4+5$.

17. The number of squares in the Swastika, which by shape is Aleph, א. Hence 17 recalls 1. Also IAV, IAO, the triune Father. See 32 and 358.

18. ChI, Life. An "elaboration" of 9.

20. IVD, Yod, the letter of the Father.

21. AHIH, existence, a title of Kether, Note $3 \times 7 = 21$. Also IHV, the first 3 (active) letters of IHVH. Mystic number of Tiphereth.

22. The number of letters in the Hebrew Alphabet; and of the paths on the Tree. Hence suggests completion of imperfection. Finality, and fatal finality. Note $2 \times 11 = 22$, the accursed Dyad at play with the Shells.

24. Number of the Elders; and $= 72 \div 3$. 72 is the "divided Name."

26. IHVH. Jehovah, as the Dyad expanded, the jealous and terrible God, the lesser Countenance. The God of Nature, fecund, cruel, beautiful, relentless.

28. Mystic number of Netzach, KCh, "Power."

31. LA, "not"; and AL, "God." In this Part I. ("Nature as it is") the number is rather forbidding. For AL is the God-name of Chesed, mercy; and so the number seems to deny that Name.

32. Number of Sephiroth and Paths, $10+22$. Hence is completion of perfection. Finality: things as they are in their totality. AHIHVH, the combined AHIH and IHVH, Macroprosopus and Microprosopus, is here. If we suppose the 3 female letters H to conceal the 3 mothers A, M, Sh, we obtain the number 358, Messiach, q.v. Note $32=2^5$, the divine Will extended through motion. $64=2^6$, will be the perfect number of matter, for it is 8, the first cube, squared. So we find it a Mercurial number, as if the solidity of matter was in truth eternal change.

35. AGLA, a name of God = Ateh Gibor Le Olahm Adonai. "To Thee be the Power unto the Ages, O my Lord!" $35=5\times7$. $7=$Divinity, $5=$Power.

36. A Solar Number. ALH. Otherwise unimportant, but is the mystic number of Mercury.

37. IChIDH. The highest principle of the Soul, attributed to Kether. Note $37=111\div3$.

38. Note $38\times11=418$ q.v. in Part II.

39. IHVH AChD, Jehovah is one. $39=13\times3$. This is then the affirmation of the aspiring soul.

40. A "dead" number of fixed law, 4×10, Tetragrammaton, the lesser countenance immutable in the heaviness of Malkuth.

41. AM, the Mother, unfertilised and unenlightened.

42. AMA, the Mother, still dark. Here are the 42 judges of the dead in Amennti, and here is the 42-fold name of the Creative God. See Liber 418.

44. DM, blood. See Part II. Here $4\times11=$the corruption of the created world.

45. MH, a secret title of Yetzirah, the Formative World. ADM, Adam, man, the species (not "the first man"). A is Air, the divine breath which stirs DM, blood, into being.

49. A number useful in the calculations of Dr Dee, and a mystic number of Venus.

50. The number of the Gates of Binah, whose name is Death (50=נ =by Tarot, "Death").

51. AN, pain. NA, failure. ADVM, Edom, the country of the demon kings. There is much in the Qabalah about these kings and their dukes; it never meant much to me, somehow. But 51 is 1 short of 52.

52. AIMA, the fertilised Mother, the Phallus (י) thrust into AMA. Also BN, the Son. Note $52=13\times4$, 4 being Mercy and the influence of the Father.

60. Samekh, which in full spells $60\times2=120$ (q.v.), just as Yod, 10, in full spells $10\times2=20$. In general, the tens are "solidifications" of the ideas of the units which they multiply. Thus 50 is Death, the Force of Change in its final and most earthy aspect. Samekh is "Temperance" in the Tarot: the 6 has little evil possible to it; the worst name one can call 60 is "restriction."

61. AIN, the Negative. ANI, Ego. A number rather like 31, q.v.

64. DIN and DNI, intelligences (the twins) of Mercury. See also 32.

65. ADNI. In Roman characters LXV=LVX, the redeeming light. See the $5^\circ=6^\circ$ ritual and "Konx om Pax." Note $65=13\times5$, the most spiritual form of force, just as 10×5 was its most material form. Note HS, "Keep silence!" and HIKL, the palace; as if it were said "Silence is the House of Adonai."

67. BINH the Great Mother. Note $6+7=13$, uniting the ideas of Binah and Kether. A number of the aspiration.

70. The Sanhedrin and the precepts of the Law. The Divine 7 in its most material aspect.

72. ChSD, Mercy. The number of the Shemhamphorasch, as if affirming God as merciful. For details of Shemhamphorasch, see 777 and other classical books of reference. Note especially I+IH+IHV+IHVH=72.

73. ChKMH, Wisdom. Also GML, Gimel, the path uniting Kether and Tiphereth. But Gimel, "the Priestess of the Silver Star," is the Female Hierophant, the Moon; and Chokmah is the Logos, or male initiator. See Liber 418 for much information on these points, though rather from the standpoint of Part II.

78. MZLA, the influence from Kether. The number of the cards of the Tarot, and of the the 13 paths of the Beard of Macroprosopus. Note $78=13\times6$. Also AIVAS, the messenger. See Part II.

80. The number of פ, the "lightning-struck Tower" of the Tarot. 8=Intellect, Mercury; its most material form is Ruin, as Intellect in the end is divided against itself.

81. A mystic number of the Moon.

84. A number chiefly important in Buddhism. $84=7\times12$.

85. PH, the letter Pé. $85=5\times17$: even the highest unity, if it move or energise, means War.

86. ALHIM. See "A Note on Genesis," EQUINOX, No. II.

90. Number of Tzaddi, a fishhook=Tanha, the clinging of man to life (9), the trap in which man is caught as a fish is caught by a hook. The most material aspect of animal life; its final doom decreed by its own lust. Also MIM, Water.

91. $91=7\times13$, the most spiritual form of the Septenary. AMN, Amen, the holiest title of God; the Amoun of the Egyptians. It equals IHVH ADNI (IAHDVNHI, interlaced), the eight-lettered name, thus linking the 7 to the 8. Note that AMN (reckoning N as final, 700) $=741=$ AMThSh, the letters of the elements; and is thus a form of Tetragrammaton, a form unveiled.

100. The number of ק, the perfect illusion, 10×10. Also כף, Kaph, the Wheel of Fortune. The identity is that of matter, fatality, change, illusion. It seems the Buddhist view of the Samsara-Çakkram.

106. NVN, Nun, a fish. The number of death. Death in the Tarot bears a cross-handled scythe; hence the Fish as the symbol of the Redeemer. ΙΧΘΥΣ = Jesus Christ, Son of God, Saviour.

108. Chiefly interesting because $108=2\times2\times3\times3\times3=$ the square of 2 playing with the cube of 3. Hence the Buddhists hailed it with acclamation, and make their rosaries of this number of beads.

111. AChD HVA ALHIM, "He is One God."

ALP, Aleph, an ox, a thousand. The redeeming Bull. By shape the Swastika, and so the Lightning. "As the lightning lighteneth out of the East even unto the West, so shall be the coming of the Son of Man." An allusion to the descent of Shiva upon Shakti in Samahdi. The Roman A shows the same through the shape of the Pentagram, which it imitates.

ASN, ruin, destruction, sudden death. *Scil.*, of the personality in Samadhi.

APL, thick darkness. *Cf.* St John of the Cross, who describes these phenomena in great detail.

AOM, the Hindu Aum or Om.

MHVLL, mad—the destruction of Reason by Illumination.

OVLH, a holocaust. *Cf.* ASN.

PLA, the Hidden Wonder, a title of Kether.

114. DMO, a tear. The age of Christian Rosencreutz.

120. SMK, Samech, a prop. Also MVSDI, basis, foundation. $120=1\times2\times3\times4\times5$, and is thus a synthesis of the power of the pentagram. [Also $1+2+\ldots+15=120$.] Hence its importance in the $5=6$ ritual, q.v. *supra* EQUINOX, No. III. I however disagree in part; it seems to me to symbolise a lesser redemption than that associated with Tiphereth. Compare at least the numbers 0.12 and 210 in Liber Legis and Liber 418, and extol their superiority. For while the first is the sublime formula of the infinite surging into finity, and the latter the supreme rolling-up of finity into infinity, the 120 can symbolise at the best a sort of intermediate condition of stability. For how can one proceed from the 2 to the 0? 120 is also ON, a very important name of God.

124. ODN, Eden.

131. SMAL, Satan so-called, but really only Samael, the accuser of the

brethren, unpopular with the Rabbis because their consciences were not clear. Samael fulfils a most useful function; he is scepticism, which accuses intellectually; conscience, which accuses morally; and even that spiritual accuser upon the Threshold, without whom the Sanctuary might be profaned. We must defeat him, it is true; but how should we abuse and blame him, without abuse and blame of Him that set him there?

136. A mystic number of Jupiter; the sum of the first 16 natural numbers.

144. A square and therefore a materialisation of the number 12. Hence the numbers in the Apocalpyse. 144,000 only means 12 (the perfect number in the Zodiac or houses of heaven and tribes of Israel) × 12, *i.e.* settled × 1000, *i.e.* on the grand scale.

148. MAZNIM, Scales of Justice.

156. BABALON. See Liber 418. This number is chiefly important for Part II. It is of no account in the orthodox dogmatic Qabalah. Yet it is 12 × 13, the most spiritual form, 13, of the most perfect number, 12, HVA. [It is TZIVN, Zion, the City of the Pyramids.—Ed.]

175. A mystic number of Venus.

203. ABR, initials of AB, BN, RVCh, the Trinity.

206. DBR, Speech, "the Word of Power."

207. AVR, Light. Contrast with AVB, 9, the astral light, and AVD, 11, the Magical Light. Aub is an illusory thing of witchcraft (*cf.* Obi, Obeah); Aud is almost = the Kundalini force ("Odic" force). This illustrates well the difference between the sluggish, viscous 9, and the keen, ecstastic 11.

210. Pertains to Part II. See Liber 418.

214. RVCh, the air, the mind.

220. Pertains to Part II. The number of verses in Liber Legis.

231. The sum of the first 22 numbers, 0 to 21; the sum of the Key-Numbers of the Tarot cards; hence an extension of the idea of 22, q.v.

270. I.N.R.I. See 5 = 6 ritual.

280. The sum of the "five letters of severity," those which have a final form—Kaph, Mem, Nun, Pe, Tzaddi. Also the number of the squares on the sides of the Vault 7 × 40; see 5 = 6 ritual. Also RP = terror.

300. The letter ש, meaning "tooth," and suggesting by its shape a triple flame. Refers Yetziratically to fire, and is symbolic of the Holy Spirit, RVCh ALHIM = 300. Hence the letter of the Spirit. Descending into the midst of IHVH, the four inferior elements, we get IHShVH Jeheshua, the Saviour, symbolised by the Pentagram.

301. ASH, Fire.

314. ShDI, the Almighty, a name of God attributed to Yesod.

325. A mystic number of Mars. BRTzBAL, the spirit of Mars, and GRAPIAL, the intelligence of Mars.

326. IHShVH, Jesus—see 300.

333. ChVRVNZVN, see Liber 418, 10th Aethyr. It is surprising that this large scale 3 should be so terrible a symbol of dispersion. There is doubtless a venerable arcanum here connoted, possibly the evil of Matter summó. 333 = 37 × 9 the accurséd.

340. ShM—the Name.

341. The sum of the "3 mothers," Aleph, Mem, and Shin.

345. MShH, Moses. Note that by transposition we have 543, AHIH AShR AHIH, "Existence is Existence," "I am that I am," a sublime title of Kether. Moses is therefore regarded as the representative of this particular manifestation of deity, who declared himself under this special name.

358. See 32. MShICh, Messiah, and NChSh, the serpent of Genesis. The dogma is that the head of the serpent (N) is "bruised," being replaced by M, the letter of Sacrifice, and God, the letter alike of virginity (י = ♍) and of original deity (י = the foundation or type of all the letters). Thus the word may be read:

"The Sacrifice of the Virgin-born Divine One triumphant (ח, the Chariot) through the Spirit," while NChSh reads "Death entering the (realm of the) Spirit."

But the conception of the Serpent as the Redeemer is truer. See my explanation of 5 = 6 ritual (EQUINOX, No. III.).

361. ADNI HARTz, the Lord of the Earth. Note 361 denotes the 3 Supernals, the 6 members of Ruach, and Malkuth. This name of God therefore embraces all the 10 Sephiroth.

365. An important number, though not in the pure Qabalah. See "The Canon." ΜΕΙΘΡΑΣ and ΑΒΡΑΞΑΣ in Greek.

370. Really more important for Part II. OSh, Creation. The Sabbatic Goat in his highest aspect. This shows the whole of Creation as matter and spirit. The material 3, the spiritual 7, and all cancelling to Zero. Also ShLM = peace.

400. The letter ת, "The Universe." It is the square of 20, "The Wheel of Fortune," and shows the Universe therefore as the Sphere of Fortune—the Samsara-Cakkram, where Karma, which fools call chance, rules.

400 is the total number of the Sephiroth, each of the 10 containing 10 in itself and being repeated in the 4 worlds of Atziluth, Briah, Yetzirah, and Assiah. These four worlds are themselves attributed to IHVH, which is therefore not the name of a tribal fetish, but the formula of a system.

401. ATh, "the" emphatic, meaning "essence of," for A and Th are first and last letters of the Hebrew Alphabet, as A and Ω are of the Greek, and A and Z of the Latin. Hence the Word Azoth, not to be confused with Azote

(lifeless, azotos), the old name for nitrogen. Azoth means the sum and essence of all, conceived as One.

406. ThV, the letter Tau (see 400), also AThH, "Thou." Note that AHA (7), the divine name of Venus (7), gives the initials of Ani, Hua, Ateh—I, He, Thou; three different aspects of a deity worshipped in three persons and in three ways: viz. (1) with averted face; (2) with prostration; (3) with identification.

418. Pertains principally to Part II., q.v.

419. TITh, the letter Teth.

434. DLTh, the letter Daleth.

440. ThLI, the great dragon.

441. AMTh, Truth. Note 441 = 21 × 21. 21 is AHIH, the God of Kether, whose Will is Truth.

450. ThN, the great dragon.

463. MTH HShQD, Moses' Wand, a rod of Almond. 3+60+400, the paths of the middle pillar.

474. DVTh, Knowledge, the Sephira that is not a Sephira. In one aspect the child of Chokmah and Binah; in another the Eighth Head of the Stooping Dragon, raised up when the Tree of Life was shattered, and Macroposopus set cherubim against Microposopus. See 4=7 ritual *supra*. Also, and very specially, Liber 418. It is the demon that purely intellectual or rational religions take as their God. The special danger of Hinayana Buddhism.

480. LILITh, the demon-queen of Malkuth.

543. AHIH AShR AHIH, "I am that I am."

666. Last of the mystic numbers of the sun. SVRTh, the spirit of Sol. Also OMMV SThN, Ommo Satan, the Satanic Trinity of Typhon, Apophis, and Besz; also ShM IHShVH, the name of Jesus. The names of Nero, Napoleon, W. E. Gladstone, and any person that you may happen to dislike, add up to this number. In reality it is the final extension of the number 6, both because 6 × 111 (ALPh = 111 = 1) = 6 and because the Sun, whose greatest number it is, is 6.

(I here interpolate a note on the "mystic numbers" of the planets. The first is that of the planet itself, *e.g.* Saturn, 3. The second is that of the number of squares in the square of the planet, *e.g.* Saturn 9. The third is that of the figures in each line of the "magic square" of the planet, *e.g.* Saturn 15. A 'magic square" is one in which each file, rank, and diagonal add to the same number, *e.g.* Saturn is 816, 357, 492, each square being filled in with the numbers from 1 upwards.

The last of the Magic numbers is the sum of the whole of the figures in the square, *e.g.* Saturn 45. The complete list is thus:

Saturn 3, 9, 15, 45.
Jupiter 4, 16, 34, 136.

Mars 5, 25, 65, 325.
Sol 6, 36, 111, 666.
Venus 7, 49, 175, 1225.
Mercury 8, 64, 260, 2080.
Luna 9, 81, 369, 3321.

Generally speaking, the first number gives a divine name, the second an archangelic or angelic name, the third a name pertaining to the Formative world, the fourth a name of a "spirit" or "blind force." For example, Mercury has AZ and DD (love) for 8, DIN and DNI for 64, TIRIAL for 260, and ThPThRThRTh for 2080. But in the earlier numbers this is not so well carried out. 136 is both IVPhIL, the Intelligence of Jupiter, and HSMAL, the Spirit.

The "mystic numbers" of the Sephiroth are simply the sums of the numbers from 1 to their own numbers.

Thus (1) Kether = 1.
(2) Chokmah = 1 + 2 = 3.
(3) Binah = 1 + 2 + 3 = 6.
(4) Chesed = 1 + 2 + 3 + 4 = 10.
(5) Geburah = 1 + 2 + 3 + 4 + 5 = 15.
(6) Tiphereth = 1 + 2 + 3 + 4 + 5 + 6 = 21.
(7) Netzach = 1 + 2 + 3 + 4 + 5 + 6 + 7 = 28.
(8) Hod = 1 + 2 + 3 + 4 + 5 + 6 + 7 + 8 = 36.
(9) Yesod = 1 + 2 + 3 + 4 + 5 + 6 + 7 + 8 + 9 = 45.
(10) Malkuth = 1 + 2 + 3 + 4 + 5 + 6 + 7 + 8 + 9 + 10 = 55.

The most important attributions of 666, however, pertain to the second part, q. v.

671. ThORA the Law, ThROA the Gate, AThOR the Lady of the Path of Daleth, ROThA the Wheel. Also ALPH, DLTh, NUN, IVD, Adonai (see 65) spelt in full.

This important number marks the identity of the Augoeides with the Way itself (" I am the Way, the Truth, and the Life ") and shows the Taro as a key; and that the Law itself is nothing else than this. For this reason the outer College of the A∴ A∴ is crowned by this "knowledge and conversation of the Holy Guardian Angel."

This number too is that of the Ritual of Neophyte. See Liber XIII.

741. AMThSh, the four letters of the elements. AMN, counting the N final as 700, the supreme Name of the Concealed One. The dogma is that the Highest is but the Four Elements; that there is nothing beyond these, beyond Tetragrammaton. This dogma is most admirably portrayed by Lord Dunsany in a tale called "The Wanderings of Shaun."

777. *Vide supra.*

800. QShTh, the Rainbow. The Promise of Redemption (8)—8 as Mercury, Intellect, the Ruach, Microprosopus, the Redeeming Son—in its most material form.

811. IAΩ (Greek numeration).

888. Jesus (Greek numeration).

913. BRAShITh, the Beginning. See "A Note on Genesis." This list * will enable the student to follow most of the arguments of the dogmatic Qabalah. It is useful for him to go through the arguments by which one can prove that any given number is the supreme. It is the case, the many being but veils of the One; and the course of argument leads one to knowledge and worship of each number in turn. For example.

Thesis. The Number Nine is the highest and worthiest of the numbers.

Scholion α. "The number nine is sacred, and attains the summits of philosophy," Zoroaster.

Scholion β. Nine is the best symbol of the Unchangeable One, since by whatever number it is multiplied, the sum of the figures is always 9, *e.g.* 9 ×487 = 4383. 4+3+8+3 = 18. 1+8 = 9.

Scholion γ. 9 = ט, a serpent. And the Serpent is the Holy Uraeus, upon the crown of the Gods.

Scholion δ. 9 = IX = the Hermit of the Tarot, the Ancient One with Lamp (Giver of Light) and Staff (the Middle Pillar of the Sephiroth). This, too, is the same Ancient as in 0, Aleph.

"The Fool" and Aleph = 1.

Scholion ε. 9 = ISVD = 80 = P = Mars = 5 = ה =

the Mother = Binah = 3 { = G = GML = 73 = ChKMH =
= AB = The Father =
= (1+2) Mystic Number of Chokmah =

= Chokmah = 2 = B = the Magus = I = 1.

Scholion F. 9 = the Foundation of all things = the Foundation of the alphabet = Yod = 10 = Malkuth = Kether = 1.

Scholion ζ. 9 = IX = The Hermit = Yod = 10 = X = The Wheel of Fortune = K = 20 = XX = The Last Judgment = Sh = 300 = 30 = L = Justice = VIII = 8 = Ch = The Chariot = VII = 7 = Z = The Lovers = VI = 6 = V (Vau) = The Pope = V = 5 = H = The Emperor = IV = 4 = D = The Empress = III = 3 = G = The High Priestess = II = 2 = B = The Magus = I = 1 = A = The Fool = 0.

---

* The complete dictionary, begun by Fra. I. A., continued by Fra. P. and revised by Fra. A. e. G. and others, will shortly be published by authority of the A.·. A.·.

Scholion η. 9 = Luna = G = 3, etc., as before.

Scholion θ. $9 = \left\{ \begin{array}{l} \text{Indigo} \\ \text{Lead} \end{array} \right\} = \text{Saturn} = 3$, etc, as before.

There are many other lines of argument. This form of reasoning reminds one of the riddle "Why is a story like a ghost?" Answer. "A story's a tale; a tail's a brush; a brush is a broom; a brougham's a carriage; a carriage is a gig; a gig's a trap; a trap's a snare; a snare's a gin; gin's a spirit; and a spirit's a ghost."

But our identities are not thus false; meditation reveals their truth. Further, as I shall explain fully later, 9 is not equal to 1 for the neophyte. These equivalences are dogmatic, and only true by favour of Him in whom All is Truth. In practice each equivalence is a magical operation to be carried out by the aspirant.

PART II

THE UNIVERSE AS WE SEEK TO MAKE IT

In the first part we have seen all numbers as Veils of the One, emanations of and therefore corruptions of the One. It is the Universe as we know it, the static Universe.

Now the Aspirant to Magic is displeased with this state of things. He finds himself but a creature, the farthest removed from the Creator, a number so complex and involved that he can scarcely imagine, much less dare to hope for, its reduction to the One.

The numbers useful to him, therefore, will be those which are subversive of this state of sorrow. So the number 2 represents to him the Magus (the great Magician Mayan who has created the illusion of Maya) as seen in the 2nd Aethyr. And considering himself as the Ego who posits the Non-Ego (Fichte) he hates this Magus. It is only the beginner who regards this Magus as the Wonder-worker—as the thing he wants to be. For the adept such little consolation as he may win is rather to be found by regarding the Magus as B = Mercury = 8 = Ch = 418 = ABRAHADABRA, the great Word, the "Word of Double Power in the Voice of the Master" which unites the 5 and the 6, the Rose and the Cross, the Circle and the Square. And also B is the Path from Binah to Kether; but that is only important for him who is already in Binah, the "Master of the Temple."

He finds no satisfaction in contemplating the Tree of Life, and the orderly arrangement of the numbers; rather does he enjoy the Qabalah as a means of juggling with these numbers. He can leave nothing undisturbed; he is the Anarchist of Philosophy. He refuses to acquiesce in merely formal proofs of the Excellence of things, "He doeth all things well," "Were the world understood Ye would see it was good," "Whatever is, is right," and so on. To him, on the contrary, whatever is, is wrong. It is part of the painful duty of a Master of the Temple to understand everything. Only he can excuse the apparent cruelty and fatuity of things. He is of the supernals; he sees things from above; yet, having come from below, he can sympathise with all. And he does not expect the Neophyte to share his views. Indeed, they are not true to a Neophyte. The silliness of the New-Thought zanies in passionately affirming "I am healthy! I am opulent! I am well-dressed! I am happy," when in truth they are "poor and miserable and blind and naked," is not a philosophical but a practical silliness. Nothing exists, says the Magister Templi, but perfection. True; yet their consciousness is imperfect. Ergo, it does not exist. For the M.T. this is so: he has "cancelled out" the complexities of the mathematical expression called existence, and the answer is zero. But for the beginner his pain and another's joy do not balance; his pain hurts him, and his brother may go hang. The Magister Templi, too, understands why Zero must plunge through all finite numbers to express itself; why it must write itself as "n – n" instead of 0; what gain there is in such writing. And this understanding will be found expressed in Liber 418 (Episode of Chaos and His Daughter) and Liber Legis (i. 28-30).

But it must never be forgotten that everyone must begin at the beginning. And in the beginning the Aspirant is a rebel, even though he feel himself to be that most dangerous type of rebel, a King Dethroned.*

Hence he will worship any number which seems to him to promise to overturn the Tree of Life. He will even deny and blaspheme the One—whom, after all, it is his ambition to be—because of its simplicity and aloofness. He is tempted to "curse God and die."

Atheists are of three kinds.

1. The mere stupid man. (Often he is very clever, as Bolingbroke, Bradlaugh and Foote were clever.) He has found out one of the minor arcana, and hugs it and despises those who see more than himself, or who regard things from a different standpoint. Hence he is usually a bigot, intolerant even of tolerance.

2. The despairing wretch, who, having sought God everywhere, and failed to find Him, thinks everyone else is as blind as he is, and that if he has failed—he, the seeker after truth!—it is because there is no goal. In his cry there is

* And of course, if his revolt succeeds, he will acquiesce in order. The first condition of gaining a grade is to be dissatisfied with the one that you have. And so when you reach the end you find order as at first; but also that the law is that you must rebel to conquer.

pain, as with the stupid kind of atheist there is smugness and self-satisfaction. Both are diseased Egos.

3. The philosophical adept, who, knowing God, says "There is No God," meaning "God is Zero," as qabalistically He is. He holds atheism as a philosophical speculation as good as any other, and perhaps less likely to mislead mankind and do other practical damage than any other.

Him you may know by his equanimity, enthusiasm, and devotion. I again refer to Liber 418 for an explanation of this mystery. The nine religions are crowned by the ring of adepts whose password is "There is No God," so inflected that even the Magister when received among them had not wisdom to interpret it.

1. Mr Daw, K.C. : M'lud, I respectfully submit that there is no such creature as a peacock.
2. Oedipus at Colonus : Alas ! there is no sun ! I, even I, have looked and found it not.
3. Dixit Stultus in corde suo : "Ain Elohim."

There is a fourth kind of atheist, not really an atheist at all. He is but a traveller in the Land of No God, and knows that it is but a stage on his journey—and a stage, moreover, not far from the goal. Daath is not on the Tree of Life ; and in Daath there is no God as there is in the Sephiroth, for Daath cannot understand unity at all. If he thinks of it, it is only to hate it, as the one thing which he is most certainly not (see Liber 418. 10th Aethyr. I may remark in passing that this book is the best known to me on Advanced Qabalah, and of course it is only intelligible to Advanced Students).

This atheist, not in-being but in-passing, is a very apt subject for initiation. He has done with the illusions of dogma. From a Knight of the Royal Mystery he has risen to understand with the members of the Sovereign Sanctuary that all is symbolic ; all, if you will, the Jugglery of the Magician. He is tired of theories and systems of theology and all such toys ; and being weary and anhungered and athirst seeks a seat at the Table of Adepts, and a portion of the Bread of Spiritual Experience, and a draught of the wine of Ecstasy.

It is then thoroughly understood that the Aspirant is seeking to solve the great Problem. And he may conceive, as various Schools of Adepts in the ages have conceived, this problem in three main forms.

1. I am not God. I wish to become God.
   This is the Hindu conception.
   I am Malkuth. I wish to become Kether.
   This is the qabalistic equivalent.

2. I am a fallen creature. I wish to be redeemed.

This is the Christian conception.

I am Malkuth, the fallen daughter. I wish to be set upon the throne of Binah my supernal mother.

This is the qabalistic equivalent.

3. I am the finite square ; I wish to be one with the infinite circle.

This is the Unsectarian conception.

I am the Cross of Extension ; I wish to be one with the infinite Rose.

This is the qabalistic equivalent.

The answer of the Adept to the first form of the problem is for the Hindu "Thou art That" (see previous chapter, "The Yogi"); for the Qabalist "Malkuth is in Kether, and Kether is in Malkuth," or "That which is below is like that which is above" or simply "Yod." (The foundation of all letters having the number 10, symbolising Malkuth.)

The answer of the Adept to the second form of the problem is for the Christian all the familiar teaching of the Song of Songs and the Apocalypse concerning the Bride of Christ.*

For the Qabalist it is a long complex dogma which may be studied in the Zohar and elsewhere. Otherwise, he may simply answer "Hé" (the letter alike of mother and daughter in IHVH). See Liber 418 for lengthy disquisitions on this symbolic basis.

The answer of the Adept to the third form of the problem is given by π, implying that an infinite factor must be employed.

For the Qabalist it is usually symbolised by the Rosy Cross, or by such formulae as $5=6$. That they concealed a Word answering this problem is also true. My discovery of this word is the main subject of this article. All the foregoing exposition has been intended to show why I sought a word to fulfil the conditions, and by what standards of truth I could measure things.

* This Christian teaching (not its qabalistic equivalent) is incomplete. The Bride (the soul) is united, though only by marriage, with the Son, who then presents her to the Father and Mother or Holy Spirit. These four then complete Tetragrammaton. But the Bride is never united to the Father. In this scheme the soul can never do more than touch Tiphereth and so receive the ray from Chokmah. Whereas even St John makes his Son say "I and my Father are one." And we all agree that in philosophy there can never be (in Truth) more than one ; this Christian dogma says "never less than four." Hence its bondage to law and its most imperfect comprehension of any true mystic teaching, and hence the difficulty of using its symbols.

But before proceeding to this Word, it is first necessary to explain further in what way one expects a number to assist one in the search for truth, or the redemption of the soul, or the formulation of the Rosy Cross. (I am supposing that the reader is sufficiently acquainted with the method of reading a name by its attributions to understand how, once a message is received, and accredited, it may be interpreted.) Thus if I ask "What is knowledge?" and receive the answer "DOTh," I read it Daleth the door, O matter, Th darkness, by various columns of *777* (To choose the column is a matter of spiritual intuition. Solvitur ambulando). But here I am only dealing with the "trying of the spirits, to know whether they be of God."

Suppose now that a vision purporting to proceed from God is granted to me. The Angel declares his name. I add it up. It comes to 65. An excellent number! a blessed angel! Not necessarily. Suppose he is of a Mercurial appearance? 65 is a number of Mars.

Then I conclude that, however beautiful and eloquent he may be, he is a false spirit. The Devil does not understand the Qabalah well enough to clothe his symbols in harmony.

But suppose an angel, even lowly in aspect, not only knows the Qabalah—your own researches in the Qabalah—as well as you do, but is able to show you truths, qabalistic truths, which you had sought for long and vainly! Then you receive him with honour and his message with obedience.

It is as if a beggar sought audience of a general, and showed beneath his rags the signet of the King. When an Indian servant shows me "chits" signed by Colonel This and Captain That written in ill-spelt Babu English, one knows what to do. On the contrary the Man Who Was Lost rose and broke the stem of his wineglass at the regimental toast, and all knew him for one of their own.

In spiritual dealings, the Qabalah, with those secrets discovered by yourself that are only known to yourself and God, forms the grip, sign, token and password that assure you that the Lodge is properly tiled.

It is consequently of the very last importance that these final secrets should never be disclosed. And it must be remembered that an obsession, even momentary, might place a lying spirit in possession of the secrets of your grade. Probably it was in this manner that Dee and Kelly were so often deceived.

A reference to this little dictionary of numbers will show that 1, 3, 5, 7, 12, 13, 17, 21, 22, 26, 32, 37, 45, 52, 65, 67, 73, 78, 91, 111, 120, 207, 231, 270, 300, 326, 358, 361, 370, 401, 406, 434, 474, 666, 671, 741, 913, were for me numbers of peculiar importance and sanctity. Most of them are venerable, referring to or harmonious with the One. Only a few—*e.g.* 120—refer to the means. There are many others—any others—just as good; but not for me. God in dealing with me would show me the signs which I should have intelligence enough to understand. It is a condition of all intellectual intercourse.

Now I preferred to formulate the practical problem in this shape: "How shall I unite the 5 and the 6, Microcosm and Macrocosm?"

And these are the numbers which seemed to me to bear upon the problem.

1. Is the goal, not the means. Too simple to serve a magician's purpose.

2. *Vide supra.*

3. Still too simple to work with, especially as 3 = 1 so easily. But, and therefore, a great number to venerate and desire.

4. The terrible number of Tetragrammaton, the great enemy. The number of the weapons of the Evil Magician. The Dyad made Law.

5. The Pentagram, symbol of the squaring of the circle by virtue of ALHIM = 3.1415, symbol of man's will, of the evil 4 dominated by man's spirit. Also Pentagrammaton, Jeheshua, the Saviour. Hence the Beginning of the Great Work.

6. The Hexagram, symbol of the Macrocosm and Microcosm interlaced, and hence of the End of the Great Work. (Pentagram on breast, Hexagram on back, of Probationer's Robe.) Yet it also symbolises the Ruach, 214, q.v., and so is as evil *in viâ* as it is good *in termino.*

7. A most evil number, whose perfection is impossible to attack.

8. The great number of redemption, because Ch = ChITh = 418, q.v. This only develops in importance as my analysis proceeds. A priori it was of n great importance.

9. Most Evil, because of its stability. AVB, witchcraft, the false moon of the sorceress.

10. Evil, memorial of our sorrow. Yet holy, as hiding in itself the return to the negative.

11. The great magical number, as uniting the antitheses of 5 and 6 etc. AVD the magic force itself.

12. Useless. Mere symbol of the Goal.

13. Helpful, since if we can reduce our formula to 13, it becomes 1 without further trouble.

17. Useful, because though it symbolises 1, it does so under the form of a thunderbolt. "Here is a magic disk for me to hurl, and win heaven by violence," says the Aspirant.

21. As bad, nearly, as 7.

26. Accursed. As bad as 4. Only useful when it is a weapon in your hand; then—"if Satan be divided against Satan," etc.

28. Attainable; and so, useful. "My victory," "My power," says the Philosophus.

30. The Balance—Truth. Most useful.

31. LA the reply to AL, who is the God of Chesed, 4. The passionate denial of God, useful when other methods fail.

32. Admirable, in spite of its perfection, because it is the perfection which all from 1 to 10 and Aleph to Tau, share. Also connects with 6, through AHIHVH.

37. Man's crown.

44. Useful to me chiefly because I had never examined it and so had acquiesced in it as accursed. When it was brought by a messenger whose words proved true, I then understood it as an attack on the 4 by the 11. "Without shedding of blood (DM = 44) there is no remission." Also since the messenger could teach this, and prophesy, it added credit to the Adept who sent the message.

45. Useful as the number of man, ADM, identified with MH, Yetzirah, the World of Formation to which man aspires as next above Assiah. Thus 45 baffles the accuser, but only by affirmation of progress. It cannot help that progress.

52. AIMA and BN. But orthodoxy conceives these as external saviours; therefore they serve no useful purpose.

60. Like 30, but weaker. "Temperance" is only an inferior balance. 120, its extension, gives a better force.

65. Fully dealt with in "Konx om Pax," q.v.

72. Almost as bad as 4 and 26; yet being bigger and therefore further from 1 it is more assailable. Also it does spell ChSD, Mercy, and this is sometimes useful.

73. The two ways to Kether, Gimel and Chokmah. Hence venerable, but not much good to the beginner.

74. LMD, Lamed, an expansion of 30. Reads "By equilibrium and self-sacrifice, the Gate!" Thus useful. Also $74 = 37 \times 2$.

So we see $37 \times 1 = 37$ Man's crown, Jechidah, the highest Soul—"in termino."
$37 \times 2 = 74$, The Balance, 2 being the symbol "in viâ."
$37 \times 3 = 111$, Aleph, etc., 3 being the Mother, the nurse of the soul.
$37 \times 4 = 148$, "The Balances," and so on. I have not yet worked out all the numbers of this important scale.

77. OZ, the Goat, *scil.* of the Sabbath of the Adepts. The Baphomet of the Templars, the idol set up to defy and overthrow the false god—though it is understood that he himself is false, not an end, but a means. Note the $77 = 7 \times 11$, magical power in perfection.

78. Most venerable because MZLA is shown as the influence descending from On High, whose key is the Tarot: and we possess the Tarot. The proper number of the name of the Messenger of the Most Exalted One. [The account of AIVAS follows in its proper place.--Ed.]

85. Good, since $85 = 5 \times 17$.

86. Elohim, the original mischief. But good, since it is a key of the Pentagram, $5 = 1 + 4 = 14 = 8 + 6 = 86$.

91. Merely venerable.

111. Priceless, because of its 37×3 symbolism, its explanation of Aleph, which we seek, and its comment that the Unity may be found in "Thick darkness" and in "Sudden death." This is the most clear and definite help we have yet had, showing Samadhi and the Destruction of the Ego as gates of our final victory.

120. See Part I. and references.

124. ODN, Eden. The narrow gate or path between Death and the Devil.

156. BABALON. This most holy and precious name is fully dealt with in Liber 418. Notice $12 \times 13 = 156$. This was a name given and ratified by Qabalah; 156 is not one of the à priori helpful numbers. It is rather a case of the Qabalah illuminating St John's intentional obscurity.

165. 11 × XV should be a number Capricorni Pneumatici. Not yet fulfilled.

201. AR, Light (Chaldee). Note $201 = 3 \times 67$, Binah, as if it were said, "Light is concealed as a child in the womb of its mother." The occult retort of the Chaldean Magi to the Hebrew sorcerers who affirmed AVR, Light, 207, a multiple of 9. But this is little more than a sectarian squabble. 207 is holy enough.

206. DBR, the Word of Power. A useful acquisition = "The Gateway of the Word of Light."

210. Upon this holiest number it is not fitting to dilate. We may refer Zelatores to Liber VII. Cap. I., Liber Legis Cap. I., and Liber 418. But this was only revealed later. At first I only had ABRAHA, the Lord of the Adepts. *Cf.* Abraha-Melin.

214. RVCh is one of the most seductive numbers to the beginner. Yet its crown is Daath, and later one learns to regard it as the great obstacle. Look at its promise 21, ending in the fearful curse of 4! Calamity!

216. I once hoped much from this number, as it is the cube of 6. But I fear it only expresses the fixity of mind. Anyhow it all came to no good.

But we have DBIR, connected with DBR, adding the Secret Phallic Power.

220. This is the number of the verses of Liber Legis. It represents 10×22,

i.e. the whole of the Law welded into one. Hence we may be sure that the Law shall stand as it is without a syllable of addition.

Note 10^{22}, the modulus of the universe of atoms, men, stars. See "Two new worlds."

222. The grand scale of 2; may one day be of value.

256. The eighth power of 2; should be useful.

280. A grand number, the dyad passing to zero by virtue of the 8, the Charioteer who bears the Cup of Babalon. See Liber 418, 12th Aethyr. See also 280 in Part I.

300. Venerable, but only useful as explaining the power of the Trident, and the Flame on the Altar. Too stable to serve a revolutionary, except in so far as it is fire.

333. See Part I.

340. Connects with 6 through ShM, the fire and the water conjoined to make the Name. Thus useful as a hint in ceremonial.

358. See Part I.

361. See Part I. Connects with the Caduceus; as 3 is the supernal fire, 6 the Ruach, 1 Malkuth. See illustration of Caduceus in EQUINOX No. II.

370. Most venerable (see Part I.). It delivers the secret of creation into the hand of the Magician. See Liber Capricorni Pneumatici.

400. Useful only as finality or material basis. Being 20×20, it shows the fixed universe as a system of rolling wheels ($20 = K$, the Wheel of Fortune).

401. See Part I. But Azoth is the Elixir prepared and perfect; the Neophyte has not got it yet.

406. See Part I.

414. HGVTh, Meditation, the 1 dividing the accursed 4. Also AIN SVP AVR, the Limitless Light.

418. CHITh, Cheth. ABRAHADABRA, the great Magic Word, the Word of the Aeon. Note the 11 letters, 5 A identical, and 6 diverse. Thus it interlocks Pentagram and Hexagram. BITh HA, the House of Hé the Pentagram; see Idra Zuta Qadisha, 694. "For H formeth K, but Ch formeth IVD." Both equal 20.

Note $4+1+8=13$, the 4 reduced to 1 through 8, the redeeming force; and $418 = Ch = 8$.

By Aiq Bkr ABRAHADABRA $= 1+2+2+1+5+1+4+1+2+2+1 = 22$. Also $418 = 22 \times 19 =$ Manifestation. Hence the word manifests the 22 Keys of Rota.

It means by translation Abraha Deber, the Voice of the Chief Seer.

It resolves into Pentagram and Hexagram as follows:—

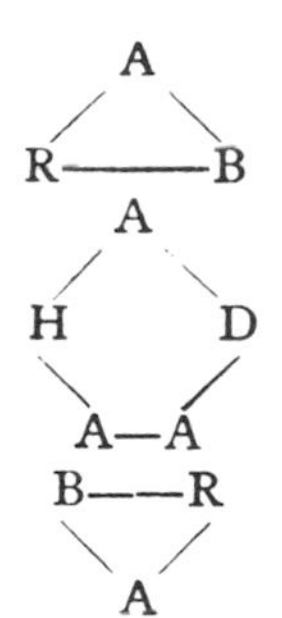

[This is by taking the 5 middle letters.]

The pentagram is 12, HVA, Macroprosopus.

The hexagram is 406, AThH, Microprosopus.

Thus it connotes the Great Work.

Note ABR, initials of the Supernals, Ab, Ben, Ruach.

(2) 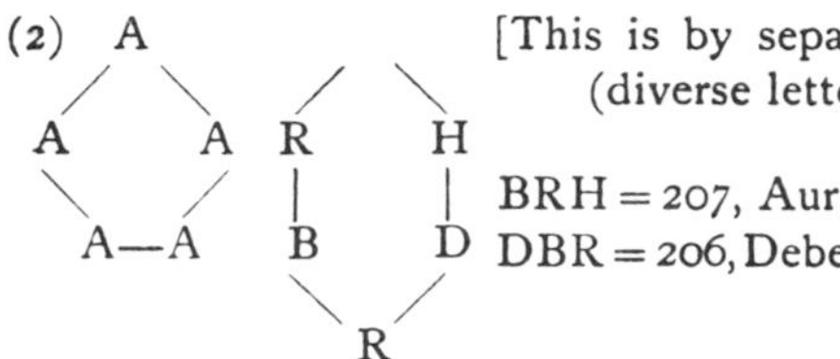

[This is by separating the One (Aleph) from the Many (diverse letters).]

BRH = 207, Aur, Light }
DBR = 206, Deber Voice } "The Vision and the Voice," a phrase which meant much to me at the moment of discovering this Word.

(3)
```
   A           A
 /   \       /   \
A     A     B     A
 \   /      |     |
  R—B       H     D
             \   /
               R
```

[By taking each alternate letter.]

205 = GBR, mighty. }
213 = ABIR, mighty. } This shows Abrahadabra as the Word of Double Power, another phrase that meant much to me at the time. AAB at the top of the Hexagram gives AB, AIMA, BN, Father, Mother, Child.

HDR by Yetzirah gives Horus, Isis, Osiris, again Father, Mother, Child This Hexagram is again the human Triad.

Dividing into 3 and 8 we get the Triangle of Horus dominating the Stooping Dragon of 8 Heads, the Supernals bursting the Head of Daath.

Also
```
   A
  R△B
```

The Supernals are supported upon two squares—

```
A—B     A—H
|  |    |  |
A—D     R—A
```

ABAD = DD, Love, 8.

AHRA = AVR, Light, 207.

Now 8 × 207 = 1656 = 18 = ChI, Living, and 207 = 9 × 23, ChIH, Life. At this time "Licht, Liebe, Leben" was the mystic name of the Mother-Temple of the G.·.D.·.

The five letters used in the word are A, the Crown; B, the Wand; D, the Cup; H, the Sword; R, the Rosy Cross; and refer further to Amoun the Father, Thoth His messenger, and Isis, Horus, Osiris, the divine-human triad.

Also 418 = ATh IAV, the Essence of IAO, q.v.

This short analysis might be indefinitely expanded; but always the symbol will remain the Expression of the Goal and the Exposition of the Path.

419. Teth, the number of the "laughing lion" on whom BABALON rideth. See Liber 418. Note $419+156=575=23\times25$, occultly signifying 24, which again signifies to them that understand the interplay of the 8 and the 3. Blessed be His holy Name, the Interpreter of his own Mystery!

434. Daleth, the holy letter of the Mother, in her glory as Queen. She saves the 4 by the 7 (D = 4 = Venus = 7), thus connects with 28. Mystic number of Netzach (Venus), Victory. Note the 3 sundering the two fours. This is the feminine victory; she is in one sense the Delilah to the divine Samson. Hence we adore her from full hearts. It ought to be remembered, by the way, that the 4 is not so evil when it has ceased to oppress us. The square identified with the circle is as good as the circle.

441. Truth, the square of 21. Hence it is the nearest that our dualistic consciousness can conceive of 21, AHIH, the God of Kether, 1. Thus Truth is our chiefest weapon, our rule. Woe to whosoever is false to himself (or to another, since in 441 that other is himself), and seven times woe to him that swerves from his magical obligation in thought, word, or deed! By my side as I write wallows in exhaustion following an age of torment one who did not understand that it is a thousand times better to die than to break the least tittle of a magical oath.

463. Shows what the Wand ought to represent. Not 364; so we should hold it by the lower end. The Wand is also Will, straight and inflexible, pertaining to Chokmah (2) as a Wand has two ends.

474. See Part I. To the beginner, though, Daath seems very helpful. He is glad that the Stooping Dragon attacks the Sanctuary. He is doing it himself. Hence Buddhists make Ignorance the greatest fetter of all the ten fetters. But in truth Knowledge implies a Knower and a Thing Known, the accursed Dyad which is the prime cause of misery.

480. Lilith. See Liber 418. So the orthodox place the legal 4 before the holy 8 and the sublime Zero. "And therefore their breaths stink."

543. Good, but only carries us back to the Mother.

666. Chosen by myself as my symbol, partly for the reasons given in Part I., partly for the reasons given in the Apocalypse. I took the Beast to be the Lion (Leo my rising sign) and Sol, 6, 666, the Lord of Leo on which Babalon should ride. And there were other more intimate considerations, unnecessary

to enter upon in this place. Note however that the Tarot card of Leo, Strength, bears the number XI., the great number of the Magnum Opus, and its interchange with Justice, VIII.; and the key of 8 is 418.

This all seemed to me so important that no qabalistic truths were so firmly implanted in my mind at the time when I was ordered to abandon the study of magic and the Qabalah as these: 8, 11, 418, 666; combined with the profoundest veneration for 1, 3, 5, 7, 13, 37, 78, 91, 111. I must insist on this at the risk of tautology and over-emphasis; for it is the key to my standard of Truth, the test-numbers which I applied to the discernment of the Messenger from the Sanctuary.

That such truths may seem trivial I am well aware; let it be remembered that the discovery of an identity may represent a year's toil. But this is the final test; repeat my researches, obtain your own holy numbers; then, and not before, will you fully understand their Validity, and the infinite wisdom of the Grand Arithmetician of the Universe.

671. Useful, as shown in Part I.

741. Useful chiefly as a denial of the Unity; sometimes employed in the hope of tempting it from its lair.

777. Useful in a similar way, as affirming that the Unity is the Qliphoth. But a dangerous tool, especially as it represents the flaming sword that drove Man out of Eden. A burnt child dreads the fire. "The devils also believe, and tremble." Worse than useless unless you have it by the hilt. Also 777 is the grand scale of 7, and this is useless to anyone who has not yet awakened the Kundalini, the female magical soul. Note 7 as the meeting-place of 3, the Mother, and 10, the Daughter; whence Netzach is the Woman, married but no more.

800. Useful only in 5=6 symbolism, q.v.

888. The grand scale of 8. In Greek numeration therefore ΙΗΣΟΥΣ the Redeemer, connecting with 6 because of its 6 letters. This links Greek and Hebrew symbolism; but remember that the mystic Iesous and Yeheshua have no more to do with the legendary Jesus of the Synoptics and the Methodists than the mystic IHVH has to do with the false God who commanded the murder of innocent children. The 13 of the Sun and the Zodiac was perhaps responsible for Buddha and his 12 disciples, Christ and his 12 disciples, Charlemagne and his 12 peers, &c., &c., but to disbelieve in Christ or Charlemagne is not to alter the number of the signs of the Zodiac. Veneration for 666 does not commit me to admiration for Napoleon and Gladstone.

I may close this paper by expressing a hope that I may have the indulgence of students. The subject is incomparably difficult; it is almost an unworked vein of thought; and my expression must be limited and thin. It is important that every identity should be most thoroughly understood. No mere perusal will serve. This paper must be studied line by line, and even to a great extent committed to memory. And that memory should already be furnished with a thorough knowledge of the chief correspondences of 777. It is hard to "suffer gladly" the particular type of fool who expects with a twenty-third-rate idle brain to assimilate in an hour the knowledge that it has cost me twelve years to acquire. I may add that nobody will ever understand this method of knowledge without himself undertaking research. Once he has experienced the joy of connecting (say) 131 and 480 through 15, he will understand. Further, it is the work itself, not merely the results, that is of service. We teach Greek and Latin, though nobody speaks either language.

And thus I close: Benedictus sit Dominus Deus Noster qui nobis dedit Scientiam Summam.

Amen!

777

777 REVISED

VEL

PROLEGOMENA SYMBOLICA AD SYSTEMAM SCEPTICO-MYSTICAE VIAE EXPLICANDAE, FUNDAMENTUM HIEROGLYPHICUM SANCTISSIMORUM SCIENTIAE SUMMAE

A REPRINT
OF 777 WITH MUCH ADDITIONAL
MATTER BY THE LATE

ALEISTER CROWLEY

TABLE OF CONTENTS

* Indicates material not in the original edition.

EDITORIAL PREFACE

777 is a qabalistic dictionary of ceremonial magic, oriental mysticism, comparative religion and symbology. It is also a handbook for ceremonial invocation and for checking the validity of dreams and visions. It is indispensable to those who wish to correlate these apparently diverse studies. It was published privately by Aleister Crowley in 1909, has long been out of print and is now practically unprocurable.

Crowley, who had a phenomenal memory, wrote it at Bournemouth in a week without reference books—or so he claimed in an unpublished section of his "Confessions." It is not, however, entirely original. Ninety per cent of the Hebrew, the four colour scales, and the order and attribution of the Tarot trumps are as taught in the Hermetic Order of the Golden Dawn with its inner circle of the Rose of Ruby and the Cross of Gold (R.R. et A.C.).

This Order is still in existence, though it has changed its name and is dormant, for it no longer accepts probationers. It was the fountain head from which Crowley and W. B. Yeats drank in their twenties. In this school they learned the traditional Western symbolism which coloured so much of their poetry and their thought. In it they were taught ceremonial magic, how to skry, and the technique for exploring the subtler realms of the mind on the so-called "astral plane."

Crowley, however, was not content with the traditional qabalistic teaching of this Western Hermetic Order with its stress on magic and demonology. He travelled eastwards, becoming a fair Arabic scholar and studying the Mahommedan secret tradition under a qualified teacher in Cairo. Going on to India he learned the elements of Shaivite Yoga at the feet of Sri Parananda, who was Solicitor-General of Ceylon before he became a sadhu. In Southern India he studied Vedanta and Raja Yoga with "the Mahatma Jnana

Guru Yogi Sabhapaty Swami." He was thus qualified to equate the Hindu and Qabalistic systems.

Allan Bennett, his friend and teacher in the Golden Dawn, had become the Burmese Buddhist bhikkhu Ananda Metteya. Crowley studied under him both in Ceylon and Burmah, and so was able to add the Hinayana Buddhist columns to 777. Although he walked eastwards into China he never found a qualified teacher of Taoism or the Yi King. His attributions of the trigrams to the Tree of Life and his explanation of the hexagrams in Appendix I to 777 were based on Legge's translation.

Crowley was only 32 when he wrote 777. Later as his knowledge and experience widened he became increasingly dissatisfied with it. He planned an enlarged edition which would correct a few errors, incorporate much new material, and bring the whole into line with The Book of the Law. He worked on this in the nineteen twenties, but never completed it. What he did finish is published here—most of it for the first time. The task of editing has been restricted for the most part to the omission of incomplete notes.

The new material, which is marked with an asterisk in the Table of Contents, consists of an essay on the magical alphabet, a short note on Qabalah and a new theory on number. Then the more important columns in Table I are explained. These explanations include a few corrections and a number of important additions to the original Table. Those who wish to work with these Tables (pp. 2-36) should extract the additions from the text, and add them to the appropriate lines of the columns concerned. Finally, some new columns and "arrangements" have been included partly from The Book of Thoth, and partly from holograph notes in Crowley's own 777. The editor has assumed that Crowley intended to incorporate these in the new edition. For the few interested in Gematria the numerical values of the Greek and Arabic alphabets have been added.

Crowley never completed 777 Revised, but he left enough material to justify its posthumous publication.

N ∴

777

VEL PROLEGOMENA SYMBOLICA AD SYSTEMAM SCEPTICO-MYSTICAE VIAE EXPLICANDAE, FUNDAMENTUM HIEROGLYPHICUM SANCTISSIMORUM SCIENTIAE SUMMAE

THE following is an attempt to systematise alike the data of mysticism and the results of comparative religion.

The sceptic will applaud our labours, for that the very catholicity of the symbols denies them any objective validity, since, in so many contradictions, something must be false; while the mystic will rejoice equally that the selfsame catholicity all-embracing proves that very validity, since after all something must be true.

Fortunately we have learnt to combine these ideas, not in the mutual toleration of sub-contraries, but in the affirmation of contraries, that transcending of the laws of intellect which is madness in the ordinary man, genius in the Overman who hath arrived to strike off more fetters from our understanding. The savage who cannot conceive of the number six, the orthodox mathematician who cannot conceive of the fourth dimension, the philosopher who cannot conceive of the Absolute—all these are one; all must be impregnated with the Divine Essence of the Phallic Yod of Macroprosopus, and give birth to their idea. True (we may agree with Balzac), the Absolute recedes; we never grasp it; but in the travelling there is joy. Am I no better than a staphylococcus because my ideas still crowd in chains?

But we digress.

The last attempts to tabulate knowledge are the *Kabbala Denudata* of Knorr von Rosenroth (a work incomplete and, in some of its parts, prostituted to the service of dogmatic interpretation), the lost symbolism of the Vault in which

Christian Rosenkreutz is said to have been buried, some of the work of Dr. Dee and Sir Edward Kelly, some very imperfect tables in Cornelius Agrippa, the "Art" of Raymond Lully, some of the very artificial effusions of the esoteric Theosophists, and of late years the knowledge of the Order Rosae Rubeae et Aureae Crucis and the Hermetic Order of the Golden Dawn. Unluckily, the leading spirit in these latter societies found that his prayer, "Give us this day our daily whisky, and just a wee drappie mair for luck!" was sternly answered, "When you have given us this day our daily Knowledge-lecture."

Under these circumstances Daath got mixed with Dewar, and Beelzebub with Buchanan.

But even the best of these systems is excessively bulky; modern methods have enabled us to concentrate the substance of twenty thousand pages in two score.

The best of the serious attempts to systematise the results of Comparative Religion is that made by Blavatzky. But though she had an immense genius for acquiring facts, she had none whatever for sorting and selecting the essentials.

Grant Allen made a very slipshod experiment in this line; so have some of the polemical rationalists; but the only man worthy of our notice is Frazer of the Golden Bough. Here, again, there is no tabulation; for us it is left to sacrifice literary charm, and even some accuracy, in order to bring out the one great point.

This: That when a Japanese thinks of Hachiman, and a Boer of the Lord of Hosts, they are not two thoughts, but one.

The cause of human sectarianism is not lack of sympathy in thought, but in speech; and this it is our not unambitious design to remedy.

Every new sect aggravates the situation. Especially the Americans, grossly and crapulously ignorant as they are of the rudiments of any human language, seize like mongrel curs upon the putrid bones of their decaying monkey-jabber, and gnaw and tear them with fierce growls and howls.

The mental prostitute, Mrs. Eddy (for example), having invented the idea which ordinary people call "God," christened it "Mind," and then by affirming a set of propositions about "Mind," which are only true of "God," set all hysterical, dyspeptic, crazy Amurrka by the ears. Personally, I don't object to people discussing the properties of four-sided triangles; but I draw the line when they use a well-known word, such as pig, or mental healer, or dungheap, to denote the object of their paranoiac fetishism.

Even among serious philosophers the confusion is very great. Such terms as God, the Absolute, Spirit, have dozens and dozens of connotations, according to the time and place of the dispute and the beliefs of the disputants.

Time enough that these definitions and their interrelation should be crystallised, even at some expense of accepted philosophical accuracy.

2. The principal sources of our tables have been the philosophers and traditional systems referred to above, as also, among many others, Pietro di Abano, Lilly, Eliphaz Levi, Sir R. Burton, Swami Vivekananda, the Hindu, Buddhist, and Chinese Classics, the Qúran and its commentators, the Book of the Dead, and, in particular, original research. The Chinese, Hindu, Buddhist, Moslem, and Egyptian systems have never before been brought into line with the Qabalah; the Tarot has never been made public.

Eliphaz Levi knew the true attributions but was forbidden to use them.*

All this secrecy is very silly. An indicible Arcanum is an arcanum that *cannot* be revealed. It is simply bad faith to swear a man to the most horrible penalties if he betray . . ., etc., and then take him mysteriously apart and confide the Hebrew Alphabet to his safe keeping. This is perhaps only ridiculous; but it is a wicked imposture to pretend to have received it from Rosicrucian manuscripts which are to be found in the British Museum. To obtain money on

* This is probably true, though in agreement with the statement of the traducer of Levi's doctrine and the vilifier of his noble personality.

these grounds, as has been done by certain moderns, is clear (and I trust, indictable) fraud.

The secrets of Adepts are not to be revealed to men. We only wish they were. When a man comes to me and asks for the Truth, I go away and practise teaching the Differential Calculus to a Bushman; and I answer the former only when I have succeeded with the latter. But to withhold the Alphabet of Mysticism from the learner is the device of a selfish charlatan. That which can be taught shall be taught, and that which cannot be taught may at last be learnt.

3. As a weary but victorious warrior delights to recall his battles—Forsitan haec olim meminisse juvabit—we would linger for a moment upon the difficulties of our task.

The question of sacred alphabets has been abandoned as hopeless. As one who should probe the nature of woman, the deeper he goes the rottener it gets; so that at last it is seen that there is no sound bottom. All is arbitrary;* withdrawing our caustics and adopting a protective treatment, we point to the beautiful clean bandages and ask the clinic to admire! To take one concrete example: the English T is clearly equivalent in sound to the Hebrew ת, the Greek τ, the Arabic ت, and the Coptic Ⲧ, but the numeration is not the same. Again, we have a clear analogy in shape (perhaps a whole series of analogies), which, on comparing the modern alphabets with primeval examples, breaks up and is indecipherable.

The same difficulty in another form permeates the question of gods.

Priests, to propitiate their local fetish, would flatter him with the title of creator; philosophers, with a wider outlook, would draw identities between many gods in order to

* All symbolism is perhaps ultimately so; there is no necessary relation in thought between the idea of a mother, the sound of the child's cry "Ma," and the combination of lines *ma*. This, too, is the extreme case, since "ma" is the sound naturally just produced by opening the lips and breathing. Hindus would make a great fuss over this true connection; but it is very nearly the only one. All these beautiful schemes break down sooner or later, mostly sooner.

obtain a unity. Time and the gregarious nature of man have raised gods as ideas grew more universal; sectarianism has drawn false distinctions between identical gods for polemical purposes.

Thus, where shall we put Isis, favouring nymph of corn as she was? As the type of motherhood? As the moon? As the great goddess Earth? As Nature? As the Cosmic Egg from which all Nature sprang? For as time and place have changed, so she is all of these!

What of Jehovah, that testy senior of early Genesis, that lawgiver of Leviticus, that war-god of Joshua, that Phallus of the depopulated slaves of the Egyptians, that jealous King-God of the times of the Kings, that more spiritual conception of the Captivity, only invented when all temporal hope was lost, that mediæval battleground of cross-chopped logic, that Being stripped of all his attributes and assimilated to Parabrahman and the Absolute of the Philosopher?

Satan, again, who in Job is merely Attorney-General and prosecutes for the Crown, acquires in time all the obloquy attaching to that functionary in the eyes of the criminal classes, and becomes a slanderer. Does any one really think that any angel is such a fool as to try to gull the Omniscient God into injustice to his saints?

Then, on the other hand, what of Moloch, that form of Jehovah denounced by those who did not draw huge profits from his rites? What of the savage and morose Jesus of the Evangelicals, cut by their petty malice from the gentle Jesus of the Italian children? How shall we identify the thaumaturgic Chauvinist of Matthew with the metaphysical Logos of John? In short, while the human mind is mobile, so long will the definitions of all our terms vary.

But it is necessary to settle on something: bad rules are better than no rules at all. We may then hope that our critics will aid our acknowledged feebleness; and if it be agreed that much learning hath made us mad, that we may receive humane treatment and a liberal allowance of rubber-cores in our old age.

4. The Tree of Life is the skeleton on which this body of truth is built. The juxtaposition and proportion of its parts should be fully studied. Practice alone will enable the student to determine how far an analogy may be followed out. Again, some analogies may escape a superficial study. The Beetle is only connected with the sign Pisces through the Tarot Trump "The Moon." The Camel is only connected with the High Priestess through the letter Gimel.

Since all things whatsoever (including no thing) may be placed upon the Tree of Life, the Table could never be complete. It is already somewhat unwieldy; we have tried to confine ourselves as far as possible to lists of Things Generally Unknown. It must be remembered that the lesser tables are only divided from the thirty-two-fold table in order to economise space; *e.g.* in the seven-fold table the entries under Saturn belong to the thirty-second part in the large table.

We have been unable for the moment to tabulate many great systems of Magic; the four lesser books of the Lemegeton, the system of Abramelin, if indeed its Qliphothic ramifications are susceptible of classification, once we follow it below the great and terrible Demonic Triads which are under the presidency of the Unutterable Name; the vast and comprehensive system shadowed in the Book called the Book of the Concourse of the Forces, interwoven as it is with the Tarot, being, indeed, on one view little more than an amplification and practical application of the Book of Thoth.

But we hope that the present venture will attract scholars from all quarters, as when the wounded Satan leaned upon his spear,

> "Forthwith on all sides to his aid was run
> By angels many and strong,"

and that in the course of time a far more satisfactory volume may result.

Many columns will seem to the majority of people to consist of mere lists of senseless words. Practice, and advance in the magical or mystical path, will enable them little by little to interpret more and more.

Even as a flower unfolds beneath the ardent kisses of the Sun, so will this table reveal its glories to the dazzling eye of illumination. Symbolic and barren as it is, yet it shall stand for the athletic student as a perfect sacrament, so that reverently closing its pages he shall exclaim, "May that of which we have partaken sustain us in the search for the Quintessence, the Stone of the Wise, the Summum Bonum, True Wisdom, and Perfect Happiness."

So mote it be!

A Brief Essay
Upon The Nature And Significance Of The
MAGICAL ALPHABET

THE book 777 has for its primary object the construction of a magical alphabet.

One of the greatest difficulties experienced by the student—a difficulty which increases rather than diminishes with his advance in knowledge—is this: he finds it impossible to gain any clear idea of the meanings of the terms which he employs. Every philosopher has his own meaning, even for such universally used terms as soul; and in most cases he does not so much as suspect that other writers use the term under a different connotation. Even technical writers and those who take the trouble to define their terms before using them are too often at variance with each other. The diversity is very great in the case of this word soul. It is sometimes used to mean Atman, an impersonal principle almost synonymous with the Absolute—itself a word which has been defined with scores of different senses. Others use it to mean the personal individual soul as distinguished from the over-soul or God. Others take it as equivalent to Neschamah, the Understanding, the intelligible essence of man, his aspiration; yet others mean the Nephesch, the animal soul, the consciousness corresponding to the senses. It has even been identified with the Ruach which is really the mechanism of the mind. Apart from these major distinctions there are literally hundreds of minor shades of meaning. We find therefore a writer predicating the soul A, B, and C, while his fellow student protests vehemently that it is none of these things—despite which the two men may be in substantial agreement.

Let us suppose for a moment that by some miracle we obtain a clear idea of the meaning of the word. The trouble has merely begun, for there immediately arises the question of the relations of one term to the others. There have been few attempts at constructing a coherent system; and those that are coherent are not comprehended.

In view of this Euroclydon of misunderstanding it is clearly necessary to establish a fundamental language. I saw this fact in my twenties. My extended travels throughout the world had brought me into contact with religious and philosophical thinkers of every shade of opinion: and the more I knew the greater became the confusion. I understood, with bitter approval, the outburst of the aged Fichte: "If I had my life to live again, the first thing I would do would be to invent an entirely new system of symbols whereby to convey my ideas." As a matter of fact certain people, notably Raymond Lully, have attempted this great work.

I discussed this question with Bhikkhu Ananda Metteya (Allan Bennett) in 1904. He professed himself completely satisfied with the Buddhist terminology. I could not concur with this opinion. Firstly, the actual words are barbarously long, impossibly so for the average European. Secondly, an understanding of the system demands complete acquiescence in the Buddhist doctrines. Thirdly, the meaning of the terms is not, as my venerable colleague maintained, as clear and comprehensive as could be wished. There is much pedantry, much confusion, and much disputed matter. Fourthly, the terminology is exclusively psychological. It takes no account of extra-Buddhistic ideas; and it bears little relation to the general order of the universe. It might be supplemented by Hindu terminology. But to do that would immediately introduce elements of controversy. We should at once be lost in endless discussions as to whether Nibbana was Nirvana or not: and so on for ever.

The system of the Qabalah is superficially open to this last objection. But its real basis is perfectly sound. We can easily discard the dogmatic interpretation of the

Rabbins. We can refer everything in the Universe to the system of pure number whose symbols will be intelligible to all rational minds in an identical sense. And the relations between these symbols are fixed by nature. There is no particular point—for most ordinary purposes—in discussing whether 49 is or is not the square of 7.

Such was the nature of the considerations that led me to adopt the Tree of Life as the basis of the magical alphabet. The 10 numbers and the 22 letters of the Hebrew Alphabet, with their traditional and rational correspondences (taking into consideration their numerical and geometrical interrelations), afford us a coherent systematic groundwork sufficiently rigid for our foundation and sufficiently elastic for our superstructure.

But we must not suppose that we know anything of the Tree a priori. We must not work towards any other type of central Truth than the nature of these symbols in themselves. The object of our work must be, in fact, to discover the nature and powers of each symbol. We must clothe the mathematical nakedness of each prime idea in a many-coloured garment of correspondences with every department of thought.

Our first task is thus to consider what we are to mean by the word number. I have dealt with this in my commentary to Verse 4, Chapter I, of The Book of the Law; "Every number is infinite: there is no difference." (See, What is a "number" or a "symbol," p. 127.)

The student should go very thoroughly into the question of transfinite number. Let him consult the "Introduction to Mathematical Philosophy" of the Hon. Bertrand Russell in a reverent but critical spirit. In particular, in the light of my note on number, the whole conception of Aleph Zero should give him a fairly clear idea of the essential paradoxes of the magical interpretation of the idea of number, and especially of the equation $0 = 2$ which I have devised to explain the universe, and to harmonise the antinomies which it presents us at every turn.

Our present state of understanding is far from perfect. It is evidently impossible to obtain a clear notion of each of the primes if only because their number is Aleph Zero.

The numbers 0 to 10, as forming the basis of the decimal system, may be considered as a microcosm of Aleph Zero. For they are endless, 10 representing the return to Unity by the reintroduction of Zero to continue the series in a manner progressively complex, each term representing not only itself in its relation with its neighbours, but the combination of two or more numbers of the first decad. That is, until we reach numbers whose factors are all (except unity) greater than 10; as 143 = (11 × 13). But this necessity to consider such numbers as altogether beyond the first decad is only apparent; each prime being itself an elaboration in some sense or other of one or more of the original 0 to 10 series.* This at least may be regarded as conventionally true for immediate purpose of study. A number such as 3299 × 3307 × 3319 may be regarded as a distant and not very important group of fixed stars. (Thus 13 is a "middle modulus" and 111 the "great modulus" of Unity. That is, the multiples of 13 and 111 explain the coefficients of their scales in terms of a more specialised idea of Unity. *E.g.* 26 = 2 × 13 represents the Dyad in a more specially connotated sense than 2 does; 888 describes the function of 8 in terms of the full meaning of 111, which is itself an elaborate account of the nature of Unity, including—for instance—the dogmatic mystery of the equation 3 = 1.)

By repercussion, again, each larger correlative of any number of 0 to 10 expresses an extended idea of that number which must immediately be included in the fundamental conception thereof. For instance, having discovered that 120 can be divided by 5, we must henceforth think of 5 as the root of those ideas which we find in 120, as well as using our previous ideas of 5 as the key to our investigation of 120.

On the surface, it would appear that this mode of working could only lead to baffling contradictions and inextricable confusion; but to the mind naturally lucid and well trained to discrimination this misfortune does not occur.

* For the meaning of the primes from 11 to 97 see p. xxv.

On the contrary, practice (which makes perfect) enables one to grasp intelligently and class coherently a far vaster congeries of facts than could possibly be assimilated by the most laborious feats of memorizing. Herbert Spencer has well explained the psychology of apprehension. The excellence of any mind, considered merely as a storehouse of information, may be gauged by its faculty of re-presenting any required facts to itself by systematic classification into groups and sub-groups.

This present attempt at a magical alphabet is, in fact, a projection, both intensive and extensive, of this system to infinity. On the one hand, all possible ideas are referred by progressive integrations to the pure numbers 0 to 10, and thence to 2, 1, and 0. On the other, the connotations of 0, 1, and 2 are extended, by progressive definitions, to include every conceivable idea on every plane of the Universe.

We are now in a position to consider the practical application of these ideas. As regards the numbers 0 to 10 of the Key-Scale, each one is a fundamental idea of a positive entity. Its nature is defined by the correspondences assigned to it in the various columns. Thus we may say that the God Hanuman, the Jackal, the Opal, Storax, Truthfulness and so on are all qualities inherent in the idea called 8.

With regard to the numbers 11 to 32 of the Key-Scale, they are not numbers at all in our sense of the word. They have been arbitrarily assigned to the 22 paths by the compiler of the Sepher Yetzirah. There is not even any kind of harmony: nothing could be much further from the idea of 29 than the sign of Pisces. The basic idea had better be considered the letter of the Hebrew Alphabet; and the correspondence of each with fairly comprehensive definitions such as the Tarot trumps is very close and necessary. (It will be noticed that certain Alphabets, especially the Coptic, have more than 22 letters. These additional symbols fill up the Tree of Life when attributed to the Sephiroth.) The numerical value of the letters does however represent a real and important relation. But these numbers are not quite the same as the original sephirotic numbers. For instance, although Beth = 2, = Mercury, and Mercury is part of the idea of Chokmah = 2, the one 2 is not identical with the other. For Mercury, in itself, is not a Sephira. It is not a positive emanation in necessary sequence in the scale 0 to 10. For Beth is the path which joins Kether and Binah, 1 and 3. Zayin = 7 is the path joining Binah, 3, and Tiphereth, 6. That is, they are not numbers in themselves, but expressions of relations between numbers according to a predetermined geometrical pattern.

Another class of number is of immense importance. It is the series usually expressed in Roman numerals which is printed on the Tarot trumps. Here, with two exceptions, the number is invariably one less than that of the letters of the alphabet, where they are numbered according to their natural order from 1 to 22. Thus Gimel, the third letter, pertains to trump II, Mem, the thirteenth letter, to No. XII. These numbers are very nearly of the same order of idea as those of the numerical value of the letters; but they represent rather the active magical energy of the number than its essential being.

To return to the pure Sephiroth, the numbers 0, 1, 2, 3, 5, and 7 are primes, the others combinations of these primes. Here we have already the principle of equilibrium between the simple and the complex. At the same time there is an inherent virtue in these compound numbers as such which makes it improper to think of them as merely combinations from their mathematical elements. Six is an idea in itself, a "Ding an sich." The fact that 6 = 2 × 3 is only one of its properties. Similar remarks apply to the numbers above 10, but here the importance of the primes as compared to that of the compound numbers is much greater. Few compound numbers appear in the present state of our knowledge in themselves as distinguished from the value of their mathematical elements. We may however instance 93, 111, 120, 210, 418, 666. But every prime is the expression of a quite definite idea. For instance 19 is the general feminine glyph, 31 the highest feminine trinity, a "great modulus" of Zero. 41 is the aspect of the feminine as a vampire force, 47 as dynamic and spasmodic, 53 as hedonogenous, 59 as claiming its complement, and so on.

Each prime number retains its peculiar significance in its multiples. Thus the number 23, a glyph of life, exhibits the life of the Dyad in 46, etc. The significance of the primes has been carefully worked out, with fair accuracy in each case, up to 97.* Above 100 only a few primes have been thoroughly investigated. This is because, by our present methods, such numbers can only be studied through their multiples. That is to say, if we wish to determine the nature of the number 17 we shall examine the series 34, 51, 68, etc., to see what words and ideas correspond to them. We shall establish a ratio 51 : 34 = 3 : 2. From our knowledge of 3 and 2 we can compare the effect produced upon them by the modulus 17. For instance, 82 is the number of the Angel of Venus and means a thing beloved; 123 means war, a plague, pleasure, violation; and 164 has the idea of cleaving, also of profane as opposed to sacred. The common element in these ideas is a dangerous fascination; whence we say that 41, the highest common factor, is the Vampire.†

But the above considerations, which would extend the letters of the magical alphabet to an infinity of symbols, are not properly pertinent to this essay. Our main object is convenience in communicating ideas. And this would be violated if we aimed too high. We can attain all our objectives for practical purposes by confining ourselves to the traditionally accepted scale of 32 paths, of 10 numbers and 22 letters. The only extension necessary is the inclusion of the three Veils of the Negative, a matter of fundamental importance in the apodeictic structure of the Tree given in the structural diagram.‡ These Veils are useful in only a very few positive lists.

* See p. xxv.

† A dictionary giving the meanings by traditional Qabalah of the numbers from 1 to 1,000 with a few higher numbers is published in *The Equinox* 1, 8, under the title "Sepher Sephiroth sub figura D."

‡ See p. xxvii.

The numbers 31 and 32 must be duplicated because the letter Shin possesses two very distinct branches of idea, one connected with the element of Fire, and the other with that of Spirit. Also the letter Tau is referred both to the planet Saturn and the element Earth. This is a great defect in the scheme, theoretically. But the traditional attributions are so numerous and well defined that no remedy seems feasible. (In practice no serious trouble of any kind is caused by the theoretical confusion.)

One further difficulty has arisen owing to the discovery of the planets Neptune and Uranus. We have however tried to turn this into an advantage by including them with Primum Mobile in a Sephirotic arrangement of the planets. And the device has justified itself by enabling us to construct a perfectly symmetrical attribution for the rulings and exaltations of the Signs of the Zodiac.

For the rest it need only be said, that, as in the case of most lines of study, the key to success is the familiarity conferred by daily practice.

THE MEANING OF THE PRIMES FROM 11 TO 97

11. The general number of magick, or energy tending to change.
13. The scale of the highest feminine unity; easily transformed to secondary masculine ideas by any male component; or, the unity resulting from love.
17. The masculine unity. (Trinity of Aleph, Vau, Yod.)
19. The feminine glyph.
23. The glyph of life—nascent life.
29. The magick force itself, the masculine current.
31. The highest feminine trinity—zero through the glyph of the circle.
37. The unity itself in its balanced trinitarian manifestation.
41. The yoni as a vampire force, sterile.
43. A number of orgasm—especially the male.
47. The yoni as dynamic, prehensile, spasmodic, etc. Esprit de travail.
53. The yoni as an instrument of pleasure.
59. The yoni calling for the lingam as ovum, menstruum, or alkali.
61. The negative conceiving itself as a positive.
67. The womb of the mother containing the twins.
71. A number of Binah. The image of nothingness and silence which is a fulfilment of the aspiration.
73. The feminine aspect of Chokmah in his phallic function.
83. Consecration: love in its highest form: energy, freedom, amrita, aspiration. The root of the idea of romance plus religion.
89. A number of sin—restriction. The wrong kind of silence, that of the Black Brothers.
97. A number of Chesed as water and as father.

THE TREE OF LIFE

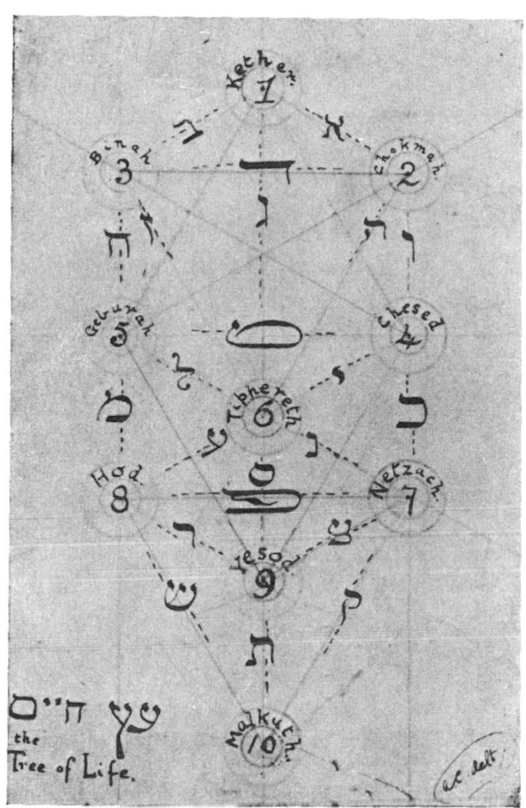

COL. XII. This arrangement is the basis of the whole system of this book. Besides the 10 numbers and the 22 letters, it is divisible into 3 columns, 4 planes, 7 planes, 7 palaces, etc., etc.

TABLE OF CORRESPONDENCES

VIII.* Orders of Qliphoth.	VII. English of Col. VI.	VI. The Heavens of Assiah.	
			0
תאומיאל (1)	Sphere of the Primum Mobile	ראשית הגלגלים	1
עוגיאל (1)	Sphere of the Zodiac or Fixed Stars	מסלות	2
סאתאריאל (1)	Sphere of Saturn	שבתאי	3
געשכלה (2)	Sphere of Jupiter	צדק	4
גולחב (3)	Sphere of Mars	מאדים	5
תגרירון (4)	Sphere of Sol	שמש	6
ערב זרק (5)	Sphere of Venus	נוגה	7
סמאל (6)	Sphere of Mercury	כוכב	8
גמליאל (7)	Sphere of Luna	לבנה	9
לילית (7)	Sphere of the Elements	חלם יסודות	10
[Elements. See Col. LXVIII.]	Air	רוח	11
[Planets follow Sephiroth]	Mercury	[Planets follow Sephiroth, corresponding]	12
	Luna		13
	Venus		14
בעירירון*	Aries 🜂	טלה	15
אדימירון	Taurus 🜃	שור	16
צללדמירון	Gemini 🜁	תאומים	17
שיחרירון	Cancer 🜄	סרטן	18
שלהבירון	Leo 🜂	אריה	19
צפרירון	Virgo 🜃	בתולה	20
	Jupiter		21
עבירירון	Libra 🜁	מאזנים	22
	Water	מים	23
נחשתירון	Scorpio 🜄	עקרב	24
נחשירון	Sagittarius 🜂	קשת	25
דגדגירון	Capricornus 🜃	גדי	26
	Mars		27
בהימירון	Aquarius 🜁	דלי	28
נשימירון	Pisces 🜄	דגים	29
	Sol		30
	Fire	אש	31
	Saturn		32
	Earth	ארץ	32 bis
	Spirit	את*	31 bis

* The asterisks (*) refer to Notes on pp. 138-146.

V.* God-Names in Assiah.	IV.* Consciousness of the Adept.	III. English of Col. II.	II.* Hebrew Names of Numbers and Letters.	I. Key Scale.
. . . .	. . . .	Nothing	. . . . . אין	0
		No Limit	. . . . אין סוף	
		Limitless L.V.X. . . .	. אין סוף אור	
. . . . אהיה	. . . . . . הוא	Crown	. . . . כתר*	1
. . . . יה	. .	Wisdom	. . . חכמה*	2
. . . יהוה אלהים	. .	Understanding	. . . . בינה*	3
. . . . אל	. .	Mercy	. . . . חסד*	4
. . . אלהים גבור	. .	Strength	. . . גבורה*	5
. יהוה אלוה ודעת	. .	Beauty	. . . תפארת*	6
. . . יהוה צבאות	. .	Victory	. . . . . נצח	7
. . אלהים צבאות	. .	Splendour	. . . . . הוד	8
. . . . שדי אל חי	. .	Foundation	. . . . יסוד*	9
. . . . אדני מלך	. .	Kingdom	. . . מלכות*	10
. . . . יהוה	. .	Ox	. . . . . אלף	11
. . . . אזבוגה (8)	. .	House	. . . . . בית	12
. . (81) אלים (9) הד	. .	Camel	. . . . . גמל	13
. . . . . . (7) אהא	. .	Door	. . . . . דלת	14
. . . .	. .	Window	. . . . . . הה	15
. . . .	. .	Nail	. . . . . . וו	16
. . . .	. .	Sword	. . . . . . זין	17
. . . .	هو الله الذي لا اله الا هو . .	Fence	. . . . . חית	18
. . . .	. .	Serpent	. . . . . טית	19
. . . .	. .	Hand	. . . . . . יוד	20
(34) אבא (4) אל אב	. .	Palm	. . . . . . כף	21
. . . .	. .	Ox Goad	. . . . . . למד	22
. . . . אל	. .	Water	. . . . . . מים	23
. . . .	. .	Fish	. . . . נון	24
. . . .	. .	Prop	. . . . . . סמך	25
. . . .	. .	Eye	. . . . עין	26
. . . . . . (65) אדני	. .	Mouth.	. . . . פה	27
. . . .	. .	Fish-hook	. . . . צדי	28
. . . .	. .	Back of Head	. . . . קוף	29
. . . . . . (36) אלה	. .	Head	. . . . ריש	30
. . . . אלהים	. .	Tooth	. . . . שין	31
. . . (15) יה (3) אב	. .	Tau (as Egyptian)	. . . . תו	32
. . . [הארץ] אדני	. .	. . . .	. . . . תו	32 bis
. . . . יהשוה	. .	. . . .	. . . . שין	31 bis

XV.* The King Scale of Colour [י].	XIV. General Attribution of Tarot.	XIII. The Paths of the Sepher Yetzirah.	
. . . .	. . . .	. . . .	0
Brilliance	The 4 Aces	Admirable or Hidden Intelligence . .	1
Pure soft blue	The 4 Twos—Kings or Knights	Illuminating I.	2
Crimson	The 4 Threes—Queens . . .	Sanctifying I.	3
Deep violet	The 4 Fours	Measuring Cohesive or Receptacular I.	4
Orange	The 4 Fives	Radical I.	5
Clear pink rose . . .	The 4 Sixes—Emperors or Princes	I. of the Mediating Influence	6
Amber	The 4 Sevens	Occult I.	7
Violet purple	The 4 Eights	Absolute or Perfect I.	8
Indigo	The 4 Nines	Pure or Clear I.	9
Yellow	The 4 Tens—Empresses or Princesses	Resplendent I.	10
Bright pale yellow . .	The Fool—[Swords] Emperors or Princes	Scintillating I.	11
Yellow	The Juggler	I. of Transparency	12
Blue	The High Priestess	Uniting I.	13
Emerald green . . .	The Empress	Illuminating I.	14
Scarlet	The Emperor	Constituting I.	15
Red orange	The Hierophant	Triumphal or Eternal One	16
Orange	The Lovers	Disposing One	17
Amber	The Chariot	I. of the House of Influence	18
Yellow, greenish . . .	Strength	I. of all the Activities of the Spiritual Being	19
Green, yellowish . . .	Hermit	I. of Will	20
Violet	Wheel of Fortune	I. of Conciliation	21
Emerald green . . .	Justice	Faithful I.	22
Deep blue	The Hanged Man — [Cups] Queens	Stable I.	23
Green blue	Death	Imaginative I.	24
Blue	Temperance	I. of Probation or Tentative One . .	25
Indigo	The Devil	Renovating I.	26
Scarlet	The House of God	Exciting I.	27
Violet	The Star	Natural I.	28
Crimson (ultra violet) .	The Moon	Corporeal I.	29
Orange	The Sun	Collecting I.	30
Glowing orange scarlet .	The Angel or Last Judgment—[Wands] Kings or Knights	Perpetual I.	31
Indigo	The Universe	Administrative I.	32
Citrine, olive, russet, and black †	Empresses [Coins]	. . . .	32 bis
White merging into grey	All 22 Trumps	. . . .	31 bis

XII.* The Tree of Life.	XI.* Elements (with their Planetary Rulers).	X. Mystic Numbers of the Sephiroth.	IX.* The Sword and the Serpent.	
. . . .	. . . .	. . 0 . .	. . . .	0
1st Plane, Middle Pillar . .	Root of 🜁 . . .	. . 1 . .	The Flaming Sword follows the downward course of the Sephiroth, and is compared to the Lightning Flash. Its hilt is in Kether and its point in Malkuth.	1
2nd Plane, Right Pillar . . .	Root of 🜂 . . .	. . 3 . .		2
2nd Plane, Left Pillar . . .	Root of 🜄 . . .	. . 6 . .		3
3rd Plane, Right Pillar . . .	. . . 🜄 . . .	. . 10 . .		4
3rd Plane, Left Pillar . . .	. . . 🜂 . . .	. . 15 . .		5
4th Plane, Middle Pillar . .	. . . 🜁 . . .	. . 21 . .		6
5th Plane, Right Pillar . . .	. . . 🜂 . . .	. . 28 . .		7
5th Plane, Left Pillar . . .	. . . 🜄 . . .	. . 36 . .		8
6th Plane, Middle Pillar . .	. . . 🜁 . . .	. . 45 . .		9
7th Plane, Middle Pillar . .	. . . 🜃 . . .	. . 55 . .		10
Path joins 1 − 2	Hot and moist 🜁 .	. . 66 . .	The Serpent of Wisdom follows the course of the paths or letters upward, its head being thus in א, its tail in ת. א, מ, and ש are the Mother letters, referring to the Elements; ב, ג, ד, כ, פ, ר, and ת, the Double letters, to the Planets; the rest, Single letters, to the Zodiac.	11
,, 1 − 3	. . . .	. . 78 . .		12
,, 1 − 6	. . . .	. . 91 . .		13
,, 2 − 3	. . . .	. . 105 . .		14
,, 2 − 6	. . ☉ 🜂 ♃ . .	. . 120 . .		15
,, 2 − 4	. . ♀ 🜄 ☽ . .	. . 136 . .		16
,, 3 − 6	. . ♄ 🜁 ☿ . .	. . 153 . .		17
,, 3 − 5	. . ♂ 🜄 . . .	. . 171 . .		18
,, 4 − 5	. . ☉ 🜂 ♃ . .	. . 190 . .		19
,, 4 − 6	. . ♀ 🜄 ☽ . .	. . 210 . .		20
,, 4 − 7	. . . .	. . 231 . .		21
,, 5 − 6	. . ♄ 🜁 ☿ . .	. . 253 . .		22
,, 5 − 8	Cold and moist 🜄 .	. . 276 . .		23
,, 6 − 7	. . ♂ 🜄 . . .	. . 300 . .		24
,, 6 − 9	. . ☉ 🜂 ♃ . .	. . 325 . .		25
,, 6 − 8	. . ♀ 🜄 ☽ . .	. . 351 . .		26
,, 7 − 8	. . . .	. . 378 . .		27
,, 7 − 9	. . ♄ 🜁 ☿ . .	. . 406 . .		28
,, 7 − 10	. . ♂ 🜄 . . .	. . 435 . .		29
,, 8 − 9	. . . .	. . 465 . .		30
,, 8 − 10	Hot and dry 🜂 . .	. . 496 . .		31
,, 9 − 10	. . . .	. . 528 . .		32
. . . .	Cold and dry 🜃 . .	. . . . . .	. . . .	32 bis
. . . .	. . . .	. . . . . .	. . . .	31 bis

XXI.* The Perfected Man.	XX. Complete Practical Attribution of Egyptian Gods.	XIX.* Selection of Egyptian Gods.	
Nu—the Hair	Heru-pa-Kraath	Harpocrates, Amoun, Nuith	0
Disk (of Ra)—the Face. [In Daath, Assi—the Neck]	Ptah	Ptah, Asar un Nefer, Hadith	1
	Isis [As Wisdom] . . .	Amoun, Thoth, Nuith [Zodiac] . . .	2
	Nephthys	Maut, Isis, Nephthys	3
Neith—the Arms . .	Amoun	Amoun, Isis	4
	Horus	Horus, Nephthys	5
The Mighty and Terrible One—the Breast	Ra	Asar, Ra	6
The Lords of Keraba—the Reins. Nuit—the Hips and Legs	Hathoor	Hathoor	7
	Thoth	Anubis	8
Asar and Asi—the Phallus and Vulva Sati—the Spine	Shu	Shu	9
The Eye of Hoor—the Buttocks and Anus	Osiris.	Seb. Lower (*i.e.* unwedded) Isis and Nephthys	10
As 6	Mout	Nu	11
Aupu—the Hips	Thoth	Thoth and Cynocephalus	12
Hathor—the Left Eye . .	Chomse	Chomse	13
Khenti-Khas — the Left Nostril	Hathoor	Hathoor	14
. . . .	Isis	Men Thu	15
Ba-Neh-Tattu—the Shoulders	Osiris.	Asar Ameshet Apis	16
. . . .	The twin Merti	Various twin Deities, Rehkt, Merti, &c.	17
. . . .	Hormakhu	Khephra	18
As 6	Horus	Ra-Hoor-Khuit, Pasht, Sekhet, Mau .	19
. . . .	Heru-pa-Kraath	Isis [as Virgin]	20
Apu-t—the Left Ear . .	Amoun-Ra	Amoun-Ra	21
. . . .	Maat	Ma	22
As 24	Ⲓⲩϧϩⲟⲩⲣⲉⲑ .	Tum Athph Auramoth (as ▽), Asar (as Hanged Man), Hekar, Isis	23
Sekhet — the Belly and Back	Hammemit	Merti goddesses, Typhon, Apep, Khephra	24
. . . .	Ⲁⲣⲏⲱⲩⲉⲣⲓⲩ .	Nephthys	25
As 10, for ע means Eye.	Set	Khem (Set)	26
Khenti-Khas — the Right Nostril	Menθu	Horus	27
The Lords of Keraba—the Reins	Nuit	Ahephi, Aroueris	28
. . . .	Anubi	Khephra (as Scarab in Tarot Trump) .	29
Hathor—the Right Eye .	Ra	Ra and many others	30
[Serget—the Teeth.] As 6	Mau	Thoum-aesh-neith, Mau, Kabeshunt Horus, Tarpesheth	31
Apu-t—the Right Ear . .	See Note *	Sebek, Mako	32
אלים חיים—the Bones. As 16	. . . .	Satem, Ahapshi, Nephthys, Ameshet .	32 bis
. . . .	. . . .	Asar	31 bis

XVIII.* The Empress Scale of Colour [ה].	XVII.* The Emperor Scale of Colour [ו].	XVI.* The Queen Scale of Colour [ה].	
. . . .	. . . .	. . . .	0
White, flecked gold	White brilliance	White brilliance	1
White, flecked red, blue, and yellow	Blue pearl grey, like mother-of-pearl	Grey	2
Grey, flecked pink	Dark brown	Black	3
Deep azure, flecked yellow	Deep purple	Blue	4
Red, flecked black	Bright scarlet	Scarlet red	5
Gold amber	Rich salmon	Yellow (gold)	6
Olive, flecked gold	Bright yellow green	Emerald	7
Yellowish brown, flecked white	Red-russet	Orange	8
Citrine, flecked azure	Very dark purple	Violet	9
Black rayed with yellow	As Queen Scale, but flecked with gold	Citrine, olive, russet, and black *	10
Emerald, flecked gold	Blue emerald green	Sky blue	11
Indigo, rayed violet	Grey	Purple	12
Silver, rayed sky blue	Cold pale blue	Silver	13
Bright rose or cerise, rayed pale green	Early spring green	Sky blue	14
Glowing red	Brilliant flame	Red	15
Rich brown	Deep warm olive	Deep indigo	16
Reddish grey inclined to mauve	New yellow leather	Pale mauve	17
Dark greenish brown	Rich bright russet	Maroon	18
Reddish amber	Grey	Deep purple	19
Plum colour	Green grey	Slate grey	20
Bright blue, rayed yellow	Rich purple	Blue	21
Pale green	Deep blue-green	Blue	22
White, flecked purple, like mother-of-pearl	Deep olive-green	Sea green	23
Livid indigo brown (like a black beetle)	Very dark brown	Dull brown	24
Dark vivid blue	Green	Yellow	25
Cold dark grey, approaching black	Blue black	Black	26
Bright red, rayed azure or emerald	Venetian red	Red	27
White, tinged purple	Bluish mauve	Sky blue	28
Stone colour	Light translucent pinkish brown	Buff, flecked silver-white	29
Amber, rayed red	Rich amber	Gold yellow	30
Vermilion, flecked crimson and emerald	Scarlet, flecked gold	Vermilion	31
Black, rayed blue	Blue black	Black	32
Black, flecked yellow	Dark brown	Amber	32 bis
White, red, yellow, blue, black (the latter outside)	The 7 prismatic colours, the violet being outside	Deep purple, nearly black	31 bis

XXXIV. Some Greek Gods.	XXXIII. Some Scandinavian Gods.	XXV.-XXXII.	XXIV. Certain of the Hindu and Buddhist Results.	
Pan			Nerodha-samapatti, Nirvikalpa-samadhi, Shiva darshana	0
Zeus, Iacchus	Wotan	We have insufficient knowledge of the attributions of Assyrian, Syrian, Mongolian, Tibetan, Mexican, Zend, South Sea, West African, &c.	Unity with Brahma, Atma darshana	1
Athena, Uranus	Odin			2
Cybele, Demeter, Rhea, Heré	Frigga			3
Poseidon	Wotan			4
Ares, Hades	Thor			5
Iacchus, Apollo, Adonis			Vishvarupa-darshana	6
Aphrodite, Niké	Freya			7
Hermes	Odin, Loki			8
Zeus (as △), Diana of Ephesus (as phallic stone)				9
Persephone, [Adonis] Psyche			Vision of the "Higher Self," the various Dhyanas or Jhanas	10
Zeus	Valkyries		Vayu-Bhawana	11
Hermes				12
Artemis, Hecate			Vision of Chandra	13
Aphrodite	Freya		Success in Bhaktiyoga	14
Athena				15
[Heré]			Success in Hathayoga, Asana and Prana-yama	16
Castor and Pollux, Apollo the Diviner				17
Apollo the Charioteer				18
Demeter [borne by lions]				19
[Attis]				20
Zeus				21
Themis, Minos, Aeacus, and Rhadamanthus				22
Poseidon			Apo-Bhawana	23
Ares				24
Apollo, Artemis (hunters)				25
Pan, Priapus, [Erect Hermes and Bacchus]				26
Ares	Tuisco			27
[Athena], Ganymede				28
Poseidon				29
Helios, Apollo			Vision of Surya	30
Hades			Agni-Bhawana	31
[Athena]				32
[Demeter]			Prithivi-Bhawana	32 bis
Iacchus			Vision of the Higher Self, Prana-yama	31 bis

XXIII.* The Forty Buddhist Meditations.		XXII. Small Selection of Hindu Deities.	
Nothing and Neither P nor p′ Space Consciousness	F F F	AUM	0
Indifference	S	Parabrahm (or any other whom one wishes to please)	1
Joy	S	Shiva, Vishnu (as Buddha avatars), Akasa (as matter), Lingam	2
Compassion	S	Bhavani (all forms of Sakti), Prana (as Force), Yoni	3
Friendliness	S	Indra, Brahma	4
Death	R	Vishnu, Varruna-Avatar	5
Buddha	R	Vishnu-Hari-Krishna-Rama	6
The Gods	R		7
Analysis into 4 Elements	A	Hanuman	8
Dhamma	R	Ganesha, Vishnu (Kurm Avatar)	9
Sangha The Body	R R	Lakshmi, &c. [Kundalini]	10
Wind	K	The Maruts [Vayu]	11
Yellow	K	Hanuman, Vishnu (as Parasa-Rama)	12
Loathsomeness of Food	P	Chandra (as ☽)	13
Dark Blue	K	Lalita (sexual aspect of Sakti)	14
Bloody Corpse	I	Shiva	15
Beaten and Scattered Corpse	I	Shiva (Sacred Bull)	16
White	K	Various twin and hybrid Deities	17
Worm-eaten Corpse	I		18
Gnawed by Wild Beasts Corpse	I	Vishnu (Nara-Singh Avatar)	19
Bloated Corpse	I	The Gopi girls, the Lord of Yoga	20
Liberality	R	Brahma, Indra	21
Hacked in Pieces Corpse	I	Yama	22
Water	K	Soma [apas]	23
Skeleton Corpse	I	Kundalini	24
Limited Aperture	K	Vishnu [Horse-Avatar]	25
Putrid Corpse	I	Lingam, Yoni	26
Blood-red	K		27
Purple Corpse	I		28
Conduct	R	Vishnu [Matsya Avatar]	29
Light	K	Surya (as ☉)	30
Fire	K	Agni [Tejas], Yama [as God of Last Judgment]	31
Quiescence	R	Brahma	32
Earth	K	[Prithivi]	32 bis
Breathing	R	[Akasa]	31 bis

XL.* Precious Stones.	XXXIX.* Plants, Real and Imaginary.	XXXVIII.* Animals, Real and Imaginary.	
. . . .	. . . .	. . . .	0
Diamond	Almond in Flower	God	1
Star Ruby, Turquoise . .	Amaranth	Man	2
Star Sapphire, Pearl. . .	Cypress, Opium Poppy	Woman	3
Amethyst and Sapphire .	Olive, Shamrock	Unicorn	4
Ruby.	Oak, Nux Vomica, Nettle . . .	Basilisk	5
Topaz, Yellow Diamond .	Acacia, Bay, Laurel, Vine . . .	Phœnix, Lion, Child.	6
Emerald.	Rose	Iynx	7
Opal, especially Fire Opal.	Moly, Anhalonium Lewinii . .	Hermaphrodite, Jackal. . . .	8
Quartz	[Banyan], Mandrake, Damiana .	Elephant	9
Rock Crystal	Willow, Lily, Ivy.	Sphinx	10
Topaz, Chalcedony . . .	Aspen	Eagle or Man (Cherub of 🜁) .	11
Opal, Agate	Vervain, Herb Mercury, Marjolane, Palm	Swallow, Ibis, Ape	12
Moonstone, Pearl, Crystal .	Almond, Mugwort, Hazel (as ☽), Moonwort, Ranunculus	Dog	13
Emerald, Turquoise . . .	Myrtle, Rose, Clover	Sparrow, Dove, Swan	14
Ruby.	Tiger Lily, Geranium	Ram, Owl	15
Topaz	Mallow	Bull (Cherub of 🜃)	16
Alexandrite, Tourmaline, Iceland Spar	Hybrids, Orchids.	Magpie. Hybrids	17
Amber	Lotus.	Crab, Turtle, Sphinx	18
Cat's Eye	Sunflower	Lion (Cherub of 🜂)	19
Peridot	Snowdrop, Lily, Narcissus . . .	Virgin, Anchorite, any solitary person or animal	20
Amethyst, Lapis Lazuli .	Hyssop, Oak, Poplar, Fig . . .	Eagle	21
Emerald.	Aloe	Elephant	22
Beryl or Aquamarine . .	Lotus, all Water Plants. . . .	Eagle-snake-scorpion (Cherub of 🜄)	23
Snakestone	Cactus	Scorpion, Beetle, Lobster or Crayfish, Wolf	24
Jacinth	Rush	Centaur, Horse, Hippogriff, Dog	25
Black Diamond	Indian Hemp, Orchis Root, Thistle	Goat, Ass	26
Ruby, any red stone. . .	Absinthe, Rue.	Horse, Bear, Wolf	27
Artificial Glass	[Olive], Cocoanut.	Man or Eagle (Cherub of 🜁), Peacock	28
Pearl.	Unicellular Organisms, Opium .	Fish, Dolphin	29
Crysoleth	Sunflower, Laurel, Heliotrope .	Lion, Sparrowhawk	30
Fire Opal	Red Poppy, Hibiscus, Nettle . .	Lion (Cherub of 🜂)	31
Onyx.	Ash, Cypress, Hellebore, Yew, Nightshade	Crocodile	32
Salt	Oak, Ivy	Bull (Cherub of) 🜃	32 bis
. . . .	Almond in flower.	Sphinx (if Sworded and Crowned)	31 bis

XXXVII. Hindu Legendary Demons.	XXXVI. Selection of Christian Gods (10); Apostles (12), Evangelists (4), and Churches of Asia (7).	XXXV. Some Roman Gods.	
. . . .	. . . .	. . . .	0
[Insufficient information.]	God, the 3 in 1	Jupiter	1
	God the Father, God who guides Parliament.	Janus	2
	The Virgin Mary	Juno, Cybele, Saturn, Hecate, &c.	3
	God the Rain-maker (*vide* Prayer-book), God the Farmer's Friend	Jupiter	4
	Christ coming to Judge the World	Mars	5
	God the Son (and Maker of Fine Weather)	Apollo	6
	Messiah, Lord of Hosts (*vide* Prayer-book, R. Kipling, &c.)	Venus	7
	God the Holy Ghost (as Comforter and Inspirer of Scripture), God the Healer of Plagues	Mercury	8
	God the Holy Ghost (as Incubus)	Diana (as ☽)	9
	Ecclesia Xsti, The Virgin Mary	Ceres	10
	Matthew	Jupiter	11
	Sardis	Mercury	12
	Laodicea	Diana	13
	Thyatira	Venus	14
	[The Disciples are too indefinite]	Mars, Minerva	15
	. . . .	Venus	16
	. . . .	Castor and Pollux, [Janus]	17
	. . . .	Mercury	18
	. . . .	Venus (repressing the Fire of Vulcan)	19
	. . . .	[Attis], Ceres, Adonis	20
	Philadelphia	Jupiter, [Pluto]	21
	. . . .	Vulcan	22
	John, Jesus as Hanged Man	Neptune	23
	. . . .	Mars	24
	. . . .	Diana (as Archer)	25
	. . . .	Pan, Vesta, Bacchus	26
	Pergamos	Mars	27
	. . . .	Juno	28
	. . . .	Neptune	29
	Smyrna	Apollo	30
	Mark	Vulcan, Pluto	31
	Ephesus	Saturn	32
	Luke	Ceres	32 bis
	The Holy Ghost	[Liber]	31 bis

XLVI.* System of Taoism.	XLV. Magical Powers [Western Mysticism].	XLIV.* Mineral Drugs.	
The Tao or Great Extreme of the Yi King	The Supreme Attainment	Carbon	0
Shang Ti (also the Tao) .	Union with God	Aur. Pot.	1
The Yang and Khien . .	The Vision of God face to face	Phosphorus . . .	2
Kwan-se-on, The Yin and Khwan	The Vision of Sorrow	Silver	3
. . . .	The Vision of Love	. . . .	4
. . . .	The Vision of Power.	Iron, Sulphur . . .	5
Li	The Vision of the Harmony of Things (also the Mysteries of the Crucifixion)	. . . .	6
. . . .	The Vision of Beauty Triumphant	Arsenic	7
. . . .	The Vision of Splendour [Ezekiel]	Mercury.	8
. . . .	The Vision of the Machinery of the Universe	Lead	9
Khan	The Vision of the Holy Guardian Angel or of Adonai	Mag. Sulph. . . .	10
Sun	Divination	. . . .	11
Sun	Miracles of Healing, Gift of Tongues, Knowledge of Sciences	Mercury.	12
Khan and Khwan . . .	The White Tincture, Clairvoyance, Divination by Dreams	. . . .	13
Tui	Love-philtres	. . . .	14
. . . .	Power of Consecrating Things	. . . .	15
. . . .	The Secret of Physical Strength	. . . .	16
. . . .	Power of being in two or more places at one time, and of Prophecy	. . . .	17
. . . .	Power of Casting Enchantments.	. . . .	18
. . . .	Power of Training Wild Beasts	. . . .	19
. . . .	Invisibility, Parthenogenesis, Initiation (?) .	. . . .	20
Li	Power of Acquiring Political and other Ascendency	. . . .	21
. . . .	Works of Justice and Equilibrium	. . . .	22
Tui	The Great Work, Talismans, Crystal-gazing, &c.	Sulphates	23
. . . .	Necromancy	. . . .	24
. . . .	Transmutations	. . . .	25
. . . .	The Witches' Sabbath so-called, the Evil Eye	. . . .	26
Kăn	Works of Wrath and Vengeance.	. . . .	27
. . . .	Astrology	. . . .	28
. . . .	Bewitchments, Casting Illusions.	. . . .	29
Li and Khien	The Red Tincture, Power of Acquiring Wealth	. . . .	30
Kăn	Evocation, Pyromancy.	Nitrates.	31
Khăn	Works of Malediction and Death	Lead	32
Kăn	Alchemy, Geomancy, Making of Pantacles .	Bismuth.	32 bis
. . . .	Invisibility, Transformations, Vision of the Genius	Carbon	31 bis

XLIII.* Vegetable Drugs.	XLII. Perfumes.	XLI. Magical Weapons.	
. . . .	. . . .	. . . .	0
Elixir Vitæ	Ambergris	Swastika or Fylfat Cross, Crown	1
Hashish	Musk	Lingam, the Inner Robe of Glory	2
Belladonna	Myrrh, Civet	Yoni, the Outer Robe of Concealment	3
Opium	Cedar	The Wand, Sceptre, or Crook	4
Nux Vomica, Nettle	Tobacco	The Sword, Spear, Scourge, or Chain	5
Stramonium, Alcohol, Digitalis, Coffee	Olibanum	The Lamen or Rosy Cross	6
Damiana	Benzoin, Rose, Red Sandal	The Lamp and Girdle	7
Anhalonium Lewinii	Storax	The Names and Versicles and Apron	8
Orchid Root	Jasmine, Jinseng, all Odoriferous Roots	The Perfumes and Sandals	9
Corn	Dittany of Crete	The Magical Circle and Triangle	10
Peppermint	Galbanum	The Dagger or Fan	11
All cerebral excitants	Mastic, White Sandal, Mace, Storax, all Fugitive Odours	The Wand or Caduceus	12
Juniper, Pennyroyal, & all emmenogogues	Menstrual Blood, Camphor, Aloes, all Sweet Virginal Odours	Bow and Arrow	13
All aphrodisiacs	Sandalwood, Myrtle, all Soft Voluptuous Odours	The Girdle	14
All cerebral excitants	Dragon's Blood	The Horns, Energy, the Burin	15
Sugar	Storax	The Labour of Preparation	16
Ergot and ecbolics	Wormwood	The Tripod	17
Watercress	Onycha	The Furnace	18
All carminatives and tonics	Olibanum	The Discipline (Preliminary)	19
All anaphrodisiacs	Narcissus	The Lamp and Wand (Virile Force reserved), the Bread	20
Cocaine	Saffron, all Generous Odours	The Sceptre	21
Tobacco	Galbanum	The Cross of Equilibrium	22
Cascara, all purges	Onycha, Myrrh	The Cup and Cross of Suffering, the Wine	23
. . . .	Siamese Benzoin, Opoponax	The Pain of the Obligation	24
. . . .	Lign-aloes	The Arrow (swift and straight application of Force)	25
Orchis [Satyrion]	Musk, civet (also ♄ ian Perfumes)	The Secret Force, Lamp	26
. . . .	Pepper, Dragon's Blood, all Hot Pungent Odours	The Sword	27
All diuretics	Galbanum	The Censer or Aspergillus	28
All narcotics	Ambergris	The Twilight of the Place and Magic Mirror	29
Alcohol	Olibanum, Cinnamon, all Glorious Odours	The Lamen or Bow and Arrow	30
. . . .	Olibanum, all Fiery Odours	The Wand or Lamp, Pyramid of △	31
. . . .	Assafœtida, Scammony, Indigo, Sulphur (all Evil Odours)	A Sickle	32
. . . .	Storax, all Dull and Heavy Odours	The Pantacle or Salt	32 bis
Stramonium	. . . .	. . . .	31 bis

LIII. The Greek Alphabet.	LII. The Arabic Alphabet.	LI. The Coptic Alphabet.	L.* Transcendental Morality. [10 Virtues (1–10), 7 Sins (Planets), 4 Magick Powers (Elements).]	
. . . .	. . . .	. . . .	. . . .	0
. . . .	Three Lost Fathers.*	. . . ⲅ . . .	Pyrrho-Zoroastrianism (Accomplishment of Great Work)	1
. . . [σ] . . .		. . . ϭ . . .	Devotion	2
. . . .		. . . ϯ . . .	Silence	3
. . . [ϲ] . . .	. . . ث . . .	. . . ⲏ . . .	Obedience	4
. . . [ϕ] . . .	. . . خ . . .	. . . ⲫ . . .	Energy	5
. . . ω . . .	. . . ذ . . .	. . . ⲱ . . .	Devotion to Great Work	6
. . . [ϵ] . . .	. . . ض . . .	. . . ⲉ . . .	Unselfishness	7
. . . .	. . . ظ . . .	. . . ϥ . . .	Truthfulness	8
. . . χ . . .	. . . غ . . .	. . . ϫ . . .	Independence	9
. . . ϡ . . .	. . . غ . . .	. . . ϩ . . .	Scepticism	10
. . . α . . .	. . . ا . . .	. . . ⲁ . . .	Noscere	11
. . . β . . .	. . . ب . . .	. . . ⲃ . . .	Falsehood, Dishonesty [Envy] . .	12
. . . γ . . .	. . . ج . . .	. . . ⲅ . . .	Contentment [Idleness]	13
. . . δ . . .	. . . د . . .	. . . ⲇ . . .	Unchastity [Lust]	14
. . . ε . . .	. . . ه . . .	. . . ⲉ . . .	. . . .	15
. . . ϝ . . .	. . . و . . .	. . . ⲩ . . .	. . . .	16
. . . ζ . . .	. . . ز . . .	. . . ⲍ . . .	. . . .	17
. . . ἡ . . .	. . . ح . . .	. . . ϧ . . .	. . . .	18
. . . θ . . .	. . . ط . . .	. . . ⲑ . . .	. . . .	19
. . . ι . . .	. . . ي . . .	. . . ⲓ . . .	. . . .	20
. . . κ . . .	. . . ك . . .	. . . ⲕ . . .	Bigotry, Hypocrisy [Gluttony] . .	21
. . . λ . . .	. . . ل . . .	. . . ⲗ . . .	. . . .	22
. . . μ . . .	. . . م . . .	. . . ⲙ . . .	Audere	23
. . . ν . . .	. . . ن . . .	. . . ⲛ . . .	. . . .	24
. . . ξ[σ] . . .	. . . س . . .	. . . ⲝ . . .	. . . .	25
. . . ο . . .	. . . ع . . .	. . . ⲟ . . .	. . . .	26
. . . π . . .	. . . ف . . .	. . . ⲡ . . .	Cruelty [Wrath]	27
. . . ψ . . .	. . . ص . . .	. . . ⲯ . . .	. . . .	28
. . . ϙ . . .	. . . ق . . .	. . . ⲭ . . .	. . . .	29
. . . ρ . . .	. . . ر . . .	. . . ⲣ . . .	[Pride]	30
. . . ϡ . . .	. . . ش . . .	. . . ϣ . . .	Velle	31
. . . τ . . .	. . . ت . . .	. . . ⲧ . . .	Envy [Avarice]	32
. . . υ . . .	. . . .	. . . .	Tacere	32 bis
. . . .	. . . .	. . . .	. . . .	31 bis

XLIX.* Lineal Figures of the Planets, &c., and Geomancy.	XLVIII. Figures related to Pure Number.	XLVII. Kings and Princes of the Jinn.	
The Circle	. . . .	. . . .	0
The Point	. . . .	. . . .	1
The Line, also the Cross .	The Cross	. . . .	2
The Plane, also the Diamond, Oval, Circle, and other Yoni Symbols	The Triangle	. . . .	3
The Solid Figure	Tetrahedron or Pyramid, Cross . .	. . . . هفيط	4
The Tessaract	The Rose	. . . . مهنط هيج	5
Sephirotic Geomantic Figures follow the Planets. Caput* and Cauda Draconis* are the Nodes of the Moon, nearly = Neptune and Herschel respectively. They belong to Malkuth.	Calvary Cross, Truncated Pyramid, Cube	. . . . . دهيجل علمص مهلع	6
	A Rose (7×7), Candlestick . . .	. . . . . سهلط مص محهلع *	7
	. . . .	. . . . . شالط نوع رزع اهموش	8
	. . . .	. . . . والخد سعلت كلت اميوز	9
	Altar, Double Cube, Calvary Cross .	. . . .	10
Those of 🜁y Triplicity .	. . . .	. . . طاهطليائل هد هبوب سمطايا	11
Octagram	Calvary Cross	. . . . . سمحاق تسيخ هليخ .	12
Enneagram	Greek Cross, Plane, Table of Shew-bread	. . . . مريخ مهلخ .	13
Heptagram	. . . .	. . . . يهاوة .	14
Puer*	. . . .	. . . . محطمتك	15
Amissio*	. . . .	. . . . . . مهطح مهلوة مليموح	16
Albus*	Swastika	. . . . . . براخ سعد بواة طنطم	17
Populus and Via* . . .	. . . .	. . . . مهيط ليلا	18
Fortuna Major and Fortuna Minor*	. . . .	. . . . نملح سمهط*	19
Conjunctio*	. . . .	. . . . . . سميحطمة مقنه كهف .	20
Square and Rhombus . .	. . . .	. . . . سويدم سبعورة .	21
Puella*	Greek Cross Solid, the Rose (3+7+12)	. . . لفطا مدبج [illegible] طمش	22
Those of 🜄y Triplicity .	. . . .	. . . . مليموح .	23
Rubeus*	. . . .	. . . . ملوم مديح .	24
Acquisitio*	The Rose (5×5)	. . . . كليل حمط مطلح .	25
Carcer*	Calvary Cross of 10, Solid . . .	. . . . . مملط or جسم مطيم	26
Pentagram	. . . .	. . . . . . عنفوالركيطم ورطش .	27
Tristitia*	. . . .	. . . . هفيط مسعود .	28
Laetitia*	. . . .	. . . . هملعش عد عقير	29
Hexagram	. . . .	. . . . . . طلجياش سطت اهيل .	30
Those of 🜂y Triplicity .	. . . .	. . . . دهيوم علسطين .	31
Triangle	. . . .	. . . . حهفاعل or معهط يمرصلو	32
Those of 🜃y Triplicity .	. . . .	. . . .	32 bis
. . . .	. . . .	. . . .	31 bis

LXIV. Secret Names of the Four Worlds.	LXIII. The Four Worlds.	LXII. Kings of the Elemental Spirits.	LXI. Angels of the Elements.	LX. The Rulers of the Elements.	
. . . . . מה	Yetzirah, Formative World	Paralda . .	. . . חסן	. . . אריאל	11
. . . . . סג	Briah, Creative World . .	Niksa . .	. . . טליהד	. . . תרשים	23
. . . . . עב	Atziluth, Archetypal World	Djin . . .	. . . אראל	. . . . שרף	31
. . . . . בן	Assiah, Material World . .	Ghob . . .	. . פורלאך	. . . כרוב	32 bis
. . . .	. . . .	. . . . . .	. . . .	. . . .	31 bis

LXXI. The Court Cards of the Tarot, with the Spheres of their Celestial Dominion—Wands.	LXX. Attribution of Pentagram.	LXIX.* The Alchemical Elements.	
The Prince of the Chariot of Fire. Rules 20° ♋ to 20° ♌, including most of Leo Minor	Left Upper Point . .	. . . ☿ . . .	11
The Queen of the Thrones of Flame. 20° ♓ to 20° ♈, includes part of Andromeda	Right Upper Point .	. . . ⊖ . . .	23
The Lord of the Flame and the Lightning. The King of the Spirits of Fire. Rules 20° ♏ to 20° ♐, including part of Hercules	Right Lower Point .	. . . 🜍 . . .	31
The Princess of the Shining Flame. The Rose of the Palace of Fire. Rules one Quadrant of Heavens round N. Pole	Left Lower Point . .	. . . ⊖ . . .	32 bis
The Root of the Powers of Fire (Ace)	Topmost Point . . .	. . . .	31 bis

LXXVI. The Five Skandhas.	LXXV. The Five Elements (Tatwas).	LXXIV. The Court Cards of the Tarot, with the Spheres of their Celestial Dominion—Pantacles.	
Sankhara .	Vayu—the Blue Circle	The Prince of the Chariot of Earth. 20° ♈ to 20° ♉	11
Vedana . .	Apas—the Silver Crescent . .	The Queen of the Thrones of Earth. 20° ♐ to 20° ♑	23
Saññā . .	Agni or Tejas—the Red Triangle	The Lord of the Wide and Fertile Land. The King of the Spirits of Earth. 20° ♌ to 20° ♍	31
Rupa . . .	Prithivi—the Yellow Square . .	The Princess of the Echoing Hills. The Lotus of the Palace of the Earth. Rules a 4th Quadrant of the Heavens about Kether	32 bis
Viññanam .	Akasa—the Black Egg	The Root of the Powers of Earth	31 bis

LIX. Archangels of the Quarters.	LVIII. Supreme Elemental Kings.	LVII.* The Four Quarters.	LVI. The Four Rivers.	LV. The Elements and Senses.	LIV. The Letters of the Name.	
. . רפאל	Tahoeloj . . .	. (E) מזרח	. . הדקל	🜁 Air, Smell .	. . ו . .	11
. גבריאל	Thahebyobeaatan	(W) מערב	. . גיחון	🜄 Water, Taste	. . ה . .	23
. מיכאל	Ohooohatan . .	. (S) דרום	. . פישון	🜂 Fire, Sight .	. . י . .	31
. . אוריאל	Thahaaotahe . .	. (N) צפון	. . . פרת	🜃 Earth, Touch	. . ה . .	32 bis
. . . . . .	. . . .	. . . . . .	. . . . . .	☸ Spirit, Hearing	. . ש . .	31 bis

LXVIII. The Demon Kings.	LXVII. The Parts of the Soul.	LXVI. Spelling of Tetragrammaton in the Four Worlds.	LXV. Secret Numbers corresponding.	
Oriens	. . . . רוח	. . . . . יוד הא ואו הא	. . 45 . .	11
Ariton	. . . . נשמה	. . . . . יוד הי ואו הי	. . 63 . .	23
Paimon	. . . . חיה	. . . . יוד היה ויו היה	. . 72 . .	31
Amaimon	. . . . נפש	. . . . . . יוד הה וו הה	. . 52 . .	32 bis
. . . .	. . . . יחידה	. . . .	. . . . . .	31 bis

LXXIII. The Court Cards of the Tarot, with the Spheres of their Celestial Dominion—Swords.	LXXII. The Court Cards of the Tarot, with the Spheres of their Celestial Dominion—Cups.	
The Prince of the Chariot of Air. 20° ♑ to 20° ♒	The Prince of the Chariot of the Waters. 20° ♎ to 20° ♏	11
The Queen of the Thrones of Air. 20° ♍ to 20° ♎	The Queen of the Thrones of the Waters. 20° ♊ to 20° ♋	23
The Lord of the Winds and the Breezes. The King of the Spirits of Air. 20° ♉ to 20° ♊	The Lord of the Waves and the Waters. The King of the Hosts of the Sea. 20° ♒ to 20° ♓, including most of Pegasus	31
The Princess of the Rushing Winds. The Lotus of the Palace of Air. Rules a 3rd Quadrant	The Princess of the Waters. The Lotus of the Palace of the Floods. Rules another Quadrant	32 bis
The Root of the Powers of Air	The Root of the Powers of Water	31 bis

LXXXIII. The Attribution of the Hexagram.	LXXXII. The Noble Eightfold Path.	LXXXI. Metals.	LXXX. Olympic Planetary Spirits.	
Left Lower Point . . .	Samma Vaca . . .	Mercury	Ophiel	12
Bottom Point	Samma Sankappo .	Silver	Phul	13
Right Lower Point . .	Samma Kammanto .	Copper	Hagith.	14
Right Upper Point . .	Samma Ajivo . . .	Tin.	Bethor.	21
Left Upper Point. . .	Samma Vayamo . .	Iron	Phaleg.	27
Centre Point	Samma Samadhi . .	Gold	Och.	30
Top Point	Samma Sati and Samaditthi	Lead	Arathron	32

<table>
<tr><th>XC.
The 42-fold Name which revolves in the Palaces of Yetzirah.</th><th>LXXXIX.*
The Revolution of אהיה in Briah.</th><th>LXXXVIII.
Translation of Col. LXXXVII.</th><th></th></tr>
<tr><td>. . . . .</td><td>. . . . .</td><td>. . . . .</td><td>0</td></tr>
<tr><td>. . . . . אב</td><td>. . . . . אהיה</td><td rowspan="3">Palatium Sancti Sanctorum . . .</td><td>1</td></tr>
<tr><td>. . . . . ני</td><td>. . . . . אההי</td><td>2</td></tr>
<tr><td>. . . . . תצ</td><td>. . . . . איהה</td><td>3</td></tr>
<tr><td>. . . . . . קרעשמן</td><td>. . . . . ההיא</td><td>P. Amoris . . . .</td><td>4</td></tr>
<tr><td>. . . . . . כגדיכש</td><td>. . . . . ההאי</td><td>P. Meriti . . . .</td><td>5</td></tr>
<tr><td>. . . . . . במרצתג</td><td>. . . . . האהי</td><td>P. Benevolentiae. . . . . . .</td><td>6</td></tr>
<tr><td>. . . . . . הקממנע</td><td>. . . . . האיה</td><td>P. Substantiae Coeli . . . .</td><td>7</td></tr>
<tr><td>. . . . . . ינלפזק</td><td>. . . . . היאה</td><td>P. Serenitatis . . . .</td><td>8</td></tr>
<tr><td>. . . . . שקי</td><td>. . . . . יאהה</td><td rowspan="4">P. Albedinis Crystalinae . . .</td><td>9</td></tr>
<tr><td rowspan="3">. . . . . עית</td><td>. . . . . . . יההא</td><td rowspan="3">10</td></tr>
<tr><td>. . . . . . . יהאה</td></tr>
<tr><td>. . . . . . . אל שדי</td></tr>
</table>

TABLE III

LXXIX. Spirits of the Planets.*	LXXVIII. Intelligences of the Planets.	LXXVII. The Planets and their Numbers.	
תפתרתרת (2080)	טיריאל (260)	☿ 8	12
חשמודאי (369)	מלכא בתרשישים ועד ברוה שהקים (3321)	☽ 9	13
קדמאל (175)	הגיאל (49)	♀ 7	14
הסמאל (136)	יופיל (136)	♃ 4	21
ברצבאל (325)	גראפיאל (325)	♂ 5	27
סורת (666)	נכיאל (111)	☉ 6	30
זזאל (45)	אגיאל (45)	♄ 3	32

TABLE IV

LXXXVII. Palaces of Briah.	LXXXVI. Choirs of Angels in Briah.	LXXXV. Angels of Briah.	LXXXIV. Divine Names of Briah.	
. . . .	. . . .	. . . .	. . . .	0
	שרפים	יהואל		1
היכל קודש קדשים	אופנים	רפאל	אל	2
	כרובים	כרוביאל		3
היכל אהבה	שיככים	צדקיאל	מצפצ (*sic*)	4
ה. זכות	תרשישים	תרשיש	יהוד	5
ה. רצון	חשמלים	מטטרון*	יהוח	6
ה. עצם שמים	מלכים	וסיאל	אלהים	7
ה. נוגה	בני אלהים	הסניאל	מצפץ	8
ה. לבנת הספיר	ישים	יהואל*	יה־אדני	9
	אראלים	מיכאל		10

XCVI.* The Revolution of יהוה in Yetzirah.	XCV. Contents of Col. XCIV.	XCIV. English of Palaces (Col. XCIII.).	
. . . .	. . . .	. . . .	0
. . . . יהוה	. . . .	. . . .	1
. . . . יההו	. . . .	. . . .	2
. . . . יוהה	. . . .	. . . .	3
. . . . הויה	Blessings, all good things . . .	Planities	4
. . . . ההוי	Snow, rain, spirit of life, blessings	Repositorium	5
. . . . ההיו	Angels singing in Divine presence	Habitaculum	6
. . . . היהו	Altar, Mikhael offering souls of just	Habitaculum	7
. . . . הוהי	Millstones where manna for just is ground for future	Locus communicationis . .	8
. . . . והיה	Sol, Luna, planets, stars, and 10 spheres	Firmamentum	9
. . . . ויהה . . . . וההי . . . . אל יהוה	Has no use. Follow 390 heavens, 18,000 worlds, Earth, Eden, and Hell	Velum sive Cortina	10

CIV. The Ten Earths in Seven Palaces.	CIII.* The Ten Divisions of the Body of God.	CII.* The Revolution of Adonai in Assiah.	CI. English of Col. C.	
. . . .	. . . .	. . . .	. . . .	0
. . . .	Cranium	. . . . . אדני	Holy living creatures	1
. . . . ארץ	Cerebrum dextrum	. . . . . אדינ	Wheels	2
. . . .	Cerebrum sinistrum	. . . . . אניד	Active ones, thrones	3
. . . . אדמה	Brachium dextrum	. . . . . אינד	Brilliant ones . . .	4
. . . . . ניא	Brachium sinistrum	. . . . . אידנ	Fiery serpents . .	5
. . . . . נשיה	Totum corpus a gutture usque ad membrum sanctum	. . . . . דניא	Kings	6
. . . . . ציה	Pes dexter	. . . . . דנאי	Gods.	7
. . . . ארקא	Pes sinister	. . . . . דינא	Sons of God . . .	8
. . . . תבל	Signum fœderis sancti . . .	. . . . . דיאנ	Angels of elements .	9
. . . . חלד	Corolla quæ est in Jesod . .	. . . . דאני . . . . דאינ . . אל אדני	Flames	10

XCIII. The Heavens of Assiah.	XCII. The Angelic Functions in the World of Yetzirah.	XCI. The Saints or Adepts of the Hebrews.	
. . . .	. . . .	. . . .	0
. . . . ⎫ ערבות	Seraphim stabant supra illud: sex alæ	Messias filius David . . .	1
. . . . ⎬ ערבות	Seraphim stabant supra illud: sex alæ	Mosheh	2
. . . . . ערבות	Seraphim stabant supra illud: sex alæ	Enoch	3
. . . . מכון	Sex alæ	Abraham	4
. . . . מעון	Uni: in duabus	Jacob	5
. . . . זבול	Velabat facies suas: et duabus velabat .	Elijah	6
. . . . שחקים	Pedes suas et	Mosheh	7
. . . . רקיע	Duabus volabat	Aaron	8
. . . . ⎫ תבל וילון שמים*	Et clamabat hic ad illum et dicebat Sanctus, sanctus, sanctus, Dominus Exercitium, plenitudo totius terræ gloria ejus	Joseph (Justus)	9
תבל וילון שמים*	Et clamabat hic ad illum et dicebat Sanctus, sanctus, sanctus, Dominus Exercitium, plenitudo totius terræ gloria ejus	David, Elisha	10

C.* Angels of Assiah.	XCIX.* Archangels of Assiah.	XCVIII. English of Col. XCVII.	XCVII. Parts of the Soul.	
. . . .	. . . .	. . . .	. . . .	0
. . . חיותהקדש	. . . . מטטרון	The Self	. . . . יחידה	1
. . . . . אופנים	. . . . . רציאל	The Life Force	. . . . . חיה	2
. . . . אראלים	. . . . צפקיאל	The Intuition	. . . . נשמה	3
. . . . חשמלים	. . . . צדקיאל	The Intellect	. . . . רוח	4
. . . . . שרפים	. . . . . כמאל	The Intellect	. . . . רוח	5
. . . . . מלכים	. . . . . רפאל	The Intellect	. . . . רוח	6
. . . . . אלהים	. . . . האניאל	The Intellect	. . . . רוח	7
. . . בני אלהים	. . . . . מיכאל	The Intellect	. . . . רוח	8
. . . . . כרבים	. . . . גבריאל	The Intellect	. . . . רוח	9
. . . . . . אשים	. (מטטרון) סנדלפון	The Animal Soul, which perceives and feels	. . . . . נפש	10

CXI. Sephirotic Colours [Dr. Jellinek].	CX. Elements and Quarters (Sepher Yetzirah).	CIX.* The Dukes and Kings of Edom.	
. . . .	. . . .	. . . .	0
Concealed Light . . .	. . רוה אלהים היים	. . . .	1
Sky Blue	Air	. . . .	2
Yellow	Water and Earth . . .	. . . .	3
White	Fire	⊙ יובב of בצרה and ♀ אהליבמה .	4
Red	Height	⊙ השסה תימבי ♀ אלה	5
White-red	Depth	⊙ הדד עוית ♀ פיכן	6
Whitish-red	East	⊙ שמלה משרקה ♀ קנז	7
Reddish-white . . .	West	⊙ שאול רהבית ♀ תימן . . .	8
White-red-whitish-red-reddish-white	South.	⊙ בעל חנן ♀ מנדיאל and מבצר	9
The Light reflecting all colours	North	⊙ הדר פעו ♀ עירם . .	10

CXIX. The Ten Fetters (Buddhism).	CXVIII. The Chakkras or Centres of Prana (Hinduism).	CXVII. The Soul (Hindu).	CXVI. Egyptian Attribution of Parts of the Soul.	
. . . .	. . . .	. . . .	Hammemit	0
Aruparaga	Sahasara (above Head) .	Atma	Kha. or Yekh . . .	1
Vi*kk*iki*k*a	Ajna (Pineal Gland) . .	Buddhi . . .	Khai. or Ka	2
Ruparaga	Visuddhi (Larynx) . .	Higher Manas .	Ba. or Baie	3
Silabata Paramesa .	. . . .	. . . . . .		4
Patigha	Anahata (Heart) . .	Lower Manas .		5
Uda*kk*ha	. . . .	. . . .	Aib	6
Mano	Manipura (Solar Plexus)	Kama		7
Sakkya-ditti . . .	Svadistthana (Navel) .	Prana		8
Kama	Muladhara (Lingam and Anus)	Linga Sharira .	Hati	9
Avi*gg*a	. . . .	Sthula Sharira .	Kheibt, Khat, Tet, Sahu .	10

CVIII.* Some Princes of the Qliphoth.	CVII. Translation of Hells.	CVI.* The Ten Hells in Seven Palaces.	CV. English of Col. CIV.	
. . . .	. . . .	. . . .	. . . .	0
Satan and Moloch	. . . . }	. . . . }	Earth (dry) . . {	1
. . . . *סמאל	Grave . . . . . }	. . . . שאול }	Earth (dry) . . {	2
. . . . . . אשת זנונים	. . . . }	. . . . }	Earth (dry) . . {	3
Lucifuge	Perdition	. . . . אבדון	Red earth . . .	4
. . . . עשתרות	Clay of Death	. . . . בארשחת	Undulating ground	5
Belphegor . . . . חיוא	Pit of Destruction . .	. . . . טיטהיון	Pasture	6
. . . . אשמדאי	Shadow of Death . .	. . . . שערימרת	Sandy earth . .	7
Adramelek . . . . בליאל	Gates of Death . . .	. . . . צלמות	Earth	8
. . . . לילית	Hell . . . . }	. . . . ניהנם }	Wet Earth . . {	9
. . . . נעמה	. . . . }	. . . . ניהנם }	Wet Earth . . {	10

CXV.* Officers in a Masonic Lodge.	CXIV. Passwords of the Grades.	CXIII. Alchemical Metals (ii.).	CXII. Alchemical Tree of Life (i.).	
. . . .	. . . .	. . . .	. . . .	0
P.M. . . . . {	Silence *	Metallic Radix . . .	. . . . ☿	1
P.M. . . . . {	. . . . . . אב	. . . . ♄	. . . . 🜍	2
P.M. . . . . {	. . . . . . דב	. . . . ♃	. . . . 🜔	3
W.M.	. . . . . . אט	. . . . ☽	. . . . ☽	4
S.W.	. . . . . . יה	. . . . ☉	. . . . ☉	5
J.W.	. . . . . אהיה	. . . . ♂	. . . . ♂	6
S.D.	. . . . . . כת	. . . . ☿♀	. . . . ♃	7
J.D.	. . . . . . אלה	. . . . ♁☿	. . . . ♀	8
I.G.	. . . . . . מה	. . . . ☿	. . . . ♄	9
T. and Candidate . . .	. . . . . . נה	Medicina Metallorum	Mercurius Philosophorum	10

CXXVI. Their Inhabitants.	CXXV.* Seven Hells of the Arabs.	CXXIV. The Heavenly Hexagram.	CXXIII. English of Col. VIII., Lines 1–10.	
. . . .	. . . .	. . . .	. . . .	0
		. . . . ♃	Dual Contending Forces	1
Hypocrites	Háwiyah . . }	. . . . ☿	Hinderers	2
		. ☽ [♄ Daath] .	Concealers	3
Pagans or Idolaters . .	Jahim	. . . . ♀	Breakers in Pieces . .	4
Guebres	Sakar	. . . . ♂	Burners	5
Sabians	Sa'ir	. . . . ☉	Disputers	6
Jews	Hutamah . . .	. . . .	Dispersing Ravens .	7
Christians	Laza	. . . .	Deceivers	8
		. . . .	Obscene Ones	9
Moslems	Jehannam . . }	. . . .	The Evil Woman or (simply) The Woman	10

CXXXII. Pairs of Angels ruling Coins.	CXXXI. Pairs of Angels ruling Swords.	CXXX. Pairs of Angels ruling Cups.	
. . . .	. . . .	. . . .	0
. . . .	. . . .	. . . .	1
. . . . . . ושריה לכבאל	. . . . . מבהאל יזלאל	. . . . . חבויה איעאל	2
. . . . . . להחיה יחויה	. . . . . הקמיה הריאל	. . . . . יבמיה ראהאל	3
. . . . . . מנדאל כוקית	. . . . . כליאל לאויה	. . . . . מומיה הייאל	4
. . . . . . פניאל מבהיה	. . . . . חעמיה אניאל	. . . . . פהליה לוויה	5
. . . . . . יילאל נממיה	. . . . . ייזאל רהעאל	. . . . . וייאל נלכאל	6
. . . . . . מצראל הרחאל	. . . . . מיכאל ההחאל	. . . . . חהויה מלהאל	7
. . . . . . כהתאל אכאיה	. . . . . יההאל ומבאל	. . . . . ילהיה וליה	8
. . . . . . הזיאל אלדיה	. . . . . מחיאל ענואל	. . . . . עריאל סאליה	9
. . . . . . ההעיה לאויה	. . . . . מנקאל דמביה	. . . . . מיהאל עשליה	10

	CXXII. The Ten Plagues of Egypt.	CXXI.* The Grades of the Order.		CXX. Magical Images of the Sephiroth.
0	. . . .	$0^{\square} = 0^{\circ}$	3rd Order	. . . .
1	Death of First-born	$10^{\circ} = 1^{\square}$ Ipsissimus . . .	3rd Order	Ancient bearded king seen in profile
2	Locusts . . .	$9^{\circ} = 2^{\square}$ Magus	3rd Order	Almost any male image shows some aspect of Chokmah
3	Darkness . .	$8^{\circ} = 3^{\square}$ Magister Templi .	3rd Order	Almost any female image shows some aspect of Binah
4	Hail and Fire .	$7^{\circ} = 4^{\square}$ Adeptus Exemptus	2nd Order	A mighty crowned and enthroned king
5	Boils	$6^{\circ} = 5^{\square}$ Adeptus Major . .	2nd Order	A mighty warrior in his chariot, armed and crowned
6	Murrain . . .	$5^{\circ} = 6^{\square}$ Adeptus Minor . .	2nd Order	A majestic king, a child, a crucified god
7	Flies	$4^{\circ} = 7^{\square}$ Philosophus . . .	1st Order	A beautiful naked woman . . .
8	Lice	$3^{\circ} = 8^{\square}$ Practicus	1st Order	An Hermaphrodite . . . . .
9	Frogs . . .	$2^{\circ} = 9^{\square}$ Theoricus . . .	1st Order	A beautiful naked man, very strong
10	Water turned to Blood	$1^{\circ} = 10^{\square}$ Zelator; $0^{\circ} = 0^{\square}$ Neophyte . . .	1st Order	A young woman crowned and veiled

	CXXIX. Pairs of Angels ruling Wands.	CXXVIII. Meaning of Col. CXXVII.	CXXVII.* Seven Heavens of the Arabs.
0	. . . .	. . . .	. . . .
1	. . . .	. . . .	. . . .
2	דניאל והואל . .	House of Glory, made of pearls	Dar al-Jalal . . . .
3	עממיה החשיה .	. . . .	. . . .
4	ניתאל ננאאל . .	House of Rest or Peace, made of rubies and jacinths	Dar as-Salam . . . . .
5	יליאל והויה . . .	Garden of Mansions, made of yellow copper .	Jannat al-Maawa . . .
6	עלמיה סיטאל . .	Garden of Eternity, made of yellow coral .	Jannat al-Khuld . . . .
7	ללהאל מהשיה .	Garden of Delights, made of white diamond .	Jannat al-Naim . . . .
8	האאיה נתהיה .	Garden of Paradise, made of red gold . . .	Jannat al-Firdaus . .
9	שאהיה ירתאל .	. . . .	. . . .
10	אומאל רייאל . .	Garden of Eden, or Everlasting Abode, made of red pearls or pure musk	Jannat al-'Adn or al-Karar

CXXXVI. Titles and Attributions of the Coin, Disc, or Pantacle Suit [Diamonds].	CXXXV. Titles and Attributions of the Sword Suit [Spades].	
. . . .	. . . .	0
The Root of the Powers of Earth	The Root of the Powers of Air	1
♃ in ♑ The Lord of Harmonious Change .	☽ in ♎ The Lord of Peace restored . . .	2
♂ in ♑ Material Works	♄ in ♎ Sorrow	3
☉ in ♑ Earthly Power	♃ in ♎ Rest from Strife	4
☿ in ♉ Material Trouble	♀ in ♒ Defeat	5
☽ in ♉ Material Success	☿ in ♒ Earned Success	6
♄ in ♉ Success Unfulfilled	☽ in ♒ Unstable Effort	7
☉ in ♍ Prudence	♃ in ♊ Shortened Force	8
♀ in ♍ Material Gain	♂ in ♊ Despair and Cruelty	9
☿ in ♍ Wealth	☉ in ♊ Ruin	10

CXLIV. Angels Lords of the Triplicity in the Signs by Day.	CXLIII. Twelve Lesser Assistant Angels in the Signs.	CXLII. Angels ruling Houses.	CXLI. The Twelve Tribes.	
סטרעטן	שרהיאל	איאל	גד	15
ראידאל	ארזיאל	טואל	אפראים	16
סערש	סראיאל	ניאל	מנשה	17
רעדר	פכיאל	כעאל	יששכר	18
סנהם	שרטיאל	עואל	יהודה	19
לסלרא	שלתיאל	ויאל	נפתלי	20
תרגבון	חדקיאל	יהאל	אשר	22
ביתחון	סאיציאל	סוסול	דן	24
אהוז	סריטיאל	סויעסאל	בנימן	25
סנדלעי	סמקיאל	כשויעיה	זבולן	26
עתור	צכמקיאל	אנסואל	ראובן	28
רמרא	וכביאל	פשיאל	שמעון	29

CXXXIV. Titles and Attributions of the Cup or Chalice Suit [Hearts].	CXXXIII.* Titles and Attributions of the Wand Suit [Clubs].	
. . . .	. . . .	0
The Root of the Powers of Water	The Root of the Powers of Fire	1
♀ in ♋ Love	♂ in ♈ Dominion	2
☿ in ♋ Abundance	☉ in ♈ Established Strength	3
☽ in ♋ Pleasure	♀ in ♈ Perfected Work	4
♂ in ♏ Loss in Pleasure	♄ in ♌ Strife*	5
☉ in ♏ Pleasure	♃ in ♌ Victory	6
♀ in ♏ Illusionary Success	♂ in ♌ Valour	7
♄ in ♓ Abandoned Success	☿ in ♐ Swiftness	8
♃ in ♓ Material Happiness	☽ in ♐ Great Strength	9
♂ in ♓ Perfected Success	♄ in ♐ Oppression	10

TABLE V

CXL. Twelve Banners of The Name.	CXXXIX. Planets exalted in Col. CXXXVII.	CXXXVIII.* Planets ruling Col. CXXXVII.	CXXXVII. Signs of the Zodiac.	
. . . . יהוה	. . . ☉ . . .	. . . ♂ . . .	. . . ♈ . . .	15
. . . . יההו	. . . ☽ . . .	. . . ♀ . . .	. . . ♉ . . .	16
. . . . יוהה	. . . .	. . . ☿ . . .	. . . ♊ . . .	17
. . . . הוהי	. . . ♃ . . .	. . . ☽ . . .	. . . ♋ . . .	18
. . . . הויה	. . . .	. . . ☉ . . .	. . . ♌ . . .	19
. . . . ההוי	. . . ☿ . . .	. . . ☿ . . .	. . . ♍ . . .	20
. . . . והיה	. . . ♄ . . .	. . . ♀ . . .	. . . ♎ . . .	22
. . . . וההי	. . . .	. . . ♂ . . .	. . . ♏ . . .	24
. . . . ויהה	. . . .	. . . ♃ . . .	. . . ♐ . . .	25
. . . . היהו	. . . ♂ . . .	. . . ♄ . . .	. . . ♑ . . .	26
. . . . היוה	. . . .	. . . ♄ . . .	. . . ♒ . . .	28
. . . . ההיו	. . . ♀ . . .	. . . ♃ . . .	. . . ♓ . . .	29

CL. Magical Images of the Decans (Succedent).	CXLIX. Magical Images of the Decans (Ascendant).	
A green-clad woman, with one leg bare from the ankle to the knee	A tall, dark, restless man, with keen flame-coloured eyes, bearing a sword	15
A man of like figure (to the ascendant), with cloven hoofs like an ox	A woman with long and beautiful hair, clad in flame-coloured robes	16
An eagle-headed man, with a bow and arrow. Wears crowned steel helmet	A beautiful woman, with her two horses . . .	17
A beautiful woman wreathed with myrtle. She holds a lyre and sings of love and gladness	A man with distorted face and hands, a horse's body, white feet, and a girdle of leaves	18
A man crowned with a white myrtle wreath holding a bow	A man in sordid raiment, with him a nobleman on horseback, accompanied by bears and dogs	19
Tall, fair, large man, with him a woman holding a large black oil jar	A virgin clad in linen, with an apple or pomegranate	20
A man, dark, yet delicious of countenance . .	A dark man, in his right hand a spear and laurel branch and in his left a book	22
A man riding a camel, with a scorpion in his hand	A man with a lance in his right hand, in his left a human head	24
A man leading cows, and before him an ape and bear	A man with 3 bodies—1 black, 1 red, 1 white .	25
A man with an ape running before him . . .	A man holding in his right hand a javelin and in his left a lapwing	26
A man arrayed like a king, looking with pride and conceit on all around him	A man with bowed head and a bag in his hand .	28
A grave man pointing to the sky	A man with two bodies, but joining their hands	29

CLVI. Magical Images of Col. CLV.	CLV. Goetic Demons of Decans (Ascendant).	CLIV. Perfumes (Cadent).	
Cat, toad, man, or all at once	. . ☉ . . . . באל	Black Pepper . .	15
Little horse or ass	. . ☽ . . . . גמיגין	Cassia	16
(1) Wolf with serpent's tail. (2) Man with dog's teeth and raven's head	. . ☽ . . . . אמון	Cypress	17
Probably a centaur or archer	. . ☿ . . . . בואר	Anise	18
Rider on pale horse, with many musicians. [Flaming and poisonous breath]	. . ☉ . . . . בלאת	Muces Muscator .	19
A soldier in red apparel and armour . .	. . ♀ . . . . זאפר	Mastick	20
Soldier with ducal crown riding a crocodile	. . ♀ . . . . שאלוש	Mortum	22
Angel with lion's head, goose's feet, horse's tail	. . ♂ . . . . יפוש	As for Asc . . .	24
A dog with a gryphon's wings	. . ♂ and ☿ . גלאסלבול	Gaxisphilium . .	25
Gold-crowned soldier in red on a red horse. Bad breath	. . ♀ . . . . ברית	Cubel Pepper . .	26
A strong man in human shape	. . ☿ . . . . פוראש	Rhubarb . . .	28
(1) Hart with fiery tail. (2) Angel . .	. . ♂ . . . . פורפור	Santal Alb . . .	29

CXLVIII. Angels of the Decanates (Cadent).	CXLVII. Angels of the Decanates (Succedent).	CXLVI. Angels of the Decanates (Ascendant).	CXLV. Angels Lords of the Triplicity in the Signs by Night.	
סטנדר	בההמי	זזר	ספעטאוי	15
יכסגנוץ	מנחראי	כדמדי	טוטת	16
ביתון	שהדני	סגרש	עונרמען	17
אלינכיר	רהדץ	מתראוש	עכאל	18
סהיבר	זחעי	לוסנהר	זלברהית	19
משפר	ראידיה	אננאורה	ססיא	20
שחדר	סהרנץ	טרסני	אחודרזון	22
ותרודיאל	נינדוהר	כמוץ	סהקנב	24
אבוהא	והרין	משראת	לברמים	25
יסנדיברודיאל	יסיסיה	מסנין	אלויר	26
נרודיאל	אבדרון	ססםם	פלאין	23
סטריף	אורון	בהלמי	נתדורינאל	29

CLIII. Perfumes (Succedent).	CLII. Perfumes (Ascendant).	CLI. Magical Images of the Decans (Cadent).	
Stammonia	Myrtle	A restless man in scarlet robes, with golden bracelets on his hands and arms	15
Codamoms	Costum	A swarthy man with white lashes, his body elephantine, with long legs; with him, a horse, a stag, and a calf	16
Cinnamon	Mastick	A man in mail, armoured with bow, arrows, and quiver	17
Succum	Camphor	A swift-footed person, with a viper in his hand, leading dogs	18
Lyn Balsami	Olibanum	A swarthy hairy man, with a drawn sword and shield	19
Srorus	Santal Flav.	An old man leaning on a staff and wrapped in a mantle	20
Bofor [?]	Galbanum	A man riding on an ass, preceded by a wolf	22
As for Asc.	Opoponax	A horse and a wolf	24
Fol Lori	Lign-aloes	A man leading another by his hair and slaying him	25
Colophonum	Assafœtida	A man holding a book, which he opens and shuts	26
Stammonia	Euphorbium	A small-headed man dressed like a woman, and with him an old man	28
Coxium	Thyme	A man of grave and thoughtful face, with a bird in his hand, before him a woman and an ass	29

CLX. Magical Images of Col. CLIX.	CLIX. Goetia Demons, &c. (Cadent).	
Like Agares	♃ . . . . . . ושאנו	15
Lion with ass's head, bellowing	♀ . . . . . . ואלפר	16
Crowned king on dromedary, accompanied by many musicians	☉ . . . . . . פאימרן	17
Leopard's head and gryphon's wings	♃ . . . . . . שיטרי	18
A knight with a lance and banner, with a serpent	♀ . . . . . . אלינוש	19
A strong man with a serpent's tail, on a pale horse	♀ . . . . . . באתין	20
Human-faced bull	♂ and ☿ . . מאראץ	22
A black crane with a sore throat—he flutters	☽ . . . . נבר	24
A monster [probably a dolphin]	♂ and ☽ . . . רינוו	25
Sea monster	☽ . . . . . . פורנאש	26
Like a guide. To be kings	☿ . . . . נצף	28
Raven	♃ . . . . . . ישטולוש	29

CLXIV. As Col. CLVIII. by Night.	CLXIII. As Col. CLVII. by Night	
Stock-dove with sore throat	♂ . . . . . . האלף	15
Man with gryphon's wings	♀ . . . . . . פוכלור	16
Stock-dove with sore throat	☽ . . . . שיץ	17
Dromedary	♀ . . . . . . אואל	18
Cruel ancient, with long white hair and beard, rides a pale horse, with sharp weapons	♀ . . . . פוך	19
(1) Thrush. (2) Man with sharp sword seemeth to answer in burning ashes or coals of fire	☿ . . . . כאין	20
Beautiful woman, with duchess crown tied to her waist, riding great camel	♀ . . . . נמור	22
Lion on horse, with serpent's tail, carries in right hand two hissing serpents	☽ . . . . ודיאץ	24
Child with angel's wings rides a two-headed dragon	☿ . . . . ואל	25
Noisy peacock	☽ . . . . . אנדראלף	26
Two beautiful angels sitting in chariot of fire	☉ . . . . . . בליאל	28
Man with many countenances, all men's and women's, carries a book in right hand	♀ . . . . דנמאל	29

CLVIII. Magical Images of Col. CLVII.	CLVII. Goetic Demons, &c. (Succedent).	
Old man, riding a crocodile and carrying a goshawk	♀ אגאר	15
Great Lion	☿ מארב	16
Accompanied by 4 noble kings and great troops	♀ ברבטוש	17
"Like a Xenopilus"	♀ גוסיון	18
An archer in green	☽ לראיך	19
Viper (or) Human, with teeth and 2 horns, and with a sword	♂ and ☿ בוטיש	20
Lion-faced man riding a bear, carrying a viper. Trumpeter with him	☉ פורשון	22
Man with 3 heads—a serpent's, a man's (having two stars on his brow), and a calf's. Rides on viper and bears firebrand	♀ אים	24
Dragon with 3 heads—a dog's, man's, and gryphon's	♀ בים	25
Hurtful angel or infernal dragon, like Berot, with a viper [breath bad]	♀ אשתרות	26
3 heads (bull, man, ram), snake's tail, goose's feet. Rides, with lance and banner, on a dragon	☉ אסמודאי	28
Wolf with a gryphon's wings and serpent's tail. Breathes flames	☽ מרחוש	29

CLXII. As Col. CLVI. by Night.	CLXI. As Col. CLV. by Night.	
Child-voiced phœnix	☽ פאנץ	15
Crow	♂ ראום	16
Soldier with lion's head rides pale horse	☽ שבניך	17
Monster	♂ ביפרו	18
Angel	♀ כרוכל	19
Soldier with red leonine face and flaming eyes ; rides great horse	♀ אלוך	20
Horse	♃ אוראוב	22
Flaming fire	☿ און	24
Bull with gryphon's wings	☉ and ☿ זאגן	25
Leopard	♀ האור	26
(1) Unicorn. (2) Dilatory bandmaster	♀ אמדוך	28
Beautiful man on winged horse	♃ שאר	29

CLXXI. As Col. CLXVII. (Cadent).	CLXX. As Col. CLXVIII. (Succedent).	CLXIX. As Col. CLXVII. (Succedent).	CLXVIII. Egyptian Names of Asc. Decans.	CLXVII. Egyptian Gods of Zodiac (Asc. Decans).	
Horus	Lencher	Anubis	Assicean	Aroueris	**15**
Apophis	Virvaso	Helitomenos	Asicath	Serapis	**16**
Titan	Verasua	Cyclops	Thesogar	Taautus	**17**
Mercophta	Syth	Hecate	Sothis	Apoltun	**18**
Nephthe	Sitlacer	Perseus	Aphruimis	Typhon	**19**
Cronus	Thopitus	Pi-Osiris	Thumis	Isis	**20**
Ophionius	Aterechinis	Omphta	Serucuth	Zeuda	**22**
Panotragus	Tepiseuth	Merota	Sentacer	Arimanius	**24**
Zeraph	Sagen	Tomras	Eregbuo	Tolmophta	**25**
Monuphta	Epima	Riruphta	Themeso	Soda	**26**
Proteus	Astiro	Vucula	Oroasoer	Brondeus	**28**
Phallophorus	Thopibui	Sourut	Archatapias	Rephan	**29**

CLXXIV. The Mansions of the Moon. [Hindu, *Nakshatra*] Arab, *Manazil*.	
♈ Sharatan (Ram's head), Butayn (Ram's belly), and 0°–10° Suraya (the Pleiads)	**15**
♉ 10°–30° Suraya, Dabaran (Aldeboran), and 0°–20° Hak'ah (three stars in head of Orion)	**16**
♊ 20°–30° Hak'ah, Han'ah (stars in Orion's shoulder), and Zira'a (two stars above ♊)	**17**
♋ Nasrah (Lion's nose), Tarf (Lion's eye), and 0°–10° Jabhah (Lion's forehead)	**18**
♌ 10°–30° Jabhah, Zubrah (Lion's mane), and 0°–20° Sarfah (Cor Leonis)	**19**
♍ 20°–30° Sarfah, 'Awwa (the Dog, two stars in ♍), and Simak (Spica Virginis)	**20**
♎ Ghafar (ϕ, ι, and κ in foot of ♍), Zubáni (horns of ♏), and 0°–10° Iklil (the Crown)	**22**
♏ 10°–30° Iklil, Kalb (Cor Scorpionis), and 0°–20° Shaulah (tail of ♏)	**24**
♐ 20°–30° Shaulah, Na'aim (stars in Pegasus), and Baldah (no constellation)	**25**
♑ Sa'ad al-Zábih (the Slaughterer's Luck), Sa'ad al-Bal'a (Glutton's Luck), and 0°–10° Sa'ad al-Sa'ad (Luck of Lucks, stars in ♒)	**26**
♒ 10°–30° Sa'ad al-Sa'ad, Sa'ad al-Akhbiyah (Luck of Tents), and 0°–20° Fargh the former (spout of the Urn)	**28**
♓ 20°–30° Fargh the former, Fargh the latter (hind lip of Urn), and Risháa (navel of Fish's belly)	**29**

CLXVI As Col. CLX. by Night.	CLXV. As Col. CLIX. by Night.	
Crow with sore throat	☿ מאלף	15
Mermaid	♀ ופאר	16
Lion on black horse carrying viper	♀ and ⊙ וינא	17
Bull with gryphon's wings	☿ העננת	18
3 heads (bull, man, ram), snake's tail, flaming eyes. Rides bear, carries goshawk	⊙ בעלם	19
Warrior with ducal crown rides gryphon. Trumpeters	♀ and ♂ מורם	20
Leopard	☿ ושו	22
Lion with gryphon's wings	♀ נפול	24
Angel with raven's head. Rides black wolf, carries sharp sword	☽ אנדר	25
Warrior on black horse	☽ כימאור	26
A star in a pentacle	דכאוראב	28
Man holding great serpent	♀ אנדרומאל	29

CLXXIII.* Genii of the Twelve Hours (Levi).	CLXXII. As Col. CLXVIII. (Cadent).	
Papus, Sinbuck, Rasphuia, Zahun, Heiglot, Mizkun, Haven	Asentacer	15
Sisera, Torvatus, Nitibus, Hizarbin, Sachluph, Baglis, Labezerin	Aharph	16
Hahabi, Phlogabitus, Eirneus, Mascarun, Zarobi, Butatar, Cahor	Tepistosoa	17
Phalgus, Thagrinus, Eistibus, Pharzuph, Sislau, Schiekron, Aclahayr	Thuismis	18
Zeirna, Tablibik, Tacritau, Suphlatus, Sair, Barcus, Camaysar	Phuonidie	19
Tabris, Susabo, Eirnilus, Nitika, Haatan, Hatiphas, Zaren	Aphut	20
Sialul, Sabrus, Librabis, Mizgitari, Causub, Salilus, Jazer	Arepien	22
Nantur, Toglas, Zalburis, Alphun, Tukiphat, Zizuph, Cuniali	Senciner	24
Risnuch, Suclagus, Kirtabus, Sablil, Schachlil, Colopatiron, Zeffar	Chenen	25
Sezarbil, Azeuph, Armilus, Kataris, Razanil, Buchaphi, Mastho	Homoth	26
Aiglun, Zuphlas, Phaldor, Rosabis, Adjuchas, Zophas, Halacho	Tepisatras	28
Tarab, Misran, Labus, Kalab, Hahab, Marnes, Sellen	Atembui	29

CLXXXI. Correct Designs of Tarot Trumps.	CLXXX. Titles of Tarot Trumps.	
A bearded Ancient seen in profile *	The Spirit of Αιθηρ	11
A fair youth with winged helmet and heels, equipped as a Magician, displays his art *	The Magus of Power	12
A crowned priestess sits before the veil of Isis between the pillars of Seth *	The Priestess of the Silver Star	13
Crowned with stars, a winged goddess stands upon the moon *	The Daughter of the Mighty Ones	14
A flame-clad god bearing equivalent symbols * . .	Sun of the Morning, chief among the Mighty.	15
Between the Pillars sits an Ancient *	The Magus of the Eternal	16
A prophet, young, and in the Sign of Osiris Risen *	The Children of the Voice: the Oracle of the Mighty Gods	17
A young and holy king under the starry canopy * .	The Child of the Powers of the Waters: the Lord of the Triumph of Light	18
A smiling woman holds the open jaws of a fierce and powerful lion	The Daughter of the Flaming Sword . . .	19
Wrapped in a cloke and cowl, an Ancient walketh, bearing a lamp and staff *	The Prophet of the Eternal, the Magus of the Voice of Power	20
A wheel of six shafts, whereon revolve the Triad of Hermanubis, Sphinx, and Typhon *	The Lord of the Forces of Life	21
A conventional figure of Justice with scales and balances	The Daughter of the Lords of Truth. The Ruler of the Balance	22
The figure of an hanged or crucified man * . .	The Spirit of the Mighty Waters	23
A skeleton with a scythe mowing men. The scythe handle is a Tau	The Child of the Great Transformers The Lord of the Gate of Death	24
The Figure of Diana huntress *	The Daughter of the Reconcilers, the Bringer-forth of Life	25
The figure of Pan or Priapus *	The Lord of the Gates of Matter The Child of the Forces of Time	26
A tower struck by forked lightning *	The Lord of the Hosts of the Mighty . . .	27
The figure of a water-nymph disporting herself * .	The Daughter of the Firmament: the Dweller between the Waters	28
The waning moon *	The Ruler of Flux and Reflux. The Child of the Sons of the Mighty	29
The Sun *	The Lord of the Fire of the World	30
Israfel blowing the Last Trumpet. The dead arising from their tombs *	The Spirit of the Primal Fire	31
Should contain a demonstration of the Quadrature of the Circle *	The Great One of the Night of Time . . .	32
. . . .	. . . .	32 bis
. . . .	. . . .	31 bis

CLXXIX. Numbers printed on Tarot Trumps.	CLXXVIII.* Geomantic Intelligences.	CLXXVII.* Yetziratic Attribution of Col. CLXXV.	CLXXVI. Numerical Value of Col. CLXXV.	CLXXV. Hebrew Letters.	
0		🜁	1	א	11
1	רפאל	☿	2	ב	12
2	גבריאל	☽	3	ג	13
3	אנאל	♀	4	ד	14
4	מלכידאל	♈	5	ה	15
5	אסמודאל	♉	6	ו	16
6	אמבריאל	♊	7	ז	17
7	מוריאל	♋	8	ח	18
11	ורכיאל	♌	9	ט	19
9	דמליאל	♍	10	י	20
10	סחיאל	♃	20, 500	כ ך	21
8	זוריאל	♎	30	ל	22
12		▽	40, 600	מ ם	23
13	ברכיאל	♏	50, 700	נ ן	24
14	אדנכיאל	♐	60	ס	25
15	הנאל	♑	70	ע	26
16	זמאל	♂	80, 800	פ ף	27
17	כאמבריאל	♒	90, 900	צ ץ	28
18	אמניציאל	♓	100	ק	29
19	מיכאל	☉	200	ר	30
20		△	300	ש	31
21	כשיאל	♄	400	ת	32
		🜃	400	ת	32 bis
		☸	300	ש	31 bis

CLXXXIII. Legendary Orders of Being.	CLXXXII. The Human Body.	
Sylphs	Respiratory Organs	11
"Voices," Witches and Wizards	Cerebral and Nervous System	12
Lemures, Ghosts	Lymphatic System	13
Succubi	Genital System	14
Mania, Erinyes [Eumenides]	Head and Face	15
Gorgons, Minotaurs	Shoulders and Arms	16
Ominous Appearances, Banshees	Lungs	17
Vampires	Stomach	18
Horror, Dragons	Heart	19
Mermaids (and ♓, its Zodiacal Opposite), Banshees	The Back	20
Incubi, Nightmares	Digestive System	21
Fairies, Harpies	Liver	22
Nymphs and Undines, Nereids, &c.	Organs of Nutrition	23
Lamiæ, Stryges, Witches	Intestines	24
Centaurs	Hips and Thighs	25
Satyrs and Fauns, Panic-demons	Genital System	26
Furies, Chimæras, Boars (as in Calydon), &c.	Muscular System	27
Water Nymphs, Sirens, Lorelei, Mermaids (*cf.* ♍)	Kidneys, Bladder, &c.	28
Phantoms, Were-wolves	Legs and Feet	29
Will o' the Wisp	Circulatory System	30
Salamanders	Organs of Circulation	31
Ghuls, Larvæ, Corpse Candles	Excretory System	32
The Dweller of the Threshold, Gnomes	Excretory Organs, Skeleton	32 bis
[Socratic Genius]	Organs of Intelligence	31 bis

TABLE I (*continued*)

Key Scale	**CLXXXIV.** Numeration of Arabic Alphabet see Col. **LII.**	**CLXXXV.** Greek Alphabet Numeration see Col. **LIII.**	**CLXXXVI.** Diseases (Typical).	**CLXXXVII.** Magical Formulae see Col. **XLI.**
0	. . . . . .	. . . . . .	. . . .	LASTAL. M....M.
1	. . . . . .	. . 31 . .	Death	
2	. . . . . .	. . 200 . .	Insanity	VIAOV
3	. . . . . .	. . . . . .	Dementia . . . . (Amnesia)	BABALON VITRIOL
4	. . 500 . .	. . . . . .	Dropsy	IHVH
5	. . 600 . .	. . 500 . .	Fever	AGLA ALHIM
6	. . 700 . .	. . 800 . .	Heart Lesions . .	ABRAHADABRA IAO : INRI
7	. . 800 . .	. . . . . .	Skin Troubles . .	ARARITA
8	. . 900 . .	. . . . . .	Nerve Troubles . .	
9	. . 1000 . .	. . 600 . .	Impotence	ALIM
10	. . . . . .	. . 900 . .	Sterility	VITRIOL
11	. . 1 . .	. . 1 . .	Fluxes	
12	. . 2 . .	. . 2 . .	Ataxia	
13	. . 3 . .	. . 3 . .	Menstrual Disorders	ALIM
14	. . 4 . .	. . 4 . .	Syphilis, Gonorrhoea	AGAPE
15	. . 5 . .	. . 5 . .	Apoplexy	
16	. . 6 . .	. . 6 . .	Indigestion . . .	
17	. . 7 . .	. . 7 . .	Phthysis, Pneumonia	
18	. . 8 . .	. . 8 . .	Rheumatism . . .	ABRAHADABRA
19	. . 9 . .	. . 9 . .	Syncope, etc., Heart	TO MEGA THERION
20	. . 10 . .	. . 10 . .	Spinal weakness Paralysis . . .	
21	. . 20 . .	. . 20 . .	Gout	
22	. . 30 . .	. . 30 . .	Kidney disorders .	
23	. . 40 . .	. . 40 . .	Chill	
24	. . 50 . .	. . 50 . .	Cancer	AUMGN
25	. . 60 . .	. . 60 . .	Apoplexy, Thrombosis	ON
26	. . 70 . .	. . 70 . .	Arthritis	ON
27	. . 80 . .	. . 80 . .	Inflammation . .	
28	. . 90 . .	. . 700 . .	Cystitis	
29	. . 100 . .	. . 90 . .	Gout	
30	. . 200 . .	. . 100 . .	Repletion	IAO: INRI
31	. . 300 . .	. . 900 . .	Fever	
32	. . 400 . .	. . 300 . .	Arterio Sclerosis .	
32 bis	. . . . . .	. . 400 . .	Sluggishness . . .	
31 bis	. . . . . .	. . . . . .	Death (full Insanity)	

TABLE II (*continued*)

	CLXXXVIII. The Body	CLXXXIX. Bodily Functions	CXC.	CXCI. The Four Truths of Buddhism.
11	Breath	Speaking .	Thought .	Sorrow's Cause
23	Chyle, Lymph .	Holding .	Nutrition	Sorrow's Ceasing
31	Blood	Moving .	Moving .	Noble Eight-fold Path
32 bis	Solid structures, Tissues	Excreting	Matter . .	Sorrow
31 bis	Semen, Marrow .	Generating	Magick .	

TABLE III (*continued*)

	CXCII. The Noble Eight-fold Path. See Col. **LXXXII.**	CXCIII. Spirits of the Planets. See Col. **LXXIX.**	CXCIV. Intelligences of the Planets. See Col. **LXXVIII.**
12	Right Speech	Taphthartarath	Tiriel
13	Right Aspiration	Chasmodai . .	Malkah Be Tarshishim va A'ad Be Ruah Shehalim
14	Right Conduct	Qedemel . . .	Hagiel
21	Right Discipline	Chismael . . .	Yophiel
27	Right Energy	Bartzabel . .	Graphiel
30	Right Rapture	Sorath	Nakhiel
32	Right Recollection (in both senses of the word). Right View-point	Zazel	Agiel

VARIOUS ARRANGEMENTS

THE NAPLES ARRANGEMENT

000	Ain	= Zero Absolute.
00	Ain Soph	= Zero as undefinable.
0	Ain Soph Aur	= Zero as basis of possible vibration.
1	Kether	= The Point: positive yet indefinable.
2	Chokmah	= The Point: distinguishable from 1 other.
3	Binah	= The Point: defined by relation to 2 others.
	The Abyss	= between Ideal and Actual.
4	Chesed	= The Point: defined by 3 coordinates. Matter.
5	Geburah	= Motion.
6	Tiphereth	= The Point: now self-conscious, able to define itself in terms of above.
7	Netzach	= The Point's Idea of Bliss (Ananda).
8	Hod	= The Point's Idea of Knowledge (Chit).
9	Yesod	= The Point's Idea of Being (Sat).
10	Malkuth	= The Point's Idea of Itself fulfilled in its complement, as determined by 7, 8, and 9.

SUGGESTIVE CORRESPONDENCES FROM THE HEBREW ALPHABET

Aleph	The Holy Ghost — Fool — Knight-Errant. Folly's doom is ruin.
Beth	The Messenger. Prometheus. The Juggler with the Secret of the Universe.
Gimel	The Virgin. The Holy Guardian Angel is attained by Self-sacrifice and Equilibrium.
Daleth	The Wife. Alchemical Salt. The Gate of the Equilibrium of the Universe.
Hé	The Mother is the Daughter, the Daughter is the Mother.
Vau	The Sun. Redeemer. The Son is but the Son.
Zain	The Twins reconciled. The answer of the Oracles is always Death.
Cheth	The Chariot containing Life. The Secret of the Universe. Ark. Sangraal.
Teth	The Act of Power. She who rules the Secret Force of the Universe.
Yod	The Virgin Man. Secret Seed of All. Secret of the Gate of Initiation.
Kaph	The All-Father in 3 forms, Fire, Air, and Water. In the whirlings is War.
Lamed	The Woman justified. By Equilibrium and Self-sacrifice is the Gate.
Mem	The Man drowned in the "womb" flood. The Secret is hidden between the waters that are above and the waters that are beneath.
Nun	The putrefaction in the Athanor. Initiation is guarded on both sides by Death.
Samekh	The Womb preserving Life. Self-control and Self-sacrifice govern the Wheel.
A'ain	The exalted Phallus. The Secret of generation is Death.
Pé	The Crowned and Conquering Children emerging from the Womb. The Fortress of the Most High.

Tzaddi	The Husband. Alchemical Sulphur. The Star is the Gate of the Sanctuary.
Qoph	The Womb seething is the glamour of physiological upset while the Sun sleeps. Illusionary is the Initiator of Disorder.
Resh	The Twins shining forth and playing. The fighting of Set and Osiris. In the Sun is the Secret of the Spirit.
Shin	The Stélé. Nuit, Hadit, their God and Man twins, as a pantacle. Resurrection is hidden in Death.
Tau	The Slain God. Universe is the Hexagram.

THE VITAL TRIADS

The Three Gods I A O	Aleph	O	The Holy Ghost.
	Beth	I	The Messenger.
	Yod	IX	The Secret Seed.
The Three Goddesses	Gimel	II	The Virgin.
	Daleth	III	The Wife.
	Hé	XVII	The Mother.
The Three Demiurges	Kaph	X	The All Father 3 in 1.
	Tzaddi	IV	The Ruler.
	Vau	V	The Son (Priest).
The Children Horus and Hoor-pa-kraat	Zain	VI	The Twins Emerging.
	Resh	XIX	The Sun (Playing).
	Pé	XVI	The Crowned and Conquering Child emerging from Womb.
The Yoni Gaudens. The Woman justified	Cheth	VII	The Graal; Chariot of Life.
	Samekh	XIV	The Pregnant Womb preserving life.
	Lamed	VIII	The Woman justified by Yod.

The Slain Gods	Teth	XI	156 and 666.
	Mem	XII	The Redeemer in the Waters.
	Qoph	XIII	The Redeeming Belly which kills XV.
The Lingam, The Yoni, The Stélé. Priest Priestess, Ceremony	A'ain	XV	Erect and glad.
	Qoph	XVIII	The Witch. Yoni stagnant and waiting.
	Shin	XX	God and Man as twins from Nuit and Hadit.
The Pantacle of the Whole	Tau	XXI	The System.

Editorial Note.—The Roman numerals refer to the Atus whose titles are given in Column CLXXX of Table VI. In this arrangement, which was published in the Book of Thoth, the fourth and seventeenth Atus (Hé and Tzaddi) have been interchanged. See editorial note to Column CLXXX on p. 124 for the explanation.

THE TRIPLICITIES OF THE ZODIAC

Fire	Fire of Fire. Aries. Lightning—swift violence, of onset.
	Air of Fire. Leo. Sun—steady force of energy.
	Water of Fire. Sagittarius. Rainbow—fading spiritualized reflection of the image.
Water	Fire of Water. Cancer. Rain, Springs, etc.—swift passionate attack.
	Air of Water. Scorpio. Sea—steady force of putrefaction.
	Water of Water. Pisces. Pool—stagnant, spiritualized reflection of images.

Air	Fire of Air. Libra. Wind—swift onset (note idea of balance as in trade winds). Air of Air. Aquarius. Clouds—steady conveyors of water. Water of Air. Gemini. Vibrations—bulk unmoved, spiritualized to reflect Ruach (mind).
Earth	Fire of Earth. Capricornus. Mountains—violent pressure (due to gravitation). Air of Earth. Taurus. Plains—steady bearing of life. Water of Earth. Virgo. Fields—quiet, spiritualized to bear vegetable and animal life.

In each case the Cardinal sign represents the Birth of the Element, the Kerubic sign its Life, and the Mutable sign its passing over towards the ideal form proper to it, *i.e.* to Spirit. So also the Empresses in the Tarot are the Thrones of Spirit.

THE TRIPLE TRINITY OF THE PLANETS

Neptune	The Spiritual	Self (ego)	Alchemical Mercury
Sun	The Human (Intellectual)*		
Moon	The Sensory (Bodily)		
Herschel	The Spiritual	Will of the Self	Alchemical Sulphur
Saturn	The Human (Intellectual)*		
Mars	The Sensory (Bodily)		
Jupiter	The Spiritual	Relation with the non-ego	Alchemical Salt
Mercury	The Human (Intellectual)*		
Venus	The Sensory (Bodily)		

* For "intellectual" one might say "conscious."

Middle Pillar		
Neptune	The Spiritual	Consciousness
Sun	The Human	
Moon	The Automatic	

Pillar of Mercy		
Herschel	The Creative	Mode of action on the non-ego
Jupiter	The Paternal	
Venus	The Passionate	

Pillar of Severity		
Saturn	The Intuitive	Mode of Self-expression
Mars	The Volitional	
Mercury	The Intellectual	

THE GENETHLIAC VALUES OF THE PLANETS

Neptune	The True Self (Zeitgeist). Spiritual environment.
Herschel	The True Will. Spiritual energy.
Saturn	The Ego (ahamkara). Skeleton.
Jupiter	The Higher Love. Wesenschaund of Krause.
Mars	The Bodily Will. Muscular system.
Sun	The Human Will. Vital force. Spiritual conscious self.
Venus	The Lower Love.
Mercury	The Mind. Cerebral tissues and nerves.
Moon	The Senses. Bodily consciousness.

EXPLANATIONS OF THE ATTRIBUTIONS IN THE MORE IMPORTANT COLUMNS OF TABLES I—VI.

(See pp. 2-36)

COLUMN I. THE KEY SCALE (see p. 2)

In order to understand thoroughly the Key Scale, the student should have mastered the Essay on the Qabalah, *The Equinox*, I, 5 (pp. 72-89), and acquainted himself with the use of Liber D (*The Equinox*, I, 8, Supplement).

It should be sufficient therefore in this place to explain simply the significance of the symbols of this scale.

The numbers 000 to 10 are printed in heavy block type. They refer to the three forms of Zero and the ten Sephiroth or numbers of the decimal scale. The diagram on page xxvii shows the conventional geometrical arrangement of the symbols 1—10. The numbers 11—32 correspond to the 22 letters of the Hebrew alphabet. They are attributed to the paths which join the Sephiroth. Their arrangement is shown in the same diagram. 31 and 32 must be supplemented by 31-bis and 32-bis, as those two paths possess a definitely double attribution; viz. 31-bis to Spirit as against 31 to Fire; 32-bis to Earth as against 32 to Saturn.

The numbers 11, 23, 31, 32-bis, 31-bis are printed close to the left edge of the column for convenience of reference, they referring to the 5 elements.

12, 13, 14, 21, 27, 30, 32 are printed in the centre of the column: they refer to the planets.

15, 16, 17, 18, 19, 20, 24, 25, 26, 28, 29 are printed on the right-hand edge of the column. They refer to the signs of the Zodiac.

It should be understood that the main object of this book is to enable the student to do four things. Firstly, to analyze any idea soever in terms of the Tree of Life. Secondly, to trace the connection between every class of idea referring it thereto. Thirdly, to translate any unknown symbolism into terms of any known one by its means. Fourthly, to make a concatenation of any part of any idea with the rest by analogy with the similar concatenation of the Sephiroth and the paths.

As an extension of this last faculty, he should endeavour to treat any given attribution of anything to the Sephiroth as part of the connotation of the idea of those numbers.

In this connection, observe that the numbers (of this column) subsequent to 10 are not to be considered as real numbers. The figures have been assigned to them arbitrarily for convenience only. Thus there is no special sympathy between 11 and the letter Aleph which is referred to it. For Aleph is connected chiefly with the idea of Zero and Unity, whereas 11 is the number of Magick, and its principal alphabetical correspondencies are Beth and Teth. Further, the essential definition of a path is determined by its position on the Tree of Life as conductor of the influence of the Sephiroth which it connects.

One great difficulty in constructing this table is caused by the intimate correspondency between certain Sephiroth and paths. Thus Kether is directly reflected into Chokmah according to one mode, and into Tiphereth according to another. Further, the creative energy on a still lower plane is symbolized in Yesod. In respect of its unity, moreover, it has its analogy in the 11th path.*

In the case of Chokmah the difficulty is even greater. Chokmah, as the creative energy Chiah, is of the same nature as Chesed, and even Tiphereth as Vau shows an intimate correspondence with the final Hé of Tetragrammaton as Chokmah with her mother. Among the paths of the Serpent this creative energy is expressed according to various modes: by the 11th path, the Wandering Fool, who impregnates the King's Daughter, by the 12th path,

* Editorial Note.—The plate on p. xxvii shows the Key Scale in diagrammatic form. 1 to 10 are the ten numbered circles or Sephiroth: 11 to 32 are the twenty-two lines or paths which connect the Sephiroth with each other: the whole forms a traditional pattern known as the Tree of Life.

which creates Maya, the 15th which is definitely phallic, and even the 13th which symbolizes change through putrefaction. Lastly, he is found in this function in the 27th path, which represents Phallum Ejaculentem. Chokmah being pre-eminently the causer of change.

Again, Chokmah is the Logos, the messenger, the transmitter of the influence from Kether, and this is shown, in a lower mode, in the Sephira Hod. He is also implied in the 11th path, for the Fool also transmits the essence of Kether. He is in the 12th path as the Magician, Mercury, in the 16th as the Magus of the Eternal, in the 17th as the Oracle of the Mighty Gods, and in the 20th as the Prophet of the Eternal, the Magus of the Voice of Power. The idea of the message is also implied in the 13th and 25th paths, perhaps even in the 32nd. The 18th path, too, conveys a certain quintessence although not in a Mercurial manner. And it is just these subtle distinctions which are vital to the proper understanding of the Tree of Life.

The idea of Binah is even more complicated. Her darkness is referred to Saturn. As the Great Sea, she gives of her nature to all those paths which contain the idea of the element of Water. Binah is connected with the Azoth, not only because the Azoth is the lower Moon, but because the Azoth partakes also of the Saturnian character, being the metal lead in one of the Alchemical systems. She is also the Great Mother. She is Venus and she is the Moon, and in each aspect she sheds her influence into very various paths. We need not here go further into the cases of the other Sephiroth.

Now from a practical point of view of constructing these tables, it will evidently be very difficult in many cases to choose on which path to place any given idea. For one thing, the ideas themselves are often very far from simple. It is obvious, for instance, that the Lotus—which is also a Wheel—might be attributed to any path in respect to its femininity. In some cases it has been necessary to give several attributions to the same thing. Observe in particular the 12 different aspects of Isis. The student must not attempt to use this book as if it were Molesworth. The whole idea of these tables is to supply him with very varied information, in such a form that he can build up in himself a scheme of the Universe in an alphabet, at once literary and mathematical, which will enable him to obtain a coherent conception of the Universe in a sufficiently compact and convenient form to utilize in both his theoretical and practical working.

Columns II, III. THE HEBREW NAMES OF NUMBERS AND LETTERS

These columns indicate the principal moral ideas connected with the Sephiroth. The names of the letters indicate rather the pictorial glyph suggested by the shape of the letter. But they also conceal a secondary meaning behind that of the numerical value and the number of the Tarot trump of each. The value of the name of each letter modifies that meaning. For example, Aleph, while principally significant of Zero and Unity, explains itself further by the number 111, the value of the letters A L P. That is to say a study of the number 111 enables us to analyze the meaning of the number 1. It indicates, for instance, the trinitarian equation $1 = 3$.

Note that the letters Hé and Vau may each be spelt fully in four different ways, corresponding to the four worlds given in column LXIV.

It is to be thoroughly understood that the titles of the Sephiroth make no claim to give anything like a complete description of their nature. The glyphs of the 22 letters have some times a greater, some times a less, importance in elaborating the connotation.

Aleph means an *Ox*, principally because the shape of the letter suggests the shape of a yoke. There is also a reference to the mildness and patience of Harpocrates: indeed, to his sexual innocence. The function of ploughing is clearly the chief idea involved: herein lies a paradox—to be studied in the last act of Parsifal.

Beth is a *House*, the letter showing the roof, floor, and one wall. It is the dwelling place of man in the world of duality and illusion.

Gimel the *Camel*, reminds us of the position of the Path on the Tree of Life as joining Kether and Tiphereth, and thus the means of travelling through the wilderness of the Abyss.

Daleth a *Door*, refers to the position of the path as joining Chokmah and Binah. It is the gate of the Supernals. Again, it is the letter of Venus; and shows the sexual symbolism. The shape suggests the porch of a doorway, or a porched tent-flap.

HÉ a *Window*, reminds us that Understanding (Hé being the letter of the Mother in Tetragrammaton) is the means by which the Light reaches us. The gap between the two strokes is the window.

VAU a *Nail* (shape directly hieroglyphic) suggests the fixation of the Supernals in Tiphereth.

ZAYIN a *Sword*, refers to the attribution of the letter to Gemini, the sign corresponding to intellectual analysis. The Yod above suggests the hilt; that below, the blade.

CHETH a *Fence*. The Cross-bar on the uprights suggests a fence—more properly the Holy Graal.

TETH is a *Serpent*, as is very obvious from the shape of the letter. The symbol of Leo also resembles the Uraeus. It being the house of the Sun, the idea is to emphasize the identity of the Star and the Snake.

YOD a *Hand*, indicates the means of action. The doctrine is that the Universe is set in motion by the action of indivisible points (Hadit). The Hand being the symbol of creative and directive energy, is the polite equivalent of Spermatozoon, the true glyph.

KAPH the *Palm* of the hand, is the hub of the wheel from which the force of the 5 elements spring. The reference is particularly to Jupiter and the 10th ATU. The regular form may suggest the fist: the final, the open hand.

LAMED an *Ox-Goad*, is once more principally a matter of shape. There is, in particular, a reference to the relation of Lamed with Aleph, a matter too profound to discuss in this place. It must be studied personally in the light of The Book of the Law and of essays thereon.

MEM *Water* suggests a wave; a breaker by its initial or medial form, and still water by its final form. In this single case, the actual meaning of the word is identical with the Yetziratic attribution of the letter. Note that the letter NUN, meaning fish, is not attributed to Pisces but to Scorpio.

NUN a *Fish,* is that which lives and moves in the water: which is here a symbol of death. It therefore indicates the forces of Scorpio, generation through putrefaction. The final form suggests a tadpole.

SAMECH a *Prop,* refers to the fact that the path connects Tiphereth with Yesod and therefore serves to connect Microprosopus with his foundation. The shape may suggest a pillow, or a stone, to be thrust under some object.

A'AIN an *Eye,* refers to the meatus. This explains the application of Capricornus to the 15th ATU. The shape may suggest the two eyes and the nose.

PÉ a *Mouth,* is explained by the shape of the letter. The Yod represents the tongue.

TZADDI a *Fish Hook,* is also an obvious matter of shape.

QOPH the *Back of the Head.* The shape is fairly suggestive.

RESH a *Head reversed.* The seat of the human consciousness, which is Solar, pertaining to Tiphereth, is in the head. Resh is the Solar letter. In shape it is merely a big Yod, implying the brain as the expansion of the Spermatozoon.

SHIN a *Tooth,* plainly exhibits the three fangs of a molar. It is also a glyph of the triple tongue of flame, the letter being referred to the element of Fire. The suggestion of devouring, eating, or eating into, is also given. The idea of the ternary shown by the three Yods is borne out by the value of the letter, 300. Yet the letter being one letter, the doctrine of the Trinity is implied. Hence its secondary attribution to the element of Spirit. It is also a glyph of the God SHU, whose head and arms, separating SEB and NUIT, form the letter. This connects it with the fire of the Last Judgment (ATU XX). I may here note that SHU is the God of air and not of fire, of the firmament that separates Earth and Heaven; so that part of the idea of the letter is to establish a link between the ideas of fire and air, the two active elements. There is a similar connection between Mem and Tau. The 12th ATU shows a man hanging from a cross, which is the meaning of Tau.

TAU a *Tau* or *Cross* symbolizes the element of Earth as a solidification of the four elements. There is also a phallic meaning, whence Tau is attributed not only to Earth, but to Saturn. Tau was originally written cruciform.

I may supplement the above remarks by saying that they make clear that there is no such apodeictic connection between the letters as between the numbers. The meanings are in many cases little more than indications of certain lines on which meditation may be profitably pushed.

COLUMN V. GOD NAMES IN ASSIAH

1. EHEIEH. The God names of the Sephiroth refer, for the most part, by meaning to their characteristics. Thus EHEIEH, pure existence, belongs to I. The sound of the word represents the indrawn and outdrawn breath.
2. YAH gives the title of the Father.
3. JEHOVAH ELOHIM gives the full name of the God, as if the Supernals were collected in Binah.
4. The name AL is used in many senses. Its deepest sense is given by The Book of the Law. The excuse for writing it here is that 4 represents Jupiter, the highest possible manifestation of Deity.
5. ELOHIM GIBOR. The attribution is natural.
6. JEHOVAH ELOAH VA-DAATH. The reference is to Tiphereth as the child of Chokmah and Binah, Daäth (their first child) having failed to find a place on the Tree.

7-8. JEHOVAH TZABAOTH and ELOHIM TZABAOTH give respectively the two principal names of the Demiurge expressed in multiplicity and positive action. (Hosts.)

9. SHADDAI EL CHAI. Almighty and Every-living God: refers to his function as Pangenetor.
10. ADONAI MELEKH. "My Lord the King" is the natural inhabitant of "The Kingdom." The attributions of the Elemental Gods are somewhat arbitrary. Tetragrammaton is given to Air (11), because Jehovah is Jupiter, the Lord of Air. Al is given to Water (23), because of its attribution to Chesed, the Sephira of Water. Elohim is given to Fire (31), because the name of five letters represents the active but feminine principle Shakti of Geburah, the fiery Sephira. Adonai Ha-Aretz is the natural title of Earth (32-bis); and Adonai is the name of God particularly referred to man in his mortality. It is one title of the Holy Guardian Angel. Yeheshua is attributed to Spirit (31-bis) on account of the formation of the word from Tetragrammaton by the insertion of the letter Shin, thus forming the

Pentagram of the Elements. The planetary names refer to the sacred numbers of the planets. The Zodiacal signs are not honoured with God-names in the Hebrew system. Those referring to the planets ruling them may be used.

COLUMN VI. THE HEAVENS OF ASSIAH

This column gives the names of the astral or apparent phenomena corresponding to Column II. It must be understood that in speaking of the sphere of a planet the astrological attribution is a minor quasi-accidental and not necessarily reliable function. It depends on astrological theories. By "Tzedeq" we should understand any function of a phenomenon which partakes of the nature of Jupiter. At the same time the Heavens of Assiah do not refer directly to pure number but indirectly through the astrological and cosmographical conventions.

1. RASHITH HA-GILGALIM. The primum mobile—or "beginning of whirling motion"—tells us that Kether is the point from which we measure motion. The Sephiroth might even perhaps be considered as co-ordinate axes.
2. MASLOTH. The fixed stars are connected with the idea of Hadit as positive interruptions of the negative continuum Nuit. Neptune is attributed to this sphere as being the outpost of the Solar system. Uranus is attributed to Daäth because of its explosive nature. The Abyss is represented in Nature by the Asteroids. There is another aspect of Uranus, the Magical Will, which is assigned to Chokmah. There is also another of Neptune, whose astrological characteristics are sympathetic with Neschamah and therefore with Binah. It must be remarked that since above the Abyss a thing is only true so far as it contains its contradictions in itself, the attributions of the planets above the Abyss cannot be so definite as those below. Each of them can in a way be attributed to any of the Supernals, and each may be given to any one for contradictory reasons. It cannot be too strongly pointed out to the practical Magician that when he comes to work with ideas above the Abyss, the whole character of his operations is completely changed.
3. SHABATAI represents Saturn as the planet of repose, of darkness, and perhaps, as the category of Time. Note

that Saturn is attributed to Daäth in the hexagram of the planets. This is the creative Saturn, the hidden God, and the Daäth of the apex of the upper triangle of the hexagram is in reality a concentration of the Trinity of the Supernals. The hexagram must not be like "the Stooping Dragon," crowned with a falsity.

4. TZEDEQ means righteousness; the inexorable law of Jupiter. The connection of this with the number 4 depends on the aspect of 4 as the square of 2, the limitation of the Dyad further fixed by self-multiplication, the introduction of a new dimension. 4 is thus a number of rigidity or materiality. Hence its ideal quality is inexorable righteousness.

Yet in connection with this, remember that Chesed means Mercy and 4 is Daleth, the letter of Venus, Love. Consideration of this is very helpful in understanding the way in which a Sephira combines widely diverse ideas.

5-9. 5. MADIM. 6. SHEMESH. 7. NOGAH. 8. KOKAB. 9. LEVANAH.*

10. CHOLIM YESODOTH. The sphere of the elements is attributed to Malkuth. Of course, the elements extend through the Sephiroth. But "element" here means the composition of Nephesch and sensible matter; which pertain to Malkuth.

11. RUACH means air, also breath and mind, thought being the expression in expansion of the union of Chokmah and Binah in the subconscious. Ruach is also translated Spirit—Latin Spiritus. There must be no confusion between this "spirit" and that symbolized by the letter Shin. The distinctions are of the utmost importance, and so manifold and subtle that the subject demands a complete essay in itself.

23. MAIM is Hebrew for Water.

31. ASH is the Hebrew for Fire.

32-bis. ARETZ is the Hebrew for Earth.

* Editorial Note.—The explanatory notes on these five heavens of Assiah were never written. The typescript merely has "Look up the actual meaning."

31-bis. ATH. I have myself assigned the word Ath to the idea of Spirit as an element, it being the Alpha and Omega, or the essence which interpenetrates the other elements. It is the unformulated reality common to them, by virtue whereof they exist.

The planetary heavens follow their Sephirotic attributions; *e.g.* 27, the Heaven of Mars is Madim given above against the number 5.

The Zodiacal heavens are simply the Hebrew names of the signs.

COLUMN VII. THE ENGLISH OF COLUMN VI

The nature of the entries in this column is to be studied in the light of the traditional astrological conception.

COLUMN VIII. THE ORDERS OF QLIPHOTH

The titles of the Qliphoth, generally speaking, suggest the vice characteristic of the Sephira or other idea to which they are attributed. Thus the Thaumiel refer to Kether, because their characteristic is to possess two contending heads, and so to deny the unity of Kether. So also the Golachab are giants like volcanoes, symbolizing energy and fire, and their liability to appear as tyranny and aimless destruction. Similarly, the Qliphoth of Venus are carrion birds, as opposed to the dove, sparrow, etc.

The transliteration and meaning of the Hebrew names of the Orders of Qliphoth are as follows:—

0. { QEMETIEL. Crowd of Gods.
BELIA'AL. Worthlessness.
A'ATHIEL. Uncertainty. }

1. THAUMIEL. Twins of God.
2. GHAGIEL. Hinderers.
3. SATARIEL. Hiding.
4. GHA'AGSHEBLAH. Smiters.
5. GOLACHAB. Flaming Ones.
6. THAGIRION. The Litigation.
7. A'ARAB ZARAQ. The Raven of Dispersion.
8. SAMAEL. The False Accuser.
9. GAMALIEL. The Obscene Ass.
10. LILITH. The Woman of Night.
15. BA'AIRIRON. The Flock.
16. ADIMIRON. Bloody.
17. TZALALIMIRON. Clangers.
18. SHICHIRIRON. Black.
19. SHALEHBIRON. Flaming.
20. TZAPHIRIRON. Scratchers.
22. A'ABIRIRON. Clayey.
24. NECHESHTHIRON. Brazen.
25. NECHESHIRON. Snakey.
26. DAGDAGIRON. Fishy.
28. BAHIMIRON. Bestial.
29. NASHIMIRON. Malignant Women.

Column X. MYSTIC NUMBERS OF THE SEPHIROTH

These numbers are obtained by adding together the natural numbers up to and including the one in question. Thus, the sum of the first ten numbers is fifty-five. Their significance has been well worked-out; and is important up to the number 13. After that, the numbers 15, 20, 21, 24, 28, and 31 have repaid the study bestowed upon them.

For the meaning of the primes from 11 to 97 see page xxv.

Column XI. THE ELEMENTS, WITH THEIR PLANETARY RULERS

1-9. Kether is said to be the root of Air, because of the force of air, or the balance of Fire and Water, and, as connected, it is Aleph, with the ideas of Zero and Unity. Chokmah is said to be the root of Fire, because of its creative nature; Binah of Water, because of its receptive passivity, and its symbolism as the Great Sea. The three elements are reflected into the second triad, Water being referred to Chesed, partly because it is the recipient of the male influence of the Supernals, partly because 4 is Daleth, Venus, the feminine or watery principle. The energy and mobility of Geburah naturally suggests Fire and Air. The third member of the triad is Tiphereth, partly for the same reason as Kether just cited, partly because Tiphereth is Microprosopus, who is Vau in Tetragrammaton, Vau being the letter of Air, the result of the union of Yod and Hé, Fire and Water.

In the third triad Netzach is Fire, as representing the devouring quality of love: Hod, Water, as representing the reflecting quality of thought: and Yesod, Air, on account of the extremely important mystery expressed in Liber 418, Aethyr XI (see *The Equinox*, I, 5).* The integrity of the Sephiroth is guaranteed by the fact that each one contains its contradictory in itself. Yesod, the Foundation, the principle of stability, cannot be shaken because it is also the ideal of elasticity, and instability.

10. Earth appears for the first time in Malkuth. The three active elements are represented in three triads in a progressively diluted and impure form. There is a progressive admixture of ideas as one descends the Tree; but when the descent becomes so gross that they can no longer subsist as such, they unite to act as a trinity, to reproduce themselves by reflection or

* Also re-issued: The Vision and the Voice, with Introduction and Commentary by The Master Therion.

crystallisation as a fixed form in which their original natures are no longer perceptible as such. They merely modify the character of the compound. The analogy is to chemical elements, which are unable to manifest the natural property of the pure state in a compound. It is only their subtler qualities which influence the nature of the compound. Thus none of the physical properties of H. are directly to be observed in its combination with SO_4. It is only the subtler qualities which determine that H_2SO_4 should be an acid.

The attribution of Earth to Malkuth is important as explaining the nature of Nephesch and manifested matter. It is to be understood that the three active elements and the first 9 Sephiroth do not exist at all directly for the senses. They are to be apprehended only indirectly, by observing their function through determining the nature of sensible things. The necessary attributions of the column are extremely important as throwing light on the nature of the Heavens of Assiah. They must be studied and meditated with great care.

Thus the fiery signs Aries, Leo, and Sagittarius partake of the nature of Sol and Jupiter, because of the active, lordly, creative, paternal, generous, noble, and similar qualities. The earthy signs are sympathetic with Venus and Luna because of the passive receptivity of these planets. Airy signs correspond particularly with Saturn and Mercury, because of the connection of these planets with thought. Watery signs are sympathetic with Mars with regard to the fact that Water possesses the fiery property of breaking up and destroying solids. The student must be careful to avoid expressing himself by inventing false antinomies. There is a great danger in arguing backwards in the Qabalah, especially in the case of attributions of this sort. Thus the explanation of the martial nature of water must not be used to argue a watery nature in Mars, whose natural sympathy is evidently Fire.

It would be supremely misleading to try to obtain any information about the nature of Mars from this column. It is almost impossible to suggest any rule for avoiding errors of this sort. The best I can do is to recommend the student never to lose sight of the fact that all attributions whatsoever have no absolute quality. The object is really to remind the student of what he already knows about any given idea and its relation with the rest. He should therefore determine for himself the nature of any idea principally by meditation or direct magical investigation, such as actual visions. He may accept provisionally the validity of correspondences so far as they indicate the best methods of invocation and evocation. Having thus firmly established in his head the correspondences of any symbol, he is less likely to misinterpret it, or to assign a new importance to any known correspondence such as is found in the latter part of this column. He will take the planetary rulers here given as little more than suggestions for memorizing minor details of the nature of the Zodiac. It would evidently be absurd to set up an antinomy between the statement in this column that Saturn and Mercury are the rulers of Libra with the statement elsewhere that Libra is ruled by Venus and Saturn exalted therein. There is, however, a certain partial sympathy between the columns. Thus Sol is exalted in Aries, Luna in Taurus, Mercury rules Gemini, and Sol Leo. In the case of Virgo, however, neither Venus nor Luna appear either as its ruler or as exalted therein. A profitable meditation might develop in some such way as follows:—

Question: Why should Venus and Luna not be given as rulers of Virgo? Virgo is suggested as the Virgin Isis, Luna as sympathetic with solitude, purity, and aptitude for reflection of the Hermit, ATU IX. Venus, again, as Binah, the recipient of Wisdom, represents one aspect of Virgo. So too does the earthy nature of Venus

> in her aspect of Demeter. In this way an attribution, which at first sight is puzzling, may assist the student to harmonize many ideas which appear at first sight incompatible.

The case of Venus is germane to the argument.* Venus is astrologically used as a synthetic term for the feminine aspect of the Deity. She has then many parts, Vesta, Ceres, Cybele, Isis, etc. The main distinction to be borne in mind is that with Luna; and the task is all the more difficult in that the symbols continually overlap. It is by harmonizing and transcending such difficulties that the student arrives at a metaphysical conception which is perfectly positive and lucid on the one hand, and on the other emancipated from the bondage of the Laws of Contradiction.

Luna = Gimel = 3. Trivia is one of the titles of Diana.

The life of woman is naturally divided into three parts: before, during, and after the age of menstruation. (1) The Virgin, (2) the Wife and Mother, (3) the Hag. In (3) the woman can no longer fulfil her natural functions, which therefore turn to the malignity of despair. Hence the identification of the Hag with the Witch. (1) is represented by Diana, the virgin huntress (legends of Atalanta, Endymion, Pan, Actaeon, Persephone, etc.), Hebe, Pallas Athene, Pythia and the Sybils, etc. The function of the virgin is inspirational. (2) is connected with Venus, Ceres, Cybele, Kwannon or Kwanseon, Sekhet, Hathor, Kali, Aphrodite, Astarte, Ashtoreth, Artemis of the Ephesians, and many other female deities. (3) is a wholly malignant symbol. Hecate and Nahema are the principal representatives of the idea.

Note that there are certain demons of the nature of Venus Aversa, symbolical of the evil caused by distorting or suppressing this principle. Such are

* Note that the symbol of Venus is the only planetary symbol which includes all ten Sephiroth.

Echidna, Lilith, the outraged Aphrodite of the Hyppolytus, the Venus of the Hörsel in Tannhäuser, Melusina, Lamia, some aspects of Kali, Kundry, possibly the malicious side of Queen Mab and the Fairy nature generally.

The student is expected to have in mind all such symbols and to overcome their incompatibility, not by blurring the outline of the different figures, but by regarding each of them as representing one phenomenal manifestation of the ultimate principle which we name Nuit, Teh, Shakti, Hé, Isis, positive electricity, the infinity of space, possibility, etc., in conjunction with a particular set of circumstances. The student will note that this principle cannot be apprehended in itself, but only in combination. Just so we can only understand electricity by observing its effects in lightning, magnetism, etc. Some philosophers have attempted to construct synthetic symbols to include all aspects of this principle. Thus the Egyptians, who were the most philosophical of all schools of Theogonists, included as many functions of femininity as possible in the idea of Isis. Thus she is:—

1. Wisdom, like Pallas Athene.
2. The Physical Moon.
3. The Perpetual Virgin, twin-born with Osiris.
4. Nature (complemented by her final form Nephthys—Perfection).
5. The Builder of Cities. (As indicated by her head-dress.)
6. The Spouse of Osiris.
7. The Mother of Horus.
8. The Spirit of Corn or food in general.
9. Earth in general.
10. The Goddess of Water or the Nile, and therefore of wine in general. She is the soul of intoxication, this representing the spiritual rapture of physical love.
11. The Initiatrix; mistress of secrets. The Teacher.

12. The Restorer (the earth fertile after winter) as shown by her collecting the fragments of Osiris.

The feminine nature is evidently coextensive with a moiety of all our ideas; and this fact alone is sufficient to account for the complexity of the symbolism. Hence the necessity for a course of meditation above indicated and for the occasional apparent contradictions.

Column XIII. THE PATHS OF THE SEPHER YETZIRAH

These attributions arise from the description of the paths in the Sepher Yetzirah. This is one of the most ancient books of the Qabalah; but it is far from clear how the ideas correspond with the general scheme of symbolism. They seem of no use in practical magical work. It is doubtful whether the text of the book is accurate, or whether (in any case) the rabbin responsible for the text had any sufficient authority.

Column XIV. GENERAL ATTRIBUTIONS OF THE TAROT

This column gives merely the actual attributions which are to be taken as the basis of any investigation of the Tarot. They are the conventional terms and no more.

Column XV. THE KING SCALE OF COLOUR

The four scales of colours (Columns XV-XVIII) are attributed to the four letters of Tetragrammaton. The King Scale represents the root of colour; that is, a relation is asserted between the essential significance of colour in the Atziluthic world, and that of the path understood as well as possible, in the light especially of Columns II, VI, and XIV. But the King Scale represents an essence of equal depth with the columns mentioned. It is an attribution of the same order as they; *i.e.* it is a primary expression of the essential ideas.

1. Brilliance represents the colourless luminosity of Kether.
2. The blue is that of the sky (Masloth).
3. The crimson represents blood. Compare the symbolism of the Scarlet Woman and her Cup in Liber 418.
4. The deep violet is episcopal. It combines 2 and 3, a bishop being the manifestation of heavenly or starry existence manifested through the principle of blood or animal life.
5. The orange suggests the energy as opposed to other qualities of the Sun.
6. The rose is that of dawn. The attribution therefore asserts the identity of the Sun and Horus and is thus implicated with the doctrine of the New Aeon.
7. Amber represents the electric voluptuousness of Aphrodite. It suggests the tint of the skin of those women who are most enthusiastically consecrated to Venus.
8. Violet-purple. Should this not be lavender? Meditate.
9. The indigo is that of the Akasa (ether) and of the throat of Shiva. It represents the night sky blue of the nemyss of Thoth. This nemyss is the mysterious yet pregnant darkness which surrounds the generative process.
10. The yellow indicates Malkuth as the appearance which our senses attach to the solar radiance. In other

words, Malkuth is the illusion which we make in order to represent to ourselves the energy of the Universe.

The Elemental Colours

These may be naturally derived from what has been said about Column XI, lines 1-10. Scarlet naturally represents the activity of Fire, blue the passivity of Water, while yellow is the balance between them. Green is the middle colour of the spectrum and therefore the balanced receptacle of the totality of vibration. Observe that the complementary of each pair of the colours of the active elements is the third. Thus, red and blue make violet, whose complementary is yellow; and so on.

For the citrine, olive, russet, and black of earth, see the explanation under 10, Malkuth, in the Queen Scale (Column XVI). The pure earth, known to the ancient Egyptians in that Equinox of the Gods over which Isis presided, was green.

The Planetary Attributions

They follow the colours of the spectrum. They are the transparent as opposed to the reflected colours. They follow the order of the subtlety and spirituality of the vibration. Thus the violet of Jupiter is definitely religious and creative, while at the end of the scale the red of Mars is physical, violent, and gross. Between these we have Saturn whose indigo represents the sobriety and deep-sea calmness of meditation, Saturn being the eldest of the Gods. Luna is blue; representing purity, aspiration and unselfish love. The green of Venus suggests the vibration of vegetable growth. It is the intermediate stage between the definitely spiritual and the definitely intellectual and emotional type of vibration. In the "rods and cones" attribution green is the central colour, the pure passivity absorbing all: as Venus combines all the Sephiroth in one symbol. The yellow of Mercury suggests the balanced but articulate movement of the mind. The orange of Sol is the intense but gross physical vibration of animal life.

The above represents merely one of an indefinitely large number of interpretations which may be derived from meditation on this attribution.

THE ZODIACAL ATTRIBUTIONS

The Zodiacal colours proceed systematically from the Scarlet of Aries to the violet of Aquarius. The colour which completes the circle is described as crimson, and is attributed to Pisces, the allusion being to the relation of Pisces with Binah through the ATU XVIII, the Moon, in which also is shown the pool of midnight through which Kephra travels in his bark; and this suggests the Night of Pan which hangs over the City of the Pyramids.

Aries is scarlet, being the House of Mars and the sign of the Spring Equinox, where occurs the fiery outburst of the new year. Taurus is red-orange, suggesting the red earth of which man (who is Taurus, Vau, Microprosopus, the Son) is made, the orange indicating the Solar influence and the energy of Geburah. Gemini is orange, since ATU VI shows the Solar twins Vau Hé. Cancer is amber, the connection being with Netzach, Venus in her less spiritual form being the chariot or vehicle through which the influence of the Supernal Mother is conveyed to man. In this chariot is borne the Sangraal or Cup of Babalon; which connects the symbolism with the legend of Parsifal and the visions of Liber 418. The ideas of love and electricity are implicit in this sign, which is ruled by the Moon and in which Jupiter is exalted.

Leo is pure yellow, yet with that tinge of green which is characteristic of the purest gold. It suggests the first form of the principle of vegetable growth, implicit in the nature of the Solar ray.

Virgo has the yellowish green of young grass. The connection is evident.

Libra is emerald green, being pre-eminently the house of Venus.

Scorpio is the greenish blue—Prussian blue—whose psychological effect upon the sensitive mind is to suggest a poisonous or putrefactive vibration. It contains the idea of life and death interpenetrating each other and reproducing each other continuously; always with the accompaniment of a certain morbid pleasure. It is the identification which one finds in Swinburne's best poems: "The Garden of Proserpine," "Dolores," "Illicet," "Anactoria," and others. The natural correspondence is the blue-green sea.

Sagittarius is blue; being the House of Jupiter, which is blue in the Queen Scale. It is also the blue of the sky; for Sagittarius is the background of the Rainbow symbolism of Q Sh Th. It is further connected with the blue of religious aspiration. It continues the path of Gimel. It is the aspiration from Yesod to Tiphereth as Gimel is from Tiphereth to Kether. Note that the aspiration to Yesod from Malkuth is *dark* blue: it being so low on the Tree its purity is to some extent darkened.

Capricornus is indigo. The connection is with the colour of Yesod, implying the sexual symbolism of the Goat.

Aquarius is violet: this is connected with ATU XVII. Cf. The Book of the Law, I, 61-64. The colour violet, generally speaking, signifies a vibration which is at the same time spiritual and erotic; *i.e.* it is the most intense of the vibrations alike on the planes of Nephesch and Neschamah. Compare at the other end of the scale the connection between the vibrations of Mars and those of the Sangraal.

Column XVI. THE QUEEN SCALE

This scale represents the first positive appearance of colour: as the King Scale is transparent, the Queen is reflected. (Spectra.)

1-3. In this scale, therefore, we read the appearance of the 32 paths as they are found in Nature. Kether, being previously unconditioned brilliance, is now articulate as white. The grey of Chokmah refers to the cloudy appearance of semen, and indicates the transmission of white to black. It is the double nature of the Dyad. Binah is black, having the faculty of absorbing all colours.

In the three Supernals, therefore, we find the 3 possible modifications of light, in its wholeness. Above the abyss there is no separation into colour.

4. Chesed has the blue of water 5. Geburah the red of fire 6. Tiphereth the yellow of air	These being the 3 primary colours of reflected light as opposed to the violet, green and red of transparent light.

The colours of the 3rd triad are derived from those of the 2nd by simple admixture.

7. Netzach. Emerald is Chesed and Tiphereth mingled. It is also the colour of Venus.
8. Hod. Orange is Tiphereth and Geburah mingled.
9. Yesod. Violet is Chesed and Geburah mingled.

Netzach and Hod are naturally the resultant of the two Sephiroth which impinge on them respectively, while Yesod represents a secondary effect of the conjunction of Chesed and Geburah, Tiphereth being the primary. Emerald represents the most brilliant aspect of Venus; orange that of Mercury. Violet of the very complex formula synthesizes Yesod in the idea of Luna. Note that Sol and Luna are direct images of the masculine and feminine principles, and much more complete Macrocosms than any other planets. This is explained by their symbols in the

Yi King, ☲ and ☵. Note also that Yesod appears openly, this being the Queen Scale, in the violet robes of the spiritual-erotic vibrations referred to above.

10. Malkuth. Just as the third Triad combines the colours of the second Triad by pairs, so does Malkuth in a yet more complete manner. Citrine combines blue, red and yellow with a predominance of yellow; olive, with a predominance of blue; russet, with a predominance of red; and these represent respectively the airy, watery, and fiery sub-elements. Black is the earthy part of Earth. But here we observe a phenomenon compatible with that found in the Tarot, where the four Empresses (symbolical of Hé final) are the throne of the Spirit as well as being the ultimate recipients of the force of King, Queen, and Emperor. The black is the link between the lowest conception, the climax of the degeneration of pure colour in the final assimilation of light, and the black of Binah. It is the lowest part of the daughter which contains in darkness the identity with the Pure Mother, to set her upon whose throne is one definite image of the Great Work. See also the 27th Symbol in Liber XXVII;* the ultimate of the feminine symbols, the complete dissociation of existence, the final disappearance of all positive ideas, but this is found to be essentially identical with the perfection of the continuum.

The planetary colours are connected chiefly with the sacred metals as observed clairvoyantly, or considered in respect of their astrological and alchemical character. Mercury is purple suggesting the iridescence of quicksilver and the blue of Mercury vapour. Luna is silver, the apparent colour of the Moon in the sky, and of the metal to which she is attributed. Venus is sky-blue; this is possibly a reference to copper-sulphate, an important salt in alchemy; but principally

* Note: ☰ ☰ is the 27th and last mutation of the Tao with the Yin and the Yang. "Therefore was the end of it sorrow; yet in that sorrow a sixfold star of glory whereby they might see to return unto the Stainless Abode; yea, unto the Stainless Abode."

because sky-blue naturally suggests the more frivolous aspects of love. The blue of Jupiter refers to the blue of the sky, his dominion, and to the appropriate colour of religious aspiration. Mars is red on account of the colour of rust, and of the use of iron in executing the pure will; whether by sword, spear, or machine. Sol is yellow, the apparent colour of the sun, and of the metal gold. Saturn is black with reference to Binah, the sphere of Saturn, to the Night of Pan (see Liber 418 in *Equinox* I, 5), to the blackness of oblivion (Saturn being Time), and to the blackness of the corruption of lead (his metal), whose heaviness and dullness confirms the appropriateness of the symbolism. It refers further to the blackness of the Tamoguna, Saturn representing the inactivity of old age.

Zodiacal colours are less obvious in their attribution. In fact it will be best to take this part of the column for what it may be worth as an uninitiated tradition. I am myself unable to attach any serious and important meaning to the majority of the symbols. At most, one can say that the colour of the scale represents the degeneration of the Key Scale. *E.g.* in the case of Aries, red represents a mere dulling of the previous scarlet. The deep indigo of Taurus suggests the laborious sadness of the brute part of man; the slate-green of Virgo may refer to the apparent ennui or colourless melancholy of the hermit life. The black of Capricorn refers to the popular idea of ATU XV; while the attribution of Pisces may refer to the actual appearance of some fish, or certain phenomena characteristic of the astral plane.

Column XVII. THE EMPEROR SCALE

The scale of the Emperor is derived from the two previous scales by simple admixture, as of colours on a palette for the most part.

Column XVIII. THE EMPRESS SCALE

The scale of the Empress is, generally speaking, either a degeneration from the scale of the Emperor or a complementary attribution, Hé being the twin of Vau. But in each case there is an added brightness whose source must be discovered by meditation. This brightness is a phenomenon compatible to that described above in connection with the Empresses being the thrones of the Spirit, and Malkuth being the extreme departure from the perfection of the Supernals, and so the link through which the redemption of the whole complex subterstructure below the Abyss may be accomplished.

The colours of the Empress Scale are combinations of two or more colours. The best may be considered as derived from the three previous scales, and the flecks or rays as representative of the bridegroom who is appointed to bring the Empress to perfection thus.

1. White flecked gold. The white is a reflection of the white brilliance of Kether; but the gold is an ornament, and thus indicates the mystery of the Holy Guardian Angel, who finds added perfection when invoked by his client, the gold of Tiphereth.
2. Red, blue, and yellow are the results of the creative energy of Chokmah and their white basis signifies that Chokmah has been perfected by fulfilling his function in this way. Also, the robe of the perfected Osiris is white flecked with red, blue, and yellow.
3. As the grey of Chokmah was perfected to the white of Kether, so the black of Binah is perfected to the grey of Chokmah. The grey is flecked with the pink of Tiphereth. This is the dawn of the child with which she is heavy, for this is the symbol of her perfection.
4. Deep azure represents Jupiter and Water. It is flecked with yellow. This represents religious meditation; the yellow flecks are the first marks of ecstasy.
5. Red is the most passive shade of the scarlet of the two former scales. The black flecks show that in its per-

fection it receives the influence of Binah, the Supernal immediately above it on the Tree.

6. Gold amber suggests the mellowness of harvest, which is the perfection of the rose-pink of dawn, the spring of the day.
7. There seems a possible reference to Semele; and the general idea is that Netzach has been brought to a quiet harmonious tone and is receiving the influence of Tiphereth. Olive flecked gold.
8. This is a mystery of Mercury, improper to indicate clearly. Yellowish brown flecked white.
9. Citrine represents the final modification of Yesod, the airy nature at last appearing. The azure flecks are derived from Chesed—perhaps through Netzach; or from Sagittarius, the path joining it with Tiphereth.
10. Malkuth has been set upon the throne of Binah; and the rays of the bridegroom Tiphereth flood her with Gold. Black rayed yellow.

THE ELEMENTS

11. Air has been made fertile, so that the golden flecks of the Sun are able to illumine it. Air is naturally barren. The green represents the Lotus on which Harpocrates is seated, or from which he is born.
23. The perfection of Water is indicated by its iridescence. This is the alchemical symbolism.
31. Fire, being pure, retains its original vermilion; but it has become capable of being the home of the crimson and emerald of Binah and her sphere of joy, Venus. It is no longer a destructive element, but the proper abode of Love, both in its higher and lower forms.

32-bis. Earth is identical with Malkuth, save that the rays are now flecks. The symbolism is similar.

31-bis. Spirit manifests the scale of five colours as shown on the Uraeus Wand. (*The Equinox* I, 3, p. 211.) Its perfection is to complete itself in the Pentagram. The mystery is similar to that mentioned in connection with 1 above.

THE PLANETS

12. *Mercury's* perfection is to still and concentrate thought, until it becomes deep red through which runs the violet vibration of spiritual-erotic ecstasy. (Note that the great defect of Mercury is its cold-bloodedness.)
13. *Luna.* The original chastity of the Moon is tinged with Love.
14. *Venus.* The defect of Venus is its tendency to romance (rose or cerise)—"External Splendour" Nogah. It is perfected by reality and usefulness—the emerald of vegetable life and growth.
21. *Jupiter.* The religious devotion of Jupiter is rewarded by the yellow rays of the Holy Guardian Angel.
27. *Mars.* The energy of Mars has been subdued until it is a proper basis for the blue and green rays of vegetable and spiritual life. (Cf. under "31. Fire," above.)
30. *Sol.* The perfection of Sol is its fixation in the amber of Cancer by elevation at the summer solstice. In this it receives the adornment of pure physical energy, Fire. The red is purer than the orange, being of the incorruptible element.
32. *Saturn.* The perfection of Saturn is its identification with Binah. It has, so to speak, made good its position above the Abyss. It is adorned with the blue rays of the King Scale of Chokmah. The symbol implies that Time, the Destroyer, has been transmuted into the condition of the operation of the Great Work, *i.e.* the marriage of Chokmah and Binah.

THE ZODIAC

15. *Aries.* Controlled fire as in a furnace.
16. *Taurus.* Rich fertile earth.
17. *Gemini* is perfected by active thoughts, aimed and tinged by spiritual intention.
18. *Cancer.* See Liber 418 (*Equinox* I, 5) on the Mysteries of Magister Templi. The blood in the Cup of Babalon has dried to brown in which the vegetable, impersonal, and immortal life lurks.

19. *Leo.* Fire is infused evenly in the Lion, thus correcting his tendency to impulse.
20. *Virgo.* The perfection of virginity is fruitfulness.
22. *Libra.* Retains the love of its ruler Venus, but this is purified of its grossness.
24. *Scorpio.* The vivid watery vibration of putrefaction assumes the hue of the beetle Kephra. The perfection of Scorpio is to bring corruptibility through its midnight.
25. *Sagittarius.* The virgin huntress is brought from her superficiality by becoming the huntress Babalon. The deep vivid blue is to be connected with the ideas of water (the Great Sea of Binah) and Chesed, the image of that sea below the Abyss.
26. *Capricornus.* The colour combines Chokmah and Binah, and is very dark. The Great Attainment is symbolized by the marriage.
28. *Aquarius* is the Kerub of the Man; and his perfection is to attain the purity of Kether (white) tinged with the purple or violet vibrations explained above.
29. *Pisces* is the symbol of the Astral Plane. (See ATU XVIII.) Its defect is glamour and illusion. It has now been brought to a mental equilibrium signifying the adaptability of the ether to receive and transmit all types of vibration.

MINUTUM MUNDUM

A General Note on Columns XV-XVIII, the Four Scales of Colour

You can use the four scales of colour as you choose. The only thing to remember is the attribution, the Tetragrammaton.

The Sephiroth are given in the King's Scale and the paths in the Queen's Scale in accordance with the general law of balance. You must never have a masculine sticking out by itself without a feminine to equilibrate it.

The Sephiroth are definitely positive ideas. The numbers are "Things in Themselves," much more so than the letters of the alphabet. The paths are merely the links between the Sephiroth.

Of course the idea of balance is carried into the Sephiroth themselves. The number 4 is masculine in its relation with number 5, feminine in its relation with number 3.

You cannot go wrong as long as you keep always this idea of balance in the forefront of your mind. Whenever one thing goes on to another thing, there must always be this opposition, and equilibrium. You can apply this to every point that comes up in practical working. It is always possible to refer any system of symbols to the Tree of Life merely by Tetragrammaton, or indeed to any of the fundamental systems of classification. It is a very useful exercise to practise this type of analysis. Take, for example, the letter Daleth, and note all its correspondences. For instance you get at once the equation 4 = 7, for the numerical value of Daleth is 4, while 7 is of Venus.

The more thoroughly you practise this the nearer you will come to the completely automatic subconscious understanding of the essence of any given symbol.

Columns XIX, XX, XXI, XXXIV, XXXV. General Remarks on the Gods

Many of the so-called names of God, such as the 99 names of Allah and the poetical lists of Hinduism, are not really names at all but descriptive titles. By the true name of a God we mean that word which represents his Magical Formula; the due process of which therefore sets his energy in motion. (See J. G. Frazer for numerous legends illustrating this idea.) There cannot therefore be more true names ultimately than there are distinct sounds. For a God with a compound name would represent a complex sound, and therefore a complex energy. Such a God would lack the simplicity which is the first attribute of Godhead.

Outside the Hebrew and such other names of Gods as can be checked and corrected if necessary by the rules of Gematria, or the Yetziratic or Tarotic attribution, there is no adequate security that corruption has not taken place, *e.g.* Osiris instead of Asar; Jupiter instead of IAO-Pater.

There are numerous dialectic changes, and changes due to corruption in the course of time or to deliberate modification, with such ends in view as the identification of a local deity with an important and popular God of similar name.

The uncertainty of primitive alphabets is responsible for mispronunciations, which are then written down phonetically and again mispronounced, so that in course of time one finds a form which cannot be recognised; *e.g.* confusion has arisen from the writing of the sound S with a C, pronouncing the C hard and then (to avoid mistakes!) replacing it by K. There is also confusion between I or Y and J (Dj), soft G and hard G, so that a name originally pronounced with a Y ends by appearing with a hard G.

The popularity of a Deity leads to his or her identification with the local interests of each new group of worshippers. Thus a corn goddess might appeal, for one reason or another, to town-dwellers, who would then acclaim her as especially protectress of cities. The process in its widest possibilities is practically universal in the case of those divinities whose cult covers any considerable variety of climates, cultures, economic and social conditions and centuries. Thus a primitive God may be worshipped under a corruption of his original name, and also by his original character. The evolution of Gods proceeds pari passu with that of their devotees.

From the above it will be clear that except in the case of the Hebrews and of a few isolated instances, it is almost impossible to decide on a satisfactory attribution for any given name. It is only where the cult of the god is limited so that his symbolic form, attributes, and legend have some single or at least predominant characteristic, that one can make use even of correctness, much less of completeness. Such is Sekhet, who is uniformly represented with a lion's head and described as possessing feline qualities, so that we can assign her to Leo without hesitation. But a goddess like Isis might be given to Zero as conterminous with Nature, to 3 as Mother, to 4 as Venus, to 6 as Harmony, to 7 as Love, to 9 as the Moon, to 10 as Virgin, to 13 again as the Moon, to 14 as Venus, to 15 as connected with the letter Hé, to 16 as the Sacred Cow, to 18 as Goddess of Water, to 24 as Draco, to 28 as Giver of Rain, to 29 as the Moon, and to 32 as Lady of the Mysteries (Saturn, Binah). In such cases one must be content with a more or less arbitrary selection, and make an independent investigation in each particular case in reference to the matter immediately under consideration. The complementary confusion is that Deities of very different nature will appear against the same rank of the Key Scale for different reasons. For instance, the number 4 includes both Isis and Amoun. There is no question of identifying these. The fact of their appearing in the same place must be taken to indicate that both ideas are necessary to complete the connotation of the number 4.

Column XIX. SOME EGYPTIAN GODS

0. Against the number Zero Harpocrates is Silence and Rest, Amoun is the Concealed. For Nuit and Hadit see the Commentary to the Book of the Law.
1. Now in the number 1, Ptah is the Creator, being represented as a mummy without gestures. It signifies that Kether has no attributes. Asar-un-Nefer is the perfected Osiris; that is Osiris brought to Kether. Heru-Ra-Ha contains the twin forms of the Lord of the Aeon. He is Kether to us in this time and place as being the highest positive conception of which we are capable.
2. Amoun as the creative Chiah, Thoth as the Logos, Nuit as connected with Mazloth.
3. Maut the Mother Vulture requiring to be impregnated by Air, the Logos. Isis as the Mother. Nephthys as the Mother in her dark aspect.
4. Amoun as the Father; Isis as water, and Hathoor the Nile Goddess.
5. Horus as the Lord of Force. Nephthys as the Lady of Severity balancing the mercy of Isis.
6. Asar, the prototype of man. Ra and On the Sun God. Harpocrates is of Tiphereth as being the Child. Also he is the centre, as Tiphereth is the centre of the Ruach. His body is rose-pink, as in the King Scale of Tiphereth. Hrumachis might also be placed here for the same reason.
7. Hathoor, the Egyptian Venus.
8. Anubis, the lower form of Thoth, Mercury.
9. Shu, Lord of the Firmament, supporting it as Azoth supports the Sephiroth 4—8 of the Tree of Life. Hermanubis, the Lord of the Threshold, because he is Yesod, the link between Ruach and Nephesch. All exclusively phallic Gods might be attributed here.
10. Seb as the Lord of Earth. The lower Isis and Nephthys as Virgins, imperfect until impregnated. Sphinx, as containing the 4 Elements or Kerubs.

THE ELEMENTS

11. Nu is the Lord of the Firmament, Hoor-pa-kraat is the Fool of the Tarot. Air.
23. Tum as the Sun descending into ocean. Ptah as the Mummy. Compare ATU XII. Auramoth, Goddess of Water. Asar as ATU XII. Isis as Goddess of Water. Hathoor as Goddess of Pleasure. Water.
31. Thoum-aesh-neith, Goddess of Fire. Mau the Lion—Sun in the South. Kabeshunt—Kerub of Fire. Horus, God of Fire.
32-bis. Ahapshi, Kerub of Earth. Nephthys, Goddess of Earth as Isis is of Water. Ameshet, Kerub of Earth.
31-bis. Asar represents Spirit as being the ideal God in the normal man.

THE PLANETS

12. Thoth and Cynocephalos, Mercurial gods.
13. Chomse, God of the Moon.
14. Hathoor, Goddess of Love.
21. Amoun-Ra, Jupiter as Creator.
27. Horus as Warrior God.
30. Sun gods.
32. Crocodile gods, devourers.

THE ZODIAC

15. Men Thu as a martial God.
16. Asar as the Redeemer. Ameshet as Kerub of Earth. Apis as Bull.
17. Twin Deities as pertaining to Gemini. Heru-Ra-Ha as containing the twin Horus Deities.
18. Kephra perhaps, because Cancer is in the nadir in the horoscope when Aries is rising.
19. Babalon and the Beast conjoined. Refers to ATU XI. Pasht, Sekhet and Mau are all Lions.
20. Isis is the Virgin.
22. Ma, Goddess of Truth and Justice (ATU VIII).
24. These are all Serpent or Dragon deities. Typhon especially Lord of destruction and death.

25. Nephthys. Perfection presides over Transmutation.
26. Khem the erect Phallus. Set, see ATU XV. Capricornus is the House of the Sun at the extreme southern declination.
28. Ahephi, Kerub of Air.
29. See ATU XVIII.

Column XXI. THE PERFECTED MAN

These attributions all refer to those parts of the human body on the Tree of Life.

Column XXII. SOME HINDU DEITIES

Add the following: 1. Shiva, Brahma. 7. Bhavani, etc. 18. Krishna. 24. Yama. 27. Krishna. 28. The Maruts.

Column XXXIV. SOME GREEK GODS

0. Pan is the All which is 0. He has the power of destroying all positive manifestation.
1. Zeus is the Supreme Unity, not to be confused with the Zeus who is the son of Kronos. Iacchus is the supreme unity in man reached by ecstasy, when everything else has been winnowed away by the winnowing fan.
2. Athena as the Wisdom which springs full-armed from the brain of Zeus. Uranus as the Starry Heaven. Hermes as the Messenger or Logos.
3. The Goddesses are all Mothers. Psyche is the Neschamah. Kronos is Saturn, the dark one and the limitation of Time.
4. Poseidon, Lord of Water. Zeus, the All-Father.
5. Ares, Lord of War. Hades, God of Fire in the partition between him and Zeus and Poseidon.
6. Iacchus as the Holy Guardian Angel. Apollo as the God of the Sun and male beauty. Adonis, the dying-God. Dionysus and Bacchus as different aspects of this God.
7. Aphrodite, Goddess of Love. Nike, Goddess of Victory. Netzach.
8. Hermes, Mercurial.
9. Zeus, equals Shu, God of Air. Diana as phallic stone and Luna. Eros as representing the reproductive passion.
10. Persephone, the virgin Earth. See her legend. She is Malkuth of Demeter and Binah. Adonis is a doubtful attribution, the connection being with Adonai as God of Earth. Psyche the unredeemed Soul. Compare line 3 above.

The Elements

11. Zeus, God of Air.
23. Poseidon, God of Water.
31. Hades, God of Fire.

32-bis. Demeter, Goddess of Corn. Gaia, Earth itself.
31-bis. Iacchus, Spirit, compare line 1 above.

THE PLANETS

12. Hermes, Mercurial.
13. Artemis, the virgin Moon. Hecate, the evil Moon.
14. These are all Deities of Love.
21. Zeus as Jupiter.
27. Ares, God of War, and Athene the Warrior Goddess.
30. Sun Gods.
32. Athene as the Higher Wisdom. Might also be attributed to line 3. Kronos as Saturn.

THE ZODIAC

16. Athene pertaining to the head. Here a doubtful attribution, but there may be some connection with the Heavenly Cow.
17. Castor and Pollux as Twins. Apollo was the inspirer of Oracles. Eros might be added if the topmost figure in ATU VI really represents him.
18. Apollo as the Charioteer.
19. Demeter borne by lions.
20. Attis. He is of course a dying-God but is attributed here because of his mutilation which corresponds to Virgo.
22. Themis, Goddess of Justice.
24. Ares, because Mars rules Scorpio. Apollo the Pythean because of his Serpent. Thanatos because of ATU XIII.
25. These attributions because Sagittarius is a hunting Sign.
26. Capricornus: these attributions refer to the erect phallus.
28. Ganymede, the Cup-bearer, is referred to the Water-carrier.
29. Poseidon, because of the watery nature of Pisces. Hermes psychopompos, connected with the symbolism of Kephra travelling under the earth.

Column XXXV. SOME ROMAN GODS

0. The Latin Spirit does not admit other than positive ideas.
1. Jupiter as the Supreme Creator.
2. Janus is the Dyad. Mercury as the Messenger.
3. These attributions are given because of their dark lunar, limited, or maternal character.
4. Jupiter is the Father. Libitina is connected with the amniotic fluid.
5. Mars, the War God.
6. Apollo, the Sun God. Bacchus, the inspirer of Harmony and Beauty; also called Aurora, Goddess of Dawn, rose-pink of Tiphereth.
7. Venus, Goddess of Love (Ananda).*
8. Mercury, God of Thought (Chit).*
9. Diana, Goddess of the Moon. Terminus, marking the boundary. Compare Hermanubis. Jupiter is God of Air and as the foundation (Sat).* Arrangement may be placed here.
10. Ceres, Goddess of Earth.

The Elements

11. Jupiter, Lord of Air. Bacchus connected with ATU 0. Juno, Goddess of Air. Aeolus, God of the Winds.
23. Neptune, God of Water. Rhea, Goddess who flows.
31. These are Gods of Fire.

32-bis. Ceres, Goddess of Earth.

31-bis. Bacchus, as Lord of Ecstasy. Spirit.

The Planets

These attributions are all obvious. It is, in fact, largely on the mythological and astrological conception of these Gods and Goddesses that the intelligibility of this whole Table is based. They represent the fundamental familiar ideas.

30. Ops, God of Wealth, which is solar.

* See The Naples Arrangement, p. 39.

32. Terminus, because Saturn is the end of things. Astraea is attributed here in so far as she may be taken to represent the central figure in ATU XXI.

THE ZODIAC

15. Mars, ruler of Aries. Minerva as for Artemis in Column XXXIV.
16. Venus, Lady of Taurus. Hymen is given here because of its connection with ATU V. See Catullus, Pervigillium Veneris.
17. Twin Gods. Hymen as relating to ATU VI.
18. Mercury is here attributed because the path of Cancer leads from the Supernal Binah to Geburah. This is a reference to ATU VII. But this attribution is very doubtful. The bearer of the Graal is not Hermes the Messenger. The Lares and Penates are given as Gods of the Home, Cancer being the sign of receptivity and settlement; but again this attribution is not altogether satisfactory.
19. ATU XI may be regarded as representing the Fire of Vulcan.
20. Vesta, the Virgin Goddess. Ceres, Flora and Adonis are given here because of their connection with spring, which is suggested by the yellowish-green colour in the King Scale.
22. A Goddess of Justice might be attributed here but in the higher sense of the Eighth ATU, the main idea is that of the satisfied woman; we might therefore insert Venus which rules Libra. Note that Saturn is exalted in Libra. Nemesis represents the ultimate automatic justice of Nature. ATU VIII may have some connection with the awakening of the Eld of the All-Father. See Liber 418 in *The Equinox*, I, 5.
24. Mars, as Ruler of Scorpio. Mors, because of ATU XIII.
25. Diana, as bearing bow and arrows. Iris, because of the rainbow.

26. Vesta is here attributed because of Capricorn being the secret flame. The other gods refer to the erect phallus.
28. Juno, Lady of Air. Aeolus, God of the Winds. The month of February, when the Sun is in Aquarius, was traditionally sacred to Juno.
29. Neptune, because Pisces is a watery sign.

Column XXXVIII. ANIMALS, REAL AND IMAGINARY

0. The Dragon represents Draco connected with Nuit in the Heaven; Ananta, the great serpent which surrounds the Universe. It devours its own tail, thereby reducing it to Zero.
1. The Swan as representing Aum. See Liber LXV, Cap. II, 17-25. See also Book of Lies, Cap. XVII. The Hawk pertains to Kether, as poised in the ether and beholding all things. Remember that Kether is primarily the individual point of view. The Soul beholds all things and changes the place according to its going. Thus in the Egyptian tradition the Hawk is the symbol of the highest type of Godhead.
3. The Bee is the traditional attribution of the Yoni.
4. Again, traditional. It is probably connected with the erect phallus of Amoun. The Unicorn is also Jupiterean, as connected with the horse of Sagittarius.
5. The Basilisk represents Geburah on account of its power of slaying with the flame of its glance.
6. The Phoenix, on account of its symbolism of the $5^\circ = 6^\square$ grade. Lion, as the typical animal of Sol. Child, as Vau of Tetragrammaton. The Spider is particularly sacred to Tiphereth. It is written that she "taketh hold with her hands and is in king's palaces." (The most characteristic title of Tiphereth is the "Palace of the King.") She has six legs and is in the centre of her web exactly as Tiphereth is in the centre of the Sephiroth of Ruach.

   The Pelican represents the Redeemer feeding its children with its own blood, and for this reason it has been chosen as the special symbol of the Brethren of the R & C.
7. Iynx. This attribution is traditional. See Eliphas Levi's design of the pantomorphous Iynx. The Raven pertains to Netzach because of the qliphotic attribution in Column VIII. All carrion birds may be

attributed here, because of their connection with Victory. Note that the path of Scorpio connects Tiphereth with Netzach. The idea of Venus is intimately connected with that of death, for death is in many important senses a part of love. Compare the Book of Lies, Caps. I, VIII, XV, XVI, and XVIII, etc., etc.

8. Hermaphrodite, as representing the dual nature of Mercury. Jackal, sacred to Anubis. Twin serpents. These represent the Mercurial double current as on the Caduceus. See the interpretation given in the (unpublished) Paris Working. Monokerōs dē Astris. This animal is given as the symbolical title of a Practicus. It is the swiftness of his motion which chiefly warrants the attribution. See Liber LXV, Cap. III, v. 2. He seems to combine the masculine and feminine element; on the one hand, the horn and the speed symbolism, on the other his white colour, his silver collar, and its inscription, linea viridis gyrat universa, which refers to Venus as containing the Universe.
9. Elephant, sacred to Ganesha, the god who breaks down obstacles. Hence placed in Yesod for the same reason as Anubis. Tortoise, as supporting the Elephant, hence equivalent to Atlas. (Compare Book of Lies, Cap. XXVI.) Toad, "ugly and venomous, wears yet a precious jewel in his head." This refers to his generative force.
10. The Sphinx, as containing the 4th Element, the Child, Hé final, twin of the male child Vau.

The Elements

11. The Eagle, king of the birds. Man as the Kerub of Air. Ox—actual meaning of Aleph.
23. The Eagle-Snake-Scorpion trinity is the Kerub of Water.
31. The Lion is the Kerub of Fire.

32-bis. The Beast is the Kerub of Earth.

The Planets

12. The Swallow for its swiftness. The Ibis, sacred to

Thoth; the Ape, sacred to Thoth. The Cynocephalos is the constant companion of Thoth and produces base imitations of his Wisdom and Power. The Twin Serpents for the same reason as in line 8. All fish are sacred to Mercury because of their swiftness, their cold-bloodedness, the gleaming white or iridescent colours which are characteristic of their scales, and to some extent to their method of reproduction. Hybrids may also be attributed here, as to line 17.

13. The Dog, as baying at the Moon and the natural companion of the huntress Artemis. The white Stork, perhaps as traditionally announcing childbirth. The Camel as the actual meaning of the letter. It conveys travellers across the desert as the path of Gimel crosses the Abyss from Tiphereth to Kether. See also Book of Lies, Cap. XLII.
14. The Sparrow and Dove are especially sacred to Venus. See Catullus's Ode to Lesbia, Tristram Shandy, Sappho's Ode to Venus, etc. For the Dove see Martial's ode referring to Catullus's Sparrow, the legend of the Virgin Mary, etc. The Dove is also Venusian on account of its soft amiability. The Swan, for the same reason as above. The Sow, the female of the boar of Mars; also because the sensuality of the sow suggests the lower type of Venus. All birds are primarily sacred to Venus, probably because the instinct of love enables a man to rise for a time above the earth. Also because of their great beauty of form and colour, because their flesh is tender as compared to that of animals, and because their speech is of the nature of ecstatic song and is devoid of any intellectual quality.
21. The Eagle is the sacred bird of Jupiter. The Praying Mantis suggests Jupiter by its simulation of a devotional attitude.
27. The Horse is sacred to Mars traditionally on account of his spirited nature. The Bear is martial chiefly for alchemical reasons and because of his great strength. The Wolf is sacred to Mars (see the legend of Rome),

also on account of his savage nature. The Boar is martial, as shown in the legend of Adonis. There is here a mystery of the grade of 6° = 5$^{\square}$, the overawing of Tiphereth by Geburah.

30. The Lion is the typically solar animal. The Hawk is solar as all-seeing. The Leopard is sacred to the sun on account of its black spots.
32. The Crocodile is Saturnian, as the devourer.

THE ZODIAC

15. The Ram is Aries by meaning. The attribution refers to its method of combatively butting. Note that the symbolism of the lamb is by no means the same. It pertains rather to Tiphereth in the formula of the Aeon of Osiris. This is all probably derived from the fact that lamb is the tenderest meat obtainable and therefore the priests insisted on lamb being sacrificed for their benefit. The true nature of the Lamb would be rather Venusian or Lunar, but it would be better to cut it altogether out of the symbolic scheme, because of the priestly connection which the idea has suffered. The Owl is sacred to Aries as the bird of Minerva.
16. The Bull is the Kerub of Earth. All beasts of burden and those used in agriculture may be attributed here.
17. All animals of dual nature in any respect pertain partly to Gemini. The Magpie is especially sacred to this sign because of its piebald plumage and its power of speech. The Parrot is given here for similar reasons. The Zebra is here on account of its stripes. All hybrids pertain to Gemini, both on account of their dual nature and because they are sterile like Mercury. The Penguin is here as superficially imitating man.
18. The Crab pertains to Cancer as the translation of the word. The Turtle is found among the symbols of the Court Cards of the suit of Cups. The Whale suggests Cancer because of its power of blowing water, and its faculty, in incorrect tradition, of swallowing large objects such as prophets. All beasts of transport may be attributed here in reference to ATU VII.

19. Leo means Lion and is the Kerub of Fire. The Cat is of the Lion family, so also is the Tiger. The Serpent is given to Leo because the letter Teth means Serpent. There is an important mystery concealed in ATU VIII, and Woman may be attributed to Leo in respect to her sexual ferocity through which she dominates Man; that is, the lower element in Man, especially his courage as represented by the Lion.
20. All animals which go solitary are attributed here, as also those which refuse to unite with others. This is connected not only with ATU IX but with the cold-bloodedness of Mercury. The Rhinoceros—the single horn suggests Mercury, line 8. In the Dhammapada he is taken as the emblem of the Hermit.
22. The Elephant is given to Libra because equilibrium is the basis of the Universe. The symmetry of any animal is of the nature of Libra, and so we may place in this group any animals which make symmetrical patterns; as, for instance, the Spider (see line 6). But even the Spiders which live in the earth build their houses with a great regularity.
24. Scorpio means Scorpion. The Beetle is given to Scorpio chiefly on account of the peculiar colour (see the Empress Scale, Column XVIII) and partly because of certain habits, such as its transmutation through putrefaction. All reptiles may be placed here for this reason. The Lobster and Crayfish are, so to speak, water scorpions. The Wolf is naturally appropriate to the night house of Mars. The Shark is one of the most martial inhabitants of the sea. The Crablouse refers to Scorpio both by nature and habitat.
25. The Centaur is traditionally connected with Archery, besides being partly a horse; the horse itself is connected with the idea of hunting and speed. Note that the speed of Sagittarius, which is the flickering of a dying fire, is not to be confused with the speed of Mercury, which is the speed of thought or electricity. The Hippogriff combines the Horse of Mars with the

Eagle of Jupiter. The Dog is sacred to the huntress Artemis.

26. Capricornus means Goat. The Ass and the Oyster are traditionally sacred to Priapus. An animal is sacred to Capricorn in respect of its ambition, actual or symbolic. It is the leaping of the Goat and its fondness for high and barren mountains which connect it with Capricorn, the sign which represents the zenith in the Zodiac. Note that the sexual instinct should primarily be regarded as indicative of the ambition or aspiration of the animal to higher things.

28. See line 11 for the first attribution. The Peacock is the bird of Juno as Lady of Air and especially Aquarius, but the Peacock might also be referred to Tiphereth or even to Mercury and Sagittarius on account of its plumage. The vision of the Universal Peacock is connected with the Beatific Vision, in which the Universe is perceived as a whole in every part, as the essence of joy and beauty; but in its diversity this is connected with the symbolism of the Rainbow, which refers to the middle stage in Alchemical working, when the Matter of the Work takes on a diversity of flashing colours. This, however, is connected not so much with the nature of Sagittarius in itself as an isolated constellation, but with its position on the Tree of Life as leading from Yesod to Tiphereth. Samekh must therefore be regarded in this matter as the threshold of Tiphereth, even as Gimel is the threshold of Kether, and Tau of Yesod. These three, therefore, constitute the three main balanced spiritual experiences in the way of attainment.

29. Pisces means Fish, but, as previously indicated, actual fish do not belong here so much as to Mercury. The Dolphin pertains to Pisces, principally because Venus is exalted in the sign, while its ruler, Jupiter, is also implied in that attribution of which we see the outcome in the title of the Heir-apparent to the Crown of France. The Beetle is Kephra, the Sun at midnight, who is shown travelling through the Pool of Night in

ATU XVIII. Pisces, moreover, is that greatest darkness before the dawn of the year in the parallel symbolism. There is also a mystery in the fact that the Beetle rolls up a ball of dung, thus constructing the Sun from the excrement of putrefaction. As it is written, "It is from the excrement of Choronzon that one takes the material for the creation of a God." The Jackal is shown in ATU XVIII. He also feeds on excrement. The sign Pisces represents the apparent stagnation of the Work, its final decomposition. And it is at this moment that it is brought by the Redeemer—who has descended into the lowest hell for the purpose—across the threshold into the higher sphere. Note that it is because of the condition of the experiment that the Work necessarily lends itself to every form of glamour and illusion. Its nature is certain to be misinterpreted even by the Redeemer himself, insofar as he is compelled to fix his attention upon the Matter of the Work and so to lose sight for the moment of the essential Truth which underlies its appearance.

The Dog is attributed to Pisces on account of his being sacred to the Moon, the title of ATU XVIII. The Dogs baying the Moon, with the accompanying assumption of witchcraft and all that type of phenomena which we associate with the treacherous semi-darkness of the waning moon, are shown in some version of the Trumps by artists who did not understand the deeper symbolism of Kephra and Anubis. That false representation is exactly characteristic of the sort of thing that always is to be expected to occur in connection with the work of the Magician in this sign.

Column XXXIX. THE PLANTS

0. The Lotus and Rose are attributed to 0 because they have traditionally been taken as glyphs of the circle.
1. The Almond in flower is connected with Aaron's Rod that budded. The Almond is the proper wood for the wand of the White magician, but the attribution should really be to the middle pillar as a whole. The branches of the Banyan tree take fresh roots where they touch the ground and start new main stems: this is connected with the special idea of Kether implied in the Philosophy given in the Commentary of the Book of the Law. (Part published in *The Equinox of the Gods*.)
2. The Amaranth is the flower of immortality. It is here placed in order to symbolize that quality of the Yod of Tetragrammaton, the principle of Chiah. The Mistletoe is given for a similar reason. The Bo or Pipal tree was the shelter of the Buddha at the moment of his enlightenment. Furthermore, its leaves suggest the phallus.
3. The Cypress pertains to Saturn. The Opium Poppy is connected with sleep, night and understanding. The Lotus is the general feminine symbol. The Lily suggests the purity of the Great Mother. The Ivy has dark leaves and its clinging nature reminds us of feminine or curving growth.
4. The Olive is attributed to Jupiter because of its softness and richness. Its colour furthermore suggests that of the watery part of Malkuth in the Queen Scale (Column XVI). The Shamrock of four leaves, a good-luck plant, suggests Jupiter. The Opium Poppy is Jupiterian as giving relief from pain, quiet, and olympian detachment.
5. The Oak and Hickory are attributed here because of the hardness of their wood. Nux Vomica, on account of its tonic properties and the action of strychnine in causing the contraction of muscles with convulsive violence. The Nettle, on account of its burning sting.

6. The Oak is also, and more properly, attributed to Tiphereth because it was the sacred tree of the Druids, the representative in the vegetable kingdom of the Sun. Its strength is also taken as harmonious with that quality in man. Furthermore, the Acorn is peculiarly phallic, and this is properly to be attributed to Tiphereth because in this case the phallic symbol contains in itself the essence of the being to be reproduced. The Acacia is placed here as a symbol of resurrection as in the rituals of Free Masonry. The Bay and Laurel are sacred to Apollo, the Vine to Dionysus.

   Gorse, the sacred flower of the A∴ A∴ was chosen as their heraldic emblem to be a symbol of the Great Work. Its appearance is that of the Sun in full blaze, and suggests the burning bush of Moses. Its branches are exceedingly firm, as should be the Will of the Adept, and they are covered with sharp spikes, which symbolize, on the one hand, the phallic energy of the Will and, on the other, the pains which are gladly endured by one who puts forth his hand to pluck this bloom of sunlight splendour. Note that the Great Work is here concentrated in Tiphereth, the attainment of the Grade corresponding to which is in fact the critical stage on the path of the Wise. The Ash is one of the most important of the solar trees; the wood is firm and elastic. The World-Ash represents the microcosm in legend. Yggdrasil is itself an Ash. Aswata, the World-Fig, should also be attributed here as the Tree itself in the microcosm.
7. The Rose has always been a special flower of Venus. The Laurel is included because a wreath of these leaves is a symbol of victory.
8. Moly is mentioned in Homer as having been given by Hermes to Ulysses to counteract the spells of Circe. It has a black root and white blossom, which again suggests the dual currents of energy. Anhalonium Lewinii has for one of its principal characteristics the power to produce very varied and brilliant colour visions.

9. The Banyan is given here for the same reason as that in line 1. It is, so to speak, the foundation of a system of trees as Yesod is the foundation of the branches of the Tree of Life. The Mandrake is the typically phallic plant. It is peculiarly adapted to use in sexual magic, and it does have a direct connection with the automatic consciousness which has its seat in Yesod. Damiana is reputed a powerful aphrodisiac, and so are Ginseng and Yohimba.
10. The Willow is the traditional tree of the neglected maiden, Malkuth unredeemed. The Lily suggests that maiden's purity, and the Ivy her clinging and flexible nature. All Cereals pertain to Malkuth, Wheat being the foundation of the Pentacle which represents Nephesch. The Pomegranate is sacred to Proserpine; in appearance also it is strongly suggestive of the feminine symbol.

THE ELEMENTS

11. Aspen resembles Air, by its trembling.
23. The Lotus is the traditional plant of Water. Its roots are in water and its purity further suggests the action of water in lustration.
31. The Red Poppy is given in this place only on account of its colour, and the same is true of Hibiscus. All scarlet flowers might be equally well placed here. But the attribution is not very satisfactory, as the nature of flowers in themselves is not usually fiery except as their perfume is a stimulant.
32-bis.-The Oak is given on account of its stability, and the Ivy because of the analogy of Earth with Malkuth. All Cereals pertain here, Wheat, the typical cereal, being the foundation of the Pentacle.
31-bis. For Almond see line 1. It should be generally remarked with regard to the elemental attributions in this column that the seed should be taken as representing Spirit with a slight admixture of Fire, the stem as Fire, the blossom as Water, the leaf as Air, and the

fruit as Earth. Note that the fruit usually contains the seed of the new generation exactly as the Empresses are called the Thrones of Spirit.

THE PLANETS

12. The attributions here given are traditional. The Palm is Mercurial, as being hermaphrodite. The Lime or Linden tree is Mercurial because of its pale yellow fruit with a peculiarly clean-tasting pulp.
13. These attributions are again traditional. The Hazel is suitable for the wand of the Black magician whose typical deity is the Moon just as that of the White magician is the Sun. The Pomegranate is also attributed here as a symbol with reference to menstruation. The Alder has a soft spongy wood which gives very little heat when burned. It haunts watery spots.
14. These are traditional also. The Fig is Venusian on account of its sexual symbolism. The Peach belongs to Venus on account of its soft beauty and sweetness, the external splendour of its bloom being easily brushed off, its tendency to rot and the prussic acid in its kernel. The Apple is traditionally appropriate to Venus on account of the legend of the Fall. There are however various traditions concerning the Tree of Knowledge of Good and Evil.
21. The Hyssop is Jupiterian on account of its religious use in lustration. It might perhaps be more properly attributed to Chesed. The Oak is traditionally sacred to Jupiter, perhaps because it is the king of the trees as Jupiter is king of the gods. The Poplar is given on account of its soft and easily swollen wood and because of its great height. The Fig is Jupiterian because of its soft, swollen and, so to speak, sensual pulp; and also perhaps because of its rich purple colour, suggesting episcopal vestments. Arnica is attributed to Jupiter for its use in relieving pain. Cedar has a traditional value in religious work—its perfume is devotional

according to the testimony of intuition, and it is supposed to preserve things in its neighbourhood from the attacks of moths, etc.

27. Absinthe and Rue—these attributions are traditional.
30. The three first attributions are obvious. The Nut is solar, as being a microcosm of Life, the fruit being also the seed. Galangal is specially sacred to the Sun; it is of the ginger family.
32. The Ash is given in connection with the phrase "ashen pale." (The real nature of the tree is more properly solar.) In the other cases, in connection with the ideas of death, melancholy, poison, etc. The Elm is Saturnian on account of its murderous habit of dropping boughs without warning. The wood is also traditionally the best available for coffins.

THE ZODIAC

15. The Olive is sacred to Minerva, but Geranium has a scarlet variety which is precisely the colour of Aries in the King Scale. The Tiger Lily is a traditional attribution.
16. Again traditional. We might possibly add giant trees of all species to this sign.
17. Hybrids are here for the same reason as in the previous column. Orchids might perhaps better be attributed to Yesod or to Capricorn for obvious reasons; they are found here on account of their duplex characteristics.
18. The Lotus is the typical flower of Water and the Moon.
19. The Snowdrop and Lily suggest the modest purity of the sign. Narcissus refers to the solitary tradition. Mistletoe is indicated by the macroscopic appearance of semen.
22. This attribution is traditional.
24. The Cactus has watery pulp and poisonous spikes. The Nettle is treacherously Martial. All treacherous and poisonous plants may be attributed to Scorpio.
25. The Rush is used for making arrows.

26. Yohimba—see line 9. Thistle is hard, stubborn and spikey. Orchis Root is connected with the Cult of Pan. Indian Hemp is tough and fibrous, thus used for making ropes; but see the Column XLIII dealing with vegetable drugs for other properties of the plant.
28. Cocoanut; this attribution is doubtful. There may be some connection with Juno as giving milk or with the symbol of the Waterbearer, because the tree gives us fruit from the air.
29. Opium is given because of its power to produce a peaceful dreamy condition which is liable to end in a stagnation of the mental faculties. Unicellular Organisms are possibly attributed here because they are so frequently found in pools. The Mangrove is not merely a tree of the swamp, but actually produces swamps.

Column XL. PRECIOUS STONES

0. These attributions are somewhat bold. The Star Sapphire refers to Nuit and the Black Diamond to the idea of NOX—Zero. It is invisible yet contains light and structure in itself.
1. The Diamond is white brilliance; it is pure carbon, the foundation of all living structure. The atomic weight is 12, the number of Hua, the title of Kether (but this is a reference to the Zodiac which makes the connection with Zero, on the one hand, and 2, on the other).
2. The Star Ruby represents the male energy of the Creator Star. Turquoise suggests Mazloth, so also does the Star Sapphire, but this would be the sphere of Chokmah not its positive attribution.
3. The Star Sapphire suggests the expanse of night with the Star appearing in the midst thereof. Note that this light is not in the stone itself but is due to the internal structure. The doctrine is that the stars are formed in the body of night by virtue of the form of that night by the impact of the energy of a higher plane. The Pearl is referred to Binah on account of its being the typical stone of the sea. It is formed by concentric spheres of hard brilliant substance, the centre being a particle of dust. Thus, that dust which is all that remains of the Exempt Adept after he has crossed the Abyss, is gradually surrounded by sphere after sphere of shining splendour, so that he becomes a fitting ornament for the bosom of the Great Mother.
4. Lapis Lazuli is of the blue violet of the highest form of Jupiter. The specks in it may perhaps be taken to represent those particles of dust referred to above. The Amethyst is the violet of Jupiter. It is the traditional stone of episcopal rank. Its legendary virtue of protecting its bearer from intoxication indicates its value in lustration. It is the purity of the Exempt Adept which destroys for him the illusion or drunkenness of existence, and therefore enables him to take

the great leap into the Abyss. The Sapphire pertains to Chesed because of the blue of water and of Venus (Daleth = 4) in the King Scale (Column XV) and of Jupiter in the Queen Scale (Column XVI).

5. The Ruby represents flaming energy.
6. The Topaz is of the gold of the Sun. It is also traditionally associated with Tiphereth. The Yellow Diamond suggests the reflection of Kether into Tiphereth.
7. The Emerald is of the green of Venus in the King Scale.
8. The Opal has the varied colours attributed to Mercury.
9. Quartz refers to the foundation. Note that gold is found in Quartz, suggesting the concealed glory of the sexual process.
10. Rock Crystal reminds us of the aphorism: Kether is in Malkuth and Malkuth in Kether, but after another manner.

THE ELEMENTS

11. Topaz is the pure transparent yellow of Air.
23. The Beryl is the pure transparent blue of Water.
31. The Fire Opal suggests the appearance of fire rising from the blackness of the matter which it consumes.

32-bis. Salt is traditionally sacred to Earth.

31-bis. The Black Diamond has the blackness of the Akasa: it is composed of carbon, the basis of the living elements.

THE PLANETS

12. Opal, see line 8. Agate has the Mercurial yellow, but its hardness indicates a strange Saturnian element in it. It might indeed be attributed to Geburah for its orange tinge and its hardness, but it is not sufficiently pure to rank as a precious stone, and must therefore not be placed among the Sephiroth.
13. The Moonstone is a direct image of the Moon. Pearl and Crystal are given for the suggestion of purity (see lines 3 and 10).

14. Emerald is the colour of Venus in the King Scale (Column XV). Turquoise is the blue of Venus in the Queen Scale (Column XVI), but its tendency is to fade into green. When it does this its value is destroyed, and this reminds us of the external splendour and internal corruption of Nogah.
21. See line 4.
27. See line 5.
30. Chrysolith, as the name implies, is a golden stone.
32. This attribution is traditional: it is the dullness and frequent blackness of Onyx which occasions the reference.

THE ZODIAC

15. Ruby is the scarlet of Aries. It is also one of the hardest of precious stones.
16. Topaz refers to the letter Vau. Tiphereth—see line 6.
17. These stones are given here on account of their polarization of light.
18. Amber is of the colour of Cancer in the King Scale: were it a precious stone, it might be attributed to Chokmah or Binah on account of its electrical properties.
19. The Cat's Eye suggests Leo directly.
20. The Peridot is of the colour of Virgo in the King Scale.
22. Emerald is of the colour of Libra in the King Scale.
24. Snakestone suggests Scorpio directly. Greenish Turquoise is attributed here as referring to its putrefaction.
25. Jacinth is Hyacinth, the beautiful boy accidentally killed by Apollo with a quoit, the attribution is therefore somewhat far-fetched—from the blood of the boy to the traditional weapons of his lover.
26. For Black Diamond see line 0 and 32-bis. The reference is to the letter A'ain, the eye. The Black Diamond reminds us of the pupil of the eye, and this eye is the eye of the Most Holy Ancient One; Kether. Capricorn is the zenith of the Zodiac as Kether is of the Sephiroth.

28. Artificial Glass pertains to Aquarius, as being the work of man, the Kerub of Air. Chalcedony suggests the clouds by its appearance.
29. Pearl is referred to Pisces because of its cloudy brilliance as contrasted with the transparency of the other precious stones. It thus reminds us of the astral plane with its semi-opaque visions as opposed to those of pure light which pertain to purely spiritual spheres. One must not emphasize the connection with water; because the Pearl is not found in the type of water characteristic of Pisces.

Column XLI. MAGICAL WEAPONS

The full meaning of these weapons will be found in Book 4, Part II, and in *Magick in Theory and Practice*. Here we can only give brief reasons for their attributions.

0. No magical weapons can be attributed here, for they are all positive. The reduction of the positive to Zero is the goal of magical work.
1. The Crown is the meaning of Kether. It refers to the Supreme Divinity which the magician assumes in his working. The Swastika symbolizes whirling energy, the initiation of all magical force—the Rashith-Ha-Gilgalim. There is a great deal of varied symbolism in this instrument, notably sexual; it demands a great deal of study to appreciate fully the virtue of this weapon. The Lamp is not a weapon; it is a light shining from above which illuminates the whole work.
2. The Lingam is the symbol of the Chiah, the creative energy. The Inner Robe symbolizes the true self of the magician, his "unconscious" as the psychoanalysts call Chiah. Their description, however, of its characteristic is totally incorrect. The Word is the intelligible expression of the Will of the creative energy of the Magus.
3. The Yoni represents Neschamah. The Outer Robe refers to the darkness of Binah. The A∴ A∴ Star refers to the aspiration. The Cup receives the influence from the Highest. It is the feminine symbol of Understanding. It must be distinguished emphatically from the wand or hollow tube of Chokmah which transmits the influence in its positive form in an intelligible manner but without understanding its nature.
4. The Wand is the reflection of the Lingam as the paternal power of Chesed in the solidification of the male creative energy of Chokmah. The Sceptre is the weapon of authority referring to Jupiter (Gedulah—magnificence). The Crook is the weapon of Chesed—Mercy as opposed to the scourge of Geburah.

5. The Scourge is the weapon of severity as opposed to the Crook. This is the explanation of these two weapons being crossed in the hands of the risen Osiris. The Sword is the weapon of Mars, so also is the Spear. These weapons emphasize the fiery energy in the creative Lingam. The Chain represents the severity of the restrictions which must be placed on wandering thoughts: it might more properly be attributed to Daäth. It does not really exist on the magician himself. Its function is to bind that which is above all Not-He. It is thus the only weapon which does not possess a definite unity of form and which has multiple units in its composition.
6. The Lamen represents the symbolic form of the Human Will and Consciousness of the magician. The Rosy Cross is technically pertinent to Tiphereth.
7. The Lamp carried in the hand pertains to Netzach because Love must be enkindled by the magician. It throws light as required on particular objects. This Lamp must in no wise be confused with that of Kether. The Girdle is the traditional weapon of Venus. It represents the ornament of beauty. When it is untied it can be used to bind and blindfold the candidate. It thus represents the power of fascination by love.
8. The Names and Versicles are Mercurial. They expand the Logos, explain it in three-dimensional (that is, material) terms, just as the number 8 is a three-dimensional expansion of the number 2. The Apron conceals the Splendour (Hod) of the magician. It also explains that splendour by virtue of its symbolic design.
9. The Perfumes pertain to Yesod as forming a link between earth and heaven. This link is material by virtue of the substance of the incense, and spiritual by virtue of their action through the olfactory sense upon the consciousness. The Sandals enable the magician to "travel on the firmament of Nu." The Sandal-strap is the Ankh which represents the mode of going, going being the essential faculty of every god. This strap, whose form is that of the Rosy Cross, forms a link

between the material apparatus of his going and his feet; that is to say, the formula of the Rosy Cross enables a man to go—or, in other words, endows him with Godhead.

The Altar is the foundation of the operation. Its characteristic is stability; also it resembles Yesod as supporting the Ruach; that is to say, the means of the Formative World (Ruach = Yetzirah) through which it is proposed to work. The Altar and the sacrifice might also as well have been attributed to Tiphereth. This would, in fact, be actually better in the case of certain types of operation, such as invocations of the Holy Guardian Angel, for in this case the human heart is the foundation of the work.

10. The Circle and Triangle are the spheres of operation of the magician and his work which is in Malkuth, the kingdom, the Realm of Assiah. The Triangle being outside the Circle, is the place of the Spirit, but it belongs not to him for his realm is formlessness. The Triangle is the figure into which Choronzon must be evoked in order to confer form upon him.

THE ELEMENTS

11. The Dagger, the characteristic elemental weapon of Air. The Fan—this symbolizes the power to direct the forces of Air.
23. The Cross of Suffering refers to the now superseded formula of Osiris. See the original emblem of the Hermetic Order of the Golden Dawn, a triangle surmounted by a Cross. The Cup is the traditional elemental weapon of Water. The Wine fills the Cup—it is the divine ecstasy entering the receptive part of the nature of the magician. The Water of Lustration in the Cup of the Stolistes balances the Fire in the thurible of the Dadouchos.
31. The Wand is the elemental weapon of Fire. It is not to be confused with the Wand of Chokmah or Chesed any more than the Cup of Water is to be mistaken for

that of Binah. The Elemental weapons are but vice-regents of the true weapons of the Sephiroth. The thurible or lamp is borne by the Dadouchos to consecrate the candidate with fire. The Pyramid of Fire is an altogether minor weapon and is only used in certain ceremonies of uncommon type.

32-bis. The Pantacle is the elemental weapon of Earth. The platter of bread and salt, or sometimes salt alone, is its equivalent, but is used actively to administer to the candidate sometimes to seal his obligation, sometimes to nourish him spiritually. Bread and Salt are the two principal substances traditionally sacred to Earth.

31-bis. The Winged Egg is symbolical of the spiritualized phallic energy. The Egg is Akasa, the source of all creation. There are many equivalent symbols.

THE PLANETS

12. The Wand is that of the Will or Word, the Logos. The Caduceus is the legendary wand of Mercury, and to be carefully distinguished from the hollow tube of Chokmah. It represents the Middle Pillar crowned by the Winged Globe of Kether. It is thus the plumed phallus as distinguished from the Phoenix-crowned phallus of animal-life creation through the initiation of Fire (see line 9), and the flowering phallus of the Lotus-crowned Wand of Isis, the wand of vegetable-life creation through the initiation of Water (see line 20). The Serpents of the Caduceus, the positive and negative forms of energy, resume the powers of these two wands.

13. The Bow and Arrow are traditionally the weapons of Artemis and Apollo (see line 30).

14. See line 7.

21. See line 4. The Sceptre is not a true weapon. It is the symbol of authority, an ornamental reminder of the wand which is kept in the background. The Sceptre must not be used to strike, it would break: as soon as its virtue is challenged, it must be instantly discarded for the thunderbolt.

27. This Sword is not to be confused with the Dagger of Air. It represents the active and militant energy of the magician. Its true form is the flaming sword, the lightning flash, which strikes down from Kether through the Sephiroth as a zig-zag flash. It destroys by dividing the unity of that against which its energies are directed. It is ultimately an error to identify the sword with the wand as a phallic symbol though this is often done. In the Lesser Mysteries of "John" the sword and disk represent the Wand and Cup of the Greater Mysteries of "Jesus." In the former, John the Baptist's head is removed by sword (air) and presented on a charger, the platter or dish of earth. In the latter, the heart of Jesus is pierced by the Spear, the Wand of Fire, and the blood collected in the Cup or Graal (water). But the Sword and Disk are not sufficiently sacred to be truly phallic. This is one of the subtle distinctions which afford the key to the finest spiritual comprehension.

30. The Lamen is solar, as representing the light of the human consciousness—in the Heart (Tiphereth)—of the magician to the spirit evoked. It is his statement to the spirit of his intention towards it, of the formula which he intends to employ; it must in no wise be confused with the Pantacle, which is passive as the Lamen is active. The one represents the condition of things in general, the other his method of dealing with that condition. Bow and Arrow—see line 13.

32. The Sickle is the traditional weapon of Saturn. It implies the power of time to reap the harvest of man's life and work. It may be used in actual ceremony to threaten the spirit that Choronzon will cut short his independent existence, that Choronzon will reap his Karma, and add it to the treasure of Choronzon's storehouse.

The Zodiac

15. The Horns are those of the Ram: they signify the

power of thought, the energy of Minerva. The Burin is used for engraving the Lamen, Pantacles, etc. Being a Knife, its character is martial, but also it pertains especially to Aries because it is used to indicate the creative ideas of the magician.

16. The Throne refers to Vau: the Heart must support and admit the lordship of the higher consciousness of the magician. The Altar may also be attributed to Taurus on account of its solidity and its function of bearing the higher elements of the magician. There is a mystery of Europa and Pasiphaë connected with this attribution.
17. The Tripod would appear at first sight to be Lunar; but this is wrong. The real connection is with ATU VI, the "Oracle of the Mighty Gods."
18. The Furnace is connected with the energy of the Sun in Cancer. The Cup is the Holy Graal.
19. The Phoenix Wand—see line 12.
20. The Lamp and Wand appear in ATU IX as the weapons of the Hermit. This Wand is concealed: it is the virile energy reserved. This Lamp has the same significance and is not to be confused with other lamps. The Bread is the natural product, the fertile earth; it conveys sacramentally, "every word that cometh out of the mouth of God." The Lotus Wand—see line 12.
22. The Cross of Equilibrium is implied or expressed in every part of the arrangements of the Temple. The Balances, or Witnesses, as shown in ATU XI, are in actual practice concealed with the Sword. They represent the complete phallus, the secret weapon, which alone can satisfy; that is, do justice to Nature.
24. The Oath is the formula of transmutation. The Serpent is connected with several of the magical weapons, and implies the secret kingly power of the magician, the essence of the phallic energy as employed in transmutation.
25. The Arrow is sacred to the rainbow symbolism. It represents especially the spiritualization of the magical energy, being a missile sped through the air, no longer

connected physically with the material form of the magician.

26. Compare line 20.
28. The Censer carries the perfumes as the clouds carry the distillation of the water of earth. The Aspergillus similarly sprinkles the lustral waters as the clouds shed rain.
29. Magical operations are usually performed in an artificial twilight; this represents the glamour of the astral plane which the magician proposes to illumine with the divine light. The natural attribution of this idea is evidently ATU XVIII. The Magic Mirror reflects astral forms. It is evidently cognate with the still waters of Pisces, and the entire symbolism is again obviously that of ATU XVIII.

Column XLII. PERFUMES

These attributions are founded for the most part upon tradition. Some of them are connected with legend, others are derived from clairvoyant observation. The rational basis of attribution is, therefore, less apparent in this column than in those of the Gods, Magical Weapons, etc.

0. No attribution can be made here, 0 being the goal of a magical operation by love under will, and any perfume will be an expansion of that love under will itself.
1. Ambergris has comparatively little perfume of its own, but it has a virtue of bringing out the best of any others with which it may be mixed. In the same way, Kether cannot be said to have any intrinsic qualities, but its influence brings out the highest faculties of those ideas which it illuminates.
2. The orchitic origin of Musk indicates Chokmah. This is the male aspect of the Work.
3. Civet, "the uncleanly flux of a cat," corresponds to Musk as Binah to Chokmah, its origin being feminine. Myrrh is traditionally the odour of sorrow and bitterness; it is the dark and passive side of Binah.

   "Brothers, I have brought him myrrh.
   Sorrow black and sinister
   Shall his name bring to the race."

   "My incense is of resinous woods and gums; and there is no blood therein: because of my hair the trees of Eternity."
4. See Column XXXIX.
5. Tobacco. This attribution is due to Fr. D. D. S. (who was a chemist). It seems to me not altogether satisfactory. The idea is presumably that it is the favourite perfume for men engaged in severe hard work.
6. The correctness of this should be intuitively perceived at once by every magician. Olibanum possesses a comprehensive catholic quality such as no other incense can boast.
7. The sensuous seductiveness of Benzoin is unmistakable. Contrast with line 24. Rose naturally suggests

the more physical aspects of the feminine symbol. Civet, however, is much more strongly sexual than Rose, but this implies a more intense element of spirituality. The student must eliminate completely from his mind any idea that sex is naturally gross. On the contrary, even the lowest manifestations of it in its pure form are less material than such ideas as are represented by Rose. Demonic, not material, developments follow the degradation of the instinct. Red Sandal is Venusian, intuitively by its smell, and sensibly by its colour. The attribution is further guaranteed by the usefulness of its oil as a specific of gonorrhoea.

8. Storax is chiefly Mercurial on account of its nondescript nature. It is really less valuable as a perfume itself than as a menstruum for other perfumes, in the same way as Mercury is the basis of amalgams. But Storax is really too dark and heavy to be a really adequate perfume for Hod.
9. Jasmin is traditionally sacred, especially in Persia, to the spiritual use of the generative process. Ginseng—see Column XXXIX. Roots are sacred to Yesod because Yesod is the Root of the Tree of Life exactly as the reproductive function is the root of the life of man. It is important not to suppose that Malkuth, Nephesch, is the root of reality. Malkuth is a pendant to the Tree, a sensory illusion which enables it to perceive itself.
10. Dittany of Crete was said by Blavatsky to be the most powerful of all magical perfumes. This is true in a limited sense. Its smoke is the best basis for material magical manifestations of all those menstrua which are not animal. It is quite as catholic as Olibanum in character but has no positive element in its composition. Further, its velvet softness and its silvery bloom remind one of Betulah. There are many allusions in classical traditions to Dittany, which all point to the same attribution.

THE ELEMENTS

11. Galbanum represents the element of Air in that exceedingly powerful incense of Tetragrammaton whose invention is ascribed to Moses.
23. Onycha represents Water in the incense of Moses. It is now very difficult to obtain, though at one time I possessed a supply. Its origin is somehow connected with certain shellfish. Myrrh—see line 3.
31. Olibanum is the fiery elemental incense of Moses.
32-bis. Storax is the earthy elemental incense of Moses.
31-bis. No attribution can be made here. See line 1.

THE PLANETS

At one time or another mediaeval writers on magic have attributed every possible incense to every possible planet. Tradition, therefore, gives little to us in this investigation, while the sense of smell varies enormously. One may almost say it is impossible for any two people to agree about any given perfume, and when they occur in combination, the diversity of opinion is even more striking. The spiritual bearing of the perception is naturally yet more illusive and indeterminate. The attributions given in this column may be considered perfectly reliable, being based as far as possible upon considerations of essential virtue, independent of sensation. Nevertheless, it is incumbent upon the student to undertake experimental investigations in every case. A proper comprehension of the virtues of perfumes is of the utmost importance to the work of the Adeptus Major, for they constitute the most vital link between the material and astral planes, and it is precisely this link which the Adeptus Major most intimately needs.

The method of burning the perfumes is of much greater importance than is generally understood. Except for material workings, the gross body of the incense should not be carbonized. The heat applied should be only that sufficient to drive off the essential aromatic substance. In many cases it is best to evaporate the essential oil previously extracted secundum artem.

The thurible should be of the (properly consecrated) metal appropriate to the incense; mixed perfumes should be burned on silver or gold, preferably gold. Failure to obtain the utmost possible perfection in any of these points is often sufficient to vitiate the most elaborate ceremony.

12. Mastic is pale yellow, and its perfume is singularly clean and free from any prejudice (to use a somewhat strange term) either for or against any particular moral idea. Its action on other perfumes is usually to intensify them and quicken their rate of vibration. White Sandal is free from the sensuousness of its Red twin. Note that the sympathy of Mercury and Venus is very strong, but it resembles that of the epicene adolescent, the Amazon maiden or the languishing boy, as opposed to the definitely sexualized youth in the romantic period of rose-coloured spectacles. Nutmeg is probably attributed to Mercury on account of its yellowish tinge. White Mace, the husk which covers it, is Mercurial. Red Mace is probably solar. Storax —see line 8. Fugitive odours are Mercurial for the obvious reasons.

13. The attribution of Menstrual Fluid to Luna depends not only on the periodicity, but on the fact that Luna is herself the symbolical vehicle of the solar light. Camphor—the white waxen appearance suggests Luna, so also the perfume is peculiarly cleanly. It is supposed by some to be useful as a disinfectant. It is in fact useful against moths. This is sympathetic with the idea of lustration. The Mexican Aloes furnishes an alcoholic drink, Pulque, whose cloudy whiteness suggests Luna. Lignum Aloes is a wood in powder, whose physical appearance at once suggests purity of aspiration to the sensitive observer. The connection is therefore directly with the Path of Gimel—see line 25.

Virginal odours obviously suggest the Virgin Moon. Sweet odours are also lunar, because the moon represents the physical senses and refers to the common people. Similarly sugar and sweet things generally are much liked by children (who are classed under Luna) and by that vast herd of mankind, and especially those women whose sense of taste is not sufficiently refined to appreciate real delicateness. Sweetness masks all finer qualities unless they be peculiarly violent: hence the use of sugar, chloroform water and similar compounds to conceal the unpleasant taste of certain medicines.

14. Sandalwood—see line 7. Myrtle, the traditional plant of Venus. Softness and voluptuousness are two of the principal qualities of Venus.
21. Saffron has brilliant purple filaments. An orange dye is prepared from it which indicates the solar nature. But this is sympathetic to Jupiter, and in any case refers to a watery element in its nature, whereas this column deals with the airy constituents of the substance described. The perfume of Saffron is intuitively perceived as generous, rich, and suggesting the sensuous enjoyment of devotion.
27. Pepper is evidently Martial owing to its fiery quality and its specific action on the mucous membrane of the nostrils. Dragon's Blood gives off a dark red smoke, is angry looking, unpleasant to smell, and intuitively perceived as smouldering irritability. Heat and pungency are two principal qualities of Mars.
30. Olibanum—see line 6. Cinnamon—the appearance is decidedly solar; any martial element therein is not confirmed by the perfume, which resembles that of a hot summer day, in the opinion of many sensitives. It is also solar on account of its cordial and carminative properties. "Glorious" is the prime epithet of the external character of Sol. By "glorious odours" are meant those which arouse in the percipient sensations of enjoyment of well-being, with possibly the influx of a certain quality of pride.
32. There is little difficulty in recognizing Saturnian perfumes; the difficulty in practice is to find one which is at all tolerable to the sense of smell. In magical work of the kind which borders upon the material plane,

large quantities of incense are necessary and incantation becomes difficult when the magician is being rapidly asphyxiated. The Adeptus Major can indeed cut himself off magically from such inconveniences but it is otherwise for the beginner. This is one more of the many reasons which have caused teachers to warn their pupils against attempting to work on the plane of Saturn until they are far advanced. Yet this caution exposes the disciple to an even worse danger than that of being choked, which is to formulate an incomplete and unbalanced universe.

Assafoetida—pure samples are not intolerably unpleasant. Scammony is repulsive, principally because of its suggestion of domestic cookery. Indigo furnishes a smoke of the characteristic dark blue of Saturn; the smoke is composed of very solid particles; and this perfume is accordingly both wholly in keeping with the nature of the Planet and pre-eminently suitable for material workings. Sulphur. This is the most difficult incense with which to work. It is liable to provoke fits of coughing, and may even be dangerous, but it is certainly the most useful in conjuration of the infernal powers. (By "Evil" is meant principally that quality which threatens the magician with failure and, philosophically speaking, this quality is pre-eminently the category of Time, which is Saturn.)

THE ZODIAC

15. See line 27.
16. It may be doubted whether the indifference of Storax, referred to in line 8, is really Mercurial: it might almost equally well be the neutrality of dullness, the characteristic of the passive laborious earth. The perfume of Storax suggests the patience of cattle, and even physically the peculiar sweetish scent of a cowshed.
17. Wormwood probably pertains to Gemini on account of the intellectual stimulation which it affords in such a magical preparation as Absinthe.

18. See line 23.
19. Olibanum, combining the ideas of fire and Sol, is pre-eminently suited to Leo, the Kerub of Fire, the house of the Sun.
20. See Column XXXIX.
22. See line 11. Galbanum has a peculiar scent which intuitively suggests danger or even evil. There is a hint of hidden treachery, which is nevertheless seductive. This refers to the exaltation of Saturn in Libra, the house of Venus, which refers to the impregnation of the idea of Love by that of Death. It recalls the rape of Persephone by Hades; or, more appropriately still, that tragic element in love which has formed a theme of all great poets, from Aeschylus and Homer to Shakespeare and Goethe.
24. Siamese Benzoin is to be distinguished from that found in other countries. It has a peculiar odour strongly suggestive of the treachery of the snake. It is the hidden poison not unlike that of Galbanum. The voluptuousness of the perfume is of that type of debauchery whose fascination is directly connected with the knowledge of its fatal issue. Opoponax refers even more directly to Scorpio than does Siamese Benzoin. There is in it even less of the sensuousness of pleasure; there is an overpowering richness of the deliciously abominable.
25. See line 13. The perfume of Lignum Aloes intuitively suggests horsemanship in an airy racecourse, as distinguished from charioteering, as if one's racecourse were a rainbow. One experiences the intense amazon purity of Atalanta. One's aspiration becomes winged. It is therefore to Sagittarius, not as the house of Jupiter, but as the path leading from Yesod to Tiphereth, that this perfume applies.
26. Musk and Civet are referred here on account of their sexual origin, and of their effect upon the aura of the magician. The regular Saturnian perfumes would only be employed in malefic work and in other of the baser aspects of Capricorn.

28. See lines 11 and 22. This attribution is not very satisfactory. There is more in Galbanum than the Saturnian and airy elements. Galbanum is too exciting to be a truly Aquarian perfume; it is too demonic, it lacks the element of humanity. In the humanitarianism of Aquarius there is no magician to understand that "love is the law, love under will." It is the smug aloofness of the philanthropist. Certain schools of late years have written very enthusiastically of Aquarius, but their attitude may seem to adherents of the true Rosicrucian doctrine as somewhat hypocritical and pharisaical. This is to be explained by the fact that in Aquarius the Sun is in his detriment. People who wish to reform the world (on a pattern of theoretical excellence totally unconnected with human nature) are at the very antipodes of solar life and light. They fear vitality.

29. See line 13. This Luna of ATU XVIII is to be contrasted strongly with that of ATU II. The path of Gimel leads from Tiphereth to Kether: it is the unswerving virginal aspiration of the human heart to its divine Lord. The postulant at the gate of the Holy of Holies puts off his pride of manhood and offers himself passively as a bride of his sublime Master. His starting point is the perfection of his human self, and his goal the unity of Absolute Truth, above all quantity or quality. On the contrary, the path of Qoph leads from Malkuth to Netzach. It is the fluctuating craving of the animal soul for the sensuous gratifications of illusory victory. By the treacherous light of the waning Moon, the wanderer stumbles through the swamps upon the edge of the black pool of the Abyss, along the winding path beset by the hell-hounds, up barren slopes to where two "squat turrets, blind as the fool's heart," guard a pass leading he knows not where. His starting point is the illusion of matter, his goal the sphere of external splendour and internal corruption. The path leads away from the middle pillar, to the anarchy of the unbalanced astral wilderness. It is the

essence of error. He should rather trust himself to the Bark of the Midnight Sun, the Winged Beetle, to bear him to the Dawn. He should rather follow the path of Tau, passing through the balanced Elements of the astral plane, despite their darkness and their terror.

The Menstrual Fluid is, however, the medium for the one as for the other. But on the path of Qoph there is no creative energy to fertilize the ova, no light to purify and vitalize their possibilities. The path of Qoph is that of witchcraft. The Great Work is not accomplished. The Postulant is not the ecstatic bride who knows that she will be endowed from on high with the great grace of motherhood, but the hag who clutches at the false gratifications of hysteria. Instead of the human consciousness being thrilled directly by the pure light of its One Lord, the animal sensorium is agitated by the confused jabberings of those demons who personate great souls, human or divine. It is the difference between the Knowledge and Conversation of the Holy Guardian Angel and the hideous intimacy with the débris of decaying minds, momentarily galvanized into manifestation by imbecile or malignant entities.

Column XLIII. VEGETABLE DRUGS

1. Elixir Vitae—the attribution to Kether is due to its omniform virtue.
2. Cocain pertains to Chokmah by its direct action on the deepest nervous centres.
3. Soma is said to give understanding and was sacred to the highest form of the Moon. Belladonna is here because of its virtue to dilate the pupil, thus producing a Black Sea; but this attribution seems a little fantastic.
4. Opium—its virtue is to relieve pain and to confer philosophic calm.
5. Nux Vomica, Nettle, and Cocain are given here for their power of excitation in one way or another. The attribution of the last named is doubtful as its apparently stimulating action is really due to its function as a local anæsthetic. Atropine is given here on account of its power to balance the influence of Morphia.
6. These drugs are all direct cardiac stimulants. Alcohol in particular pertains to Bacchus. Further, it is an omniform menstruum for the Astral Light.

7-8. Cannabis Indica and Anhalonium Lewinii appear to act on both these Sephiroth. Their action is very similar. They produce in one mood voluptuous visions which pertain to Venus, and in another confer the power of self-analysis, which is Mercurial.

9. This attribution refers to its alleged aphrodisiac action.
10. Corn is the typical stimulant of the Nephesch as such.

Column XLV. MAGICAL POWERS

The attributions in this column explain themselves: they are direct representations in spiritual or magical experience of the natures of the various components of the Key Scale.

Add: 0. Vision of No Difference.
2. Vision of Antinomies.
3. Vision of Wonder.
6. Beatific Vision.
25. Vision of Universal Peacock.
32. Travels on the Astral Plane.

Columns LVI-LXVIII, LXXVII-LXXXVI, XCVII

These attributions are all traditional.

Columns CLXXX and CLXXXI. THE ATUS OF THOTH

Editorial Note.—The fifty-seventh verse of the first chapter of The Book of the Law reads: "All the letters of my Book are aright, but Tzaddi is not the Star. This also is a secret: my prophet shall reveal it to the wise." As a result Crowley decided to transpose Atus IV and XVII, making Tzaddi the Emperor and Hé the Star, a reversal of the traditional attributions. In an unpublished Commentary on the Book of the Law, he wrote in 1924: "Tzaddi is the letter of the Emperor, the Trump IV, and Hé is the Star, the Trump XVII, Aquarius and Aries are therefore counter-changed, revolving on the pivot of Pisces, just as the Trumps VIII and XI, Leo and Libra, do about Virgo. This last revelation makes the Tarot attributions sublimely, perfectly, flawlessly symmetrical. The fact of its being so is a most convincing proof of the Superhuman Wisdom of the author of the Book to those who have laboured years, in vain, to elucidate the problems of the Tarot."

Incidentally, but unknown to Crowley in 1904 when the Book of the Law was dictated to him, if the signs of the Zodiac are placed on the diagram known as the Moebius Ribbon, Hé and Tzaddi, or the Emperor and the Star, change places in fact at the twist in that ribbon.

In his published work Crowley did not transpose Hé and Tzaddi until his edition of The Book of Thoth in 1944. The change, therefore, only occurs once in 777 Revised, namely in The Vital Triads on p. 41, which are taken from The Book of Thoth. Those who accept The Book of the Law should therefore alter 15 to 28 and 28 to 15 in the Key Scale throughout this book. Their tables will then agree with those published in the Book of Thoth, but will disagree with the same tables in *Magick in Theory and Practice.*

APPENDIX A

WHAT IS QABALAH ?

Qabalah is: —

(*a*) A language fitted to describe certain classes of phenomena, and to express certain classes of ideas which escape regular phraseology. You might as well object to the technical terminology of chemistry.

(*b*) An unsectarian and elastic terminology by means of which it is possible to equate the mental processes of people apparently diverse owing to the constraint imposed upon them by the peculiarities of their literary expression. You might as well object to a lexicon, or a treatise on comparative religion.

(*c*) A system of symbolism which enables thinkers to formulate their ideas with complete precision, and to find simple expression for complex thoughts, especially such as include previously disconnected orders of conception. You might as well object to algebraic symbols.

(*d*) An instrument for interpreting symbols whose meaning has become obscure, forgotten or misunderstood by establishing a necessary connection between the essence of forms, sounds, simple ideas (such as number) and their spiritual, moral, or intellectual equivalents. You might as well object to interpreting ancient art by consideration of beauty as determined by physiological facts.

(*e*) A system of classification of omniform ideas so as to enable the mind to increase its vocabulary of thoughts and facts through organizing and correlating them. You might as well object to the mnemonic value of Arabic modifications of roots.

(*f*) An instrument for proceeding from the known to the unknown on similar principles to those of mathematics. You might as well object to the use of $\sqrt{-I}$, x^4, etc.

(*g*) A system of criteria by which the truth of correspondences may be tested with a view to criticizing new discoveries in the light of their coherence with the whole body of truth. You might as well object to judging character and status by educational and social convention.

APPENDIX B

WHAT IS A "NUMBER"? OR A "SYMBOL"?

The Book of the Law* I, 4, defines the word "number." It may clarify the subject if we venture to paraphrase the text. The statement "Every number is infinite" is, on the face of it, a contradiction in terms. But that is only because of the accepted idea of a number as not being a thing in itself, but merely a term in a series homologous in character. All orthodox mathematical argument is based on definitions involving this conception. For example, it is fundamental to admit the identity of 2 plus 1 with 1 plus 2. The Book of the Law presents an altogether different conception of the nature of number.

Mathematical ideas involve what is called a continuum, which is, superficially at least, of a different character to the physical continuum. For instance, in the physical continuum, the eye can distinguish between the length of a one-inch stick and a two-inch stick, but not between those which measure respectively one thousand miles and one thousand miles and one inch, though the difference in each case is equally an inch. The inch difference is either perceptible or not perceptible, according to the conditions. Similarly, the eye can distinguish either the one-inch stick or the two-inch stick from one of one inch and a half. But we cannot continue this process indefinitely—we can always reach a point where the extremes are distinguishable from each other, but their mean from neither of the extremes. Thus, in the physical continuum, if we have three terms: A, B, and C, A appears equal to B, and B to C, yet C appears greater than A. Our reason tells us that this conclusion is an absurdity, that we have been deceived by the grossness of our perceptions. It is useless for us to

* Published in The Equinox of the Gods and also in booklet form.

invent instruments which increase the accuracy of our observations, for though they enable us to distinguish between the three terms of our series, and so restore the theoretical Hierarchy, we can always continue the process of division until we arrive at another series: A^{I}, B^{I}, C^{I}, where A^{I} and C^{I} are distinguishable from each other, but where neither is distinguishable from B^{1}.

On the above grounds, modern thinkers have endeavoured to create a distinction between the mathematical and the physical continua; yet it should surely be obvious that the defect in our organs of sense, which is responsible for the difficulty, shows that our method of observation debars us from appreciating the true nature of things by this method of observation.

However, in the case of the mathematical continuum, its character is such that we can continue indefinitely the process of division between any two mathematical expressions soever, without interfering in any way with the regularity of the process, or creating a condition in which two terms become indistinguishable from each other. The mathematical continuum, moreover, is not merely a question of series of integral numbers, but of other types of numbers, which like integers, express relation between existing ideas, yet are not measurable in terms of that series. Such numbers are themselves parts of a continuum of their own, which interpenetrates the series of integers without touching it, at least necessarily.

For example; the tangents of angles made by the separation of two lines from coincidence to perpendicularity, increase constantly from zero to infinity. But the only integral value is found at the angle of 45°, where it is unity.

It may be said that there is an infinite number of such series, each possessing the same property of infinite divisibility. The ninety tangents of angles differing by one degree between zero and ninety may be multiplied sixty-fold by taking the minute instead of the degree as the coefficient of the progression, and these again sixty-fold by introducing the second to divide the minute. So on ad infinitum.

All these considerations depend upon the assumption that every number is no more than a statement of relation. The new conception, indicated by the Book of the Law, is of course in no way contradictory of the orthodox view; but it adds to it in the most practically important manner. A statistician computing the birth-rate of the last centuries makes no special mention of the birth of Napoleon. This does not invalidate his results; but it demonstrates how exceedingly limited is their scope even with regard to their object, for the birth of Napoleon had more influence on the death-rate (and so of the birth-rate) than any other phenomenon included in his calculations.

A short digression is necessary. There may be some who are still unaware of the fact, but the mathematical and physical sciences are in no sense concerned with absolute truth, only with the relations between observed phenomena and the observer. The statement that the acceleration of falling bodies is thirty-two feet per second, is only the roughest of approximations at the best. In the first place it applies to earth. As most people know, in the Moon the rate is only one-sixth as great. But, even on earth, it differs in a marked manner between the poles and the equator, and not only so, but it is affected by so small a matter as the neighbourhood of a mountain.

It is similarly inaccurate to speak of "repeating" an experiment. The exact conditions never recur. One cannot boil water twice over. The water is not the same, and the observer is not the same. When a man says that he is sitting still, he forgets that he is whirling through space with vertiginous rapidity.

It is possibly such considerations that led earlier thinkers to admit that there was no expectation of finding truth in anything but mathematics, and they rashly supposed that the apparent ineluctability of her laws constituted a guarantee of their coherence with truth. But mathematics is entirely a matter of convention, no less so than the rules of Chess or Baccarat. When we say that "two straight lines cannot enclose a space," we mean no more than that we are unable to think of them as doing so. The truth of the statement depends, consequently, on that of the hypothesis that our minds bear witness to truth. Yet the insane man may be unable to think that he is not the victim of mysterious persecution. We find that no reason for believing him. It is useless to reply that mathematical truths receive universal consent, because they do not. It is a matter of elaborate and tedious training to persuade even the few people whom we teach of the simplest theorems in Geometry. There are very few people living who are convinced—or even aware—of the more recondite results of analysis. It is no reply to this criticism to say that all men can be convinced if they are sufficiently trained, for who is to guarantee that such training does not warp the mind?

But when we have brushed away these preliminary objections, we find that the nature of the statement itself is not, and cannot be, more than a statement of correspondences between our ideas. In the example chosen, we have five ideas: those of duality, of straightness, of a line, of enclosing, and of space. None of these are more than ideas. Each one is meaningless until it is defined as corresponding in a certain manner to certain other ideas. We cannot define any word soever, except by identifying it with two or more equally undefined words. To define it by a single word would evidently constitute tautology.

We are thus forced to the conclusion that all investigation may be stigmatized as obscurum per obscurius. Logically, our position is even worse. We define A as BC, where B is DE, and C is FG. Not only does the process increase the number of our unknown quantities in Geometrical progression at every step, but we must ultimately arrive at a point where the definition of Z involves the term A. Not only is all argument confined within a vicious circle, but so is the definition of the terms on which any argument must be based.

It might be supposed that the above chain of reasoning made all conclusions impossible. But this is only true when we investigate the ultimate validity of our propositions. We can rely on water boiling at 100° Centigrade,* although, for mathematical accuracy, water never boils twice running at precisely the same temperature, and although, logically, the term water is an incomprehensible mystery.

To return to our so-called axioms: two straight lines cannot enclose a space. It has been one of the most important discoveries of modern mathematics, that this statement, even if we assume the definition of the various terms employed, is strictly relative, not absolute; and that common sense is impotent to confirm it as in the case of the boiling water. For Bolyai, Lobatschewsky, and Riemann have shown conclusively that a consistent system of Geometry can be erected on any arbitrary axiom soever. If one chooses to assume that the sum of the interior angles of a triangle is either greater than, or less than, two right angles, instead of equal to them, we can construct two new systems of Geometry, each perfectly consistent with itself, and we possess no means soever for deciding which of the three represents truth.

I may illustrate this point by a simple analogy. We are accustomed to assert that we go from France to China, a form of expression which assumes that those countries are stationary, while we are mobile. But the fact might be equally well expressed by saying that France left us and China came to us. In either case there is no implication of absolute motion, for the course of the earth through space is not taken into account. We implicitly refer to a standard of repose which, in point of fact, we know not to exist. When I say that the chair in which I am sitting has remained stationary for the last hour, I mean only stationary in respect to myself and the house. In reality, the earth's rotation has carried it over one thousand miles,

* In revising this Comment, I note with amusement that it had escaped me that 100° C. is by definition the temperature at which water boils! I have seen it boil at about 84° C. on the Baltoro Glacier, and determined my height above sea-level by observing the boiling-point so often that I had quite forgotten the original conditions of Celsius.

and the earth's course some seventy thousand miles from its previous position. All that we can expect of any statement is that it should be coherent with regard to a series of assumptions which we know perfectly well to be false and arbitrary.

It is commonly imagined, by those who have not examined the nature of the evidence, that our experience furnishes a criterion by which we may determine which of the possible symbolic representations of Nature is the true one. They suppose that Euclidian Geometry is in conformity with Nature because the actual measurements of the interior angles of a triangle tell us that their sum is in fact equal to two right angles, just as Euclid tells us that theoretical considerations declare to be the case. They forget that the instruments which we use for our measurements are themselves conceived of as in conformity with the principles of Euclidian Geometry. In other words, they measure ten yards with a piece of wood about which they really know nothing but that its length is one-tenth of the ten yards in question.

The fallacy should be obvious. The most ordinary reflection should make it clear that our results depend upon all sorts of conditions. If we inquire, "What is the length of the thread of Quicksilver in a thermometer?", we can only reply that it depends on the temperature of the instrument. In fact, we judge temperature by the difference of the coefficients of expansion due to heat of the two substances, glass and mercury.

Again, the divisions of the scale of the thermometer depend upon the temperature of boiling water, which is not a fixed thing. It depends on the pressure of the earth's atmosphere, which varies (according to time and place) to the extent of over twenty per cent. Most people who talk of "Scientific accuracy" are quite ignorant of elementary facts of this kind.

It will be said, however, that having defined a yard as the length of a certain bar deposited in the Mint in London, under given conditions of temperature and pressure, we are at least in a position to measure the length of other objects by comparison, directly or indirectly, with that standard. In a rough and ready way that is more or less correct. But if it should occur that the length of things in general were halved or doubled, we could not possibly be aware of the fact. The same considerations apply to all the other so-called laws of Nature. We have no means soever of determining even so simple a matter as to whether one of two events happens before or after the other.

Let us take an instance. It is well known that the light of the sun requires some eight minutes to reach the earth. Simultaneous* phenomena in the two bodies would therefore appear to be separated in time to that extent; and, from a mathematical standpoint, the same discrepancy theoretically exists, even if we suppose the two bodies in question to be only a few yards one more remote than the other. Recent consideration of these facts has shown the impossibility of determining the fact of priority, so that it may be just as reasonable to assert that a dagger-thrust is caused by a wound as vice versa. Lewis Carroll has an amusing parable to this effect in *Through the Looking-Glass*, which work, by the way, with its predecessor, is packed with examples of philosophical paradox.†

We may now return to our text, "Every number is

* Simultaneity, closely considered, possesses no meaning soever. See A. S. Eddington, *Space, Time, and Gravitation*, p. 51.

† If I strike a billiard-ball, and it moves, both my will and its motion have causes long antecedent to the act. I may consider both my work and its reaction as twin effects of the eternal Universe. The moved arm and ball are part of a state of the Cosmos which resulted necessarily from its momentarily previous state, and so, back for ever.

Thus my Magical Work is only one of the cause-effects necessarily concomitant with the cause-effects which set the ball in motion. I may therefore regard the act of striking as a cause-effect of my original Will to move the ball, though necessarily previous to its motion. But the case of Magical Work is not quite analogous. For I am such that I am compelled to perform Magick in order to make my Will to prevail; so that the cause of my doing the Work is also the cause of the ball's motion, and therefore is no reason, why one should precede the other. See *Magick in Theory and Practice* for a full discussion.

Since writing the above, I have been introduced to *Space, Time, and Gravitation* where similar arguments are adduced.

infinite." The fact that every number is a term in a mathematical continuum is no more an adequate definition than if we were to describe a picture as a number so-and-so in the catalogue. Every number is a thing in itself* possessing an infinite number of properties peculiar to itself.

Let us consider, for a moment, the numbers 8 and 9. 8 is the number of cubes measuring one inch each way in a cube which measures two inches each way; while 9 is the number of squares measuring one inch each way in a square measuring three inches each way. There is a sort of reciprocal correspondence between them in this respect.

By adding 1 to 8 we obtain 9, so that we might define unity as that which has the property of transforming a three-dimensional expansion of two into a two-dimensional expansion of three. But if we add unity to 9, unity appears as that which has the power of transforming the two-dimensional expansion of three aforesaid into a mere oblong measuring 5 by 2. Unity thus appears as in possession of two totally different properties. Are we then to conclude that it is not the same unity? How are we to describe unity, how know it? Only by experiment can we discover the nature of its action on any given number. In certain minor respects, this action exhibits regularity. We know, for example, that it uniformly transforms an odd number into an even one, and vice versa; but that is practically the limit of what we can predict as to its action.

We can go further, and state that any number soever possesses this infinite variety of powers to transform any other number, even by the primitive process of addition. We observe also how the manipulation of any two numbers can be arranged so that the result is incommensurable with either, or even so that ideas are created of a character totally incompatible with our original conception of numbers as a series of positive integers. We obtain unreal and irrational expressions, ideas of a wholly different order, by a very simple juxtaposition of such apparently comprehensible and commonplace entities as integers.

* I regret to find myself in disagreement with the Hon. Bertrand Russell with regard to the conception of the nature of Number.

There is only one conclusion to be drawn from these various considerations. It is that the nature of every number is a thing peculiar to itself, a thing inscrutable and infinite, a thing inexpressible, even if we could understand it.

In other words, a number is a soul, in the proper sense of the term, an unique and necessary element in the totality of existence.

We may now turn to the second phrase of the text: "there is no difference." It must strike the student immediately that this is, on the face of it, a point blank contradiction of all that has been said above. What have we done but insist upon the essential difference between any two numbers, and shown that even their sequential relation is little more than arbitrary, being indeed rather a convenient way of regarding them for the purpose of coordinating them with our understanding than anything else? On a similar principle, we number public vehicles or telephones without implication even of necessary sequence. The appellation denotes nothing beyond membership of a certain class of objects, and is indeed expressly chosen to avoid being entangled in considerations of any characteristics of the individual so designated except that cursory designation.

When it is said that there is no difference between numbers (for in this sense I think we must understand the phrase), we must examine the meaning of the word "difference." Difference is the denial of identity in the first place; but the word is not properly applied to discriminate between objects which have no similarity. One does not ask, "What is the difference between a yard and a minute?" in practical life. We do ask the difference between two things of the same kind. The Book of the Law is trying to emphasize the doctrine that each number is unique and absolute. Its relations with other numbers are therefore in the nature of illusion. They are the forms of presentation under which we perceive their semblances; and it is to the last degree important to realize that these semblances only indicate the nature of the realities behind them in the same way in which the degrees on a thermometric scale indicate heat. It is quite unphilosophical to say that 50 degrees Centigrade is hotter than 40 degrees. Degrees of temperature are similarly conventions invented by ourselves to describe physical states of a totally different order; and, while the heat of a body may be regarded as an inherent property of its own, our measure of that heat in no way concerns it.

We use instruments of science to inform us of the nature of the various objects which we wish to study but our observations never reveal the thing as it is in itself. They only enable us to compare unfamiliar with familiar experiences. The use of an instrument necessarily implies the imposition of alien conventions. To take the simplest example: when we say that we see a thing, we only mean that our consciousness is modified by its existence according to a particular arrangement of lenses and other optical instruments, which exist in our eyes and not in the object perceived. So also, the fact that the sum of 2 and 1 is 3, affords us but a single statement of relations symptomatic of the presentation to us of those numbers.

We have, therefore, no means soever of determining the difference between any two numbers, except in respect of a particular and very limited relation. Furthermore, in view of the infinity of every number, it seems not unlikely that the apparent differences observed by us would tend to disappear with the disappearance of the arbitrary conditions which we attach to them to facilitate, as we think, our examination. We may also observe that each number being absolute, is the centre of its universe, so that all other numbers, so far as they are related to it, are its appanages. Each number, is therefore, the totality of the Universe, and there cannot be any difference between one infinite universe and another. The triangle ABC may look very different from the standpoint of A, B, and C respectively; each view is true, absolutely; yet it is the same triangle.

The above interpretation of the text is of revolutionary character, from the point of view of science and mathematics. Investigation on the lines here laid down will lead to the solution of those grave problems which have so long baffled the greatest minds of the world, on account of the initial error of attacking them on lines which involve self-contradiction. The attempt to discover the nature of things by a study of the relations between them is precisely parallel with the ambition to obtain a finite value of Π. Nobody wishes to deny the practical value of the limited investigations which have so long preoccupied the human mind. But it is only quite recently* that even the best thinkers have begun to recognize that their work was only significant within a certain order. It will soon be admitted on all hands that the study of the nature of things in themselves is a work for which the human reason is incompetent; for the nature of reason is such that it must always formulate itself in proportions which merely assert a positive or negative relation between a subject and a predicate. Men will thus be led to the development of a faculty, superior to reason, whose apprehension is independent of the hieroglyphic representations of which reason so vainly makes use.† This then will be the foundation of the true spiritual science which is the proper tendency of the evolution of man. This science will clarify, without superseding, the old; but it will free men from the bondage of mind little by little; just as the old science has freed them from the bondage of matter.

* This was written in 1924.—Editor.

† See *Eleusis*, A. Crowley Collected Works, Vol. II, Epilogue.

NOTES TO TABLE OF CORRESPONDENCES

(See pp. 2-36)

Col. II.—0-10 are the names of the Numbers or Emanations; **11-34** the Letters spelt in full.

Line **1**.—Some of the common titles of Kether are:—

נקדה פשות The Small Point.
תת זל The Profuse Giver.
נקדה ראשונה The Primordial Point.
רישא הוורה The White Head.
אמן Amen.
אור מופלא Lux occulta.
פלא Mirum occultum.
רום מעלה Inscrutable Height.
אריך אנפין Long of Nose.
אריך אפים Long of Face.
עתיק יומין The Ancient of Days.
(Also name of seven inferiors!)
אהיה אשר אהיה Existence of Existences.
עתיקא דעתיקין Ancient of Ancient Ones
עתיקא קדישא Holy Ancient One.
אור פשוט Lux simplicissima.
טמירה דטמרין Concealed of the Concealed.
רישא *The* Head.
אור פנימי Lux interna.
עליון The Most High.
הוא He.
רישא דלא The Head which is Not.

Line **2**.—Chokmah has additional titles:—

כחמה Power of Yetzirah.
י of Tetragrammaton.

אבא אב

It has also the Divine Name, יהוה.

Col. II. (*continued*)—

Line **3**.—Binah has these additional titles:—

אמא The dark sterile mother.
אימא The bright pregnant mother.
אלהים / יהוה אלהים } Divine Names.
כורסיא Throne.

Line **4**.—*Chesed* has this additional title:—

גדולה Majesty.

Line **5**.—*Geburah* has these additional titles:—

דין Justice.
פחד Fear.

Line **6**.—*Tiphereth* has these additional titles:—

זעיר אנפין Lesser Countenance.
מלך King.

Seir Anpin, שעיר אנפין:—

אדם Adam.
בן The Son.
איש The Man.
שכאנום Spare Angels.

Line **9**.—*Jesod* has this additional title:—

צדיק-יסוד-עולם The Righteous is the Foundation of the World.

Line **10**.—Malkuth has these titles (among others):—

שער The Gate (by Temurah, עשר = 10).
תרעא The Gate (Chaldee),

which has same number (671) as אדני. In full—

אלף-דלת-נון-יוד

Col. II. (*continued*)—

Also—

Gates of Death.
,, ,, Shadow of Death.
,, ,, Tears.
,, ,, Justice.
,, ,, Prayer.
Gate of Daughter of Mighty Ones.
,, ,, Garden of Eden.

Also—

Inferior Mother—

The Daughter.
The Queen. מלכה
The Bride. כלה
The Virgin. בתולה

Col. IV.—This column may be equally well symbolised by any single entry, preferably in 0. The Monistic and Nihilistic conceptions are convertible. Hua may be equally named Tao, Iao, Noumenon, and the like. All language on this subject is necessarily feeble and hieroglyphic. It is to name that which by definition has no name.

Col. V.—These God-names are the "Grand Words" of the corresponding grades (see Col. CXXI.), except for $5° = 6^{□}$, whose G.W. is יהשוה.

The Zodiacal Gods are as for the Sephira, which corresponds to the Planet ruling. Apparently, in the numeration of Azbogah, line 12, only the AZ count.

That these following are only titles of the One Ineffable Name is shown by Koran xvii. 110. But monotheism is not true for the normal consciousness, but only for that of the adept.

الملك king	الرحيم merciful	الرّحمن compassionate
المؤمن he to whom one is faithful	السلام peace	القدوس holy
الجبار le fort	العزيز le cher	المهيمن terrible
البارئ innocent	الخالق creator	المتكبر the proud
القهار vainqueur	الغفار pardoner	المصور picturer

Col. V. (*continued*)—

الفتاح opener	الرزاق bountiful	الوهاب giver
الباسط supporter	القابض holder	العليم all-wise
المعز cherisher	الرافع exalter	الخافض humbler
البصير all-seer	السميع all-hearer	المذل hater
اللطيف consoler	العدل just	الحكم judge
العظيم great	الحليم long-suffering, gracious	الخبير all-knower
العلي exalted	الشكور worthy of thanks	الغفور pardoner
المقيت exposer	الحفيظ protector	الكبير the great
الكريم genereux	الجليل glorious	الحسيب numberer
الواسع vast	المجيب hearer of complaints	الرقيب beholder of hearts
المجيد exalted	الودود reconciler	الحكيم healer, wise
الحق truth	الشهيد witness of all	الباعث sender
المتين solid	القوي strong	الوكيل advocate
المحصي reckoner	الحميد worthy of thanks	الولي foster father
المحيي giver of life	المعيد resurrector	المبدي beginner
القيوم advocate of all	الحي living	المميت stayer
الواحد sole	الماجد most holy	الواجد the only one
المقتدر most mighty	القادر of power full	الصمد unaccompanied
الاول the 1st	المؤخر retarder	المقدم first of officers, hastener

Col. V. (*continued*)—

الباطن concealed	الظاهر manifested	الاحر the last
البر charitable	المتعال highest	الوالى fosterer of all
العفو pardoner	المنتقم avenger	التواب turner of hearts
ذو الجلال والاكرام worthy of glory and honour	مالك الملك roi de l'univers	الرؤف who pitieth
الغنى rich	الجامع assembler	المقسط divider
الضار afflicter	المانع refuser	المغني enricher
الهادي peace-giver	النور la lumiere	النافع giver of advantages
الوارث inheritor	الباقي survivor	البديع inventor
	الصبور patient	الرشيد (? beginning) guide

هو الله الذي لا الله الّا هو امين

Hua is God ; and there is none other God than Hua. Amen.

Col. VI., Line 34.—Essence, *cf.* α and ω.

Col. VIII.—

Lines 1-10.—Beth Elohim gives a quite different ten Qliphoth.

Line 15.—

In the midst of the Zodiacal Qliphoth are סמאל and אסמדאי.
At SE corner, Man, Serpent, and the elder Lilith the wife of Samael.
At NE corner, the Ox and Ass, and Aggereth the daughter of Machalath.
At NW corner, the Scorpion and אסימון, the Unnameable and כעמה.
At SW angle, the Lion and Horse, and the younger Lilith the wife of Asmodai.

Col. IX.—The Cup of the Stolistes has its rim in **2** and **3** and its foot in **10**.

The Caduceus is (easily) placed on the Tree and divided into א, מ, and ש.

The Waxing Moon in **4**; Waning in **5**; Full in **6**.

Col. XI.—The elements, of whose nature the signs of the Zodiac partake, are shown by the symbol against them.

Col. XII.—Let 45 be a straight line. On 45 erect the equilateral △s 451, 459. From 4 and 5 draw straight lines 247, 358 ⊥ 45, and the straight lines 25 ⊥ 14, 43 ⊥ 15, 48 ⊥ 59, and 57 ⊥ 49, the points 2, 3, 7, and 8 marking the intersections. Join 19, 12, 13, 23, 78, 79, 89. Let 6 be the point of intersection of 19, 57, 48. On 78 erect an equilateral △ with its apex away from I. Produce 19 to 10, join 7-10, 8-10. Daath is at the junction of 25, 34. See figure, p. xxvii.

Cols. XV.-XVIII.—

Daath—Lavender, Grey-white, Pure violet, Grey flecked gold.
Herschel—Silver flecked white.

Col. XVI., Line 10.—For 🜁, ▽, △, and 🜃.

Col. XIX.—Urim and Thummim = Auramoth and Thoum Mou, Egyptian Gods. They are methods of divination by △ and 🜃.

Col. XX., Line 32.—These Gods preside over the pieces in "Rosicrucian Chess."

🜁 of △	Bishop	Ⲑⲱⲟⲩⲙ ⲙⲱⲟⲩ
▽ of △	Queen	Ⲓⲅϩⲁⲟⲩⲣⲉⲑ
△ of △	Knight	Ϧⲛⲱⲟⲩ ⲫⲱⲏϣ
🜃 of △	Pawn	ⲕⲁⲃⲉⲝⲛⲩϥ
🜃 of △	Castle	Ϣⲁⲩⲱϧⲓⲅ
⊛ of △	King	Ⲫⲁⲟⲩⲣⲱ
🜁 of ▽	Bishop	Ⲝⲟⲡⲓⲅ ⲑⲁ ⲙⲱⲟⲩ
▽ of ▽	Queen	Ⲑⲏⲱⲟⲩⲣ ⲓⲅ Ⲑⲁⲙⲱⲟⲩ
△ of ▽	Knight	ⲥⲉⲃⲁ ϧⲛⲱⲟⲩ ϩⲁⲟⲩⲣ ⲓⲅ ⲑⲁ ⲙⲱⲟⲩ

Col. **XX.** *(continued)*—

🜃 of 🜄 Pawn ϯⲱⲙⲁⲑⲫ

🜃 of 🜄 Castle Ϣⲏⲱⲉⲩ ⲑⲁ ⲓⲥ

☸ of 🜄 King Ⲡⲑⲁ Ϧⲁⲫⲏⲛ-Ϧⲏⲝ

🜁 of 🜁 Bishop ⲍⲱ ⲱⲁⲛ

🜄 of 🜁 Queen Ϧⲛⲱⲟⲩ ⲑⲁ Ⲡⲉϧⲏϯ

🜂 of 🜁 Knight Ϭⲟⲩ Ⲃⲁⲗ

🜃 of 🜁 Pawn ⲁϩⲉⲫⲓ

🜃 of 🜁 Castle ⲑⲁⲣⲫⲉϣⲥ ϥⲁ Ϧⲛⲱⲟⲩⲑⲁ ⲡⲉ

☸ of 🜁 King Ϭⲟⲩϧⲁⲟⲩⲣⲓⲥ

🜁 of 🜃 Bishop Ⲁⲣⲏⲱⲩⲉⲣⲓⲥ

🜄 of 🜃 Queen Ⲏⲓⲥⲉⲥ

🜂 of 🜃 Knight ϩⲱⲱⲣ

🜃 of 🜃 Pawn ϩⲙⲉϣⲉϯ

The Pawns refer to ת as the House of the Elements only, not to ת as 🜃.

🜃 of 🜃 Castle Ⲛⲉⲩⲫⲑⲩⲓⲉⲥ

☸ of 🜃 King Ⲏϣⲱⲱⲣⲓⲥ

Line 32.—Ⲥϥⲃⲁϧⲩⲱⲟⲩ ϩⲛⲟⲩⲉ. ⲓⲥⲑⲟⲙⲱⲟⲩ and ⲗⲩⲉⲫⲓ : ϯⲱⲙⲁⲑⲫ : ϩⲙⲉϣⲉϯ : Ⲕⲁⲃϥⲝⲛⲩϥ.

Col. **XXI.**—The perfected Egyptian exclaims, "There is no part of me that is not of the Gods." This column gives the attribution in detail. The non-cherubic Zodiacal signs are omitted; but follow their affinities.

Col. XXIII.—Formless State (F) = 4
Sublime State (S) = 4
Reflection (R) = 10
Kashina (K) = 10
Impurity (I) = 10
Analysis (A) = 1
Perception (P) = 1

40

Cols. XXXVIII.-XL.—The vagueness and extent of these attributions is shown in this table from Agrippa, who is too catholic to be quite trustworthy.

Things under the Sun which are called Solary.

Among stones—

1. The eye of the Sun.
2. Carbuncle.
3. Chrysolite.
4. Iris (stone).
5. Heliotrope (stone).
6. Hyacinth (stone).
7. Pyrophylus (stone).
8. Pantaura.
9. Topazius.
10. Chrysopassus.
11. Rubine.
12. Balagius.
13. Auripigmentum and things of a golden colour.

Among plants—

1. Marigold.
2. Lote-tree.
3. Peony.
4. Sallendine.
5. Balm.
6. Ginger.
7. Gentian.
8. Dittany.
9. Vervain.
10. Bay-tree.
11. Cedar.
12. Palm-tree.
13. Ash.
14. Ivy.
15. Vine.
16. Mint.
17. Mastic.
18. Zedoary.
19. Saffron.
20. Balsam.
21. Amber.
22. Musk.
23. Yellow honey.
24. Lignum aloes.
25. Cloves.
26. Cinnamon.
27. Calamus.
28. Aromaticus.
29. Pepper.
30. Frankincense.
31. Sweet marjoram.
32. Libanotis.

Among animals—

1. Lion.
2. Crocodile.
3. Spotted-wolf.
4. Ram.
5. Boar.
6. Bull.
7. Baboon.

Among birds—

1. Phœnix.
2. Eagle.
3. Vulture.
4. Swan.
5. Cock.
6. Crow.
7. Hawk.

Among insects—

1. Glow-worm.
2. Beetle.

Among fish—

1. Sea-calf.
2. Shell-fish.
3. Pulius.
4. Star-fish.
5. Strombi.
6. Margari.

Among metals—

1 Gold.

Col. XL.—Aaron's breastplate is very doubtful; we advise reliance on columns Stones and Tribes, we having chosen Stones on bases of physical analogy to Signs, Colours, &c.

Col. XLII.—The following table of sub-elemental perfumes is important:—

☸	of	☸	Ambergris.
🜁	of	☸	The Gall of the Rukh.
🜄	of	☸	Onycha.
🜃	of	☸	Musk.
🜂	of	☸	Civet.
☸	of	🜁	Lign-aloes.
🜁	of	🜁	Galbanum.
🜄	of	🜁	Mastick.
🜃	of	🜁	Storax.
🜂	of	🜁	Olibanum.
☸	of	🜄	Myrrh.
🜁	of	🜄	Camphor.
🜄	of	🜄	Siamese Benzoin.
🜃	of	🜄	Indigo.
🜂	of	🜄	Opoponax.
☸	of	🜃	Dittany of Crete.
🜁	of	🜃	Assafœtida.
🜄	of	🜃	Clover.
🜃	of	🜃	Storax.
🜂	of	🜁	Benzoin.
☸	of	🜂	Saffron.
🜁	of	🜂	Lign-aloes.
🜄	of	🜂	Red-sanders.
🜃	of	🜂	Red Sandalwood.
🜂	of	🜂	Olibanum.

Cols. XLIII. and XLIV.—And, generally, all drugs exciting the parts of the body corresponding. See Col. CLXXXII.

Col. XLVI.—Each Trigram combines with itself and the others to make 64 Hexagrams, which partake of the combined nature. This attribution is the true key to the Yi King. No sinologist has had any idea of it, but it is obvious enough now that O. M. has solved it.

See Appendix I.

Col. XLVII.—

Line 7.—Has a monkey.

Line 19.—Said to have a monkey.

Col. XLIX.—The Geomantic Figures of the Planets are those of the signs which they rule.

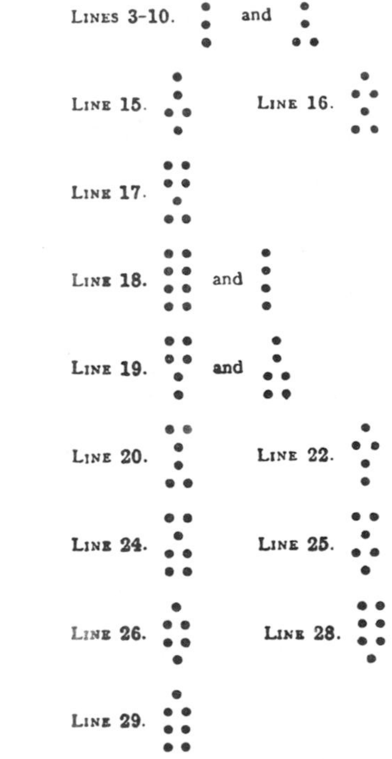

See the "Handbook of Geomancy," *The Equinox* I: 2, p. 137.

Col. L.—The Catholic "seven deadly sins" in square brackets.

Col. LVII.—Egyptian Quarters.

Cols. LVII., LIX., &c.—Beth Elohim gives:—

Michael, Leo, and South to ▽ and י.

Gabriel ♉, and North to △ and ה.

Raphael, Man, and West to 🜃 and ה.

Uriel, Eagle, and East to 🜁 and ו.

Col. LXIX.—

Sattvas,	☿	In a close analogy.
Rajas, and	🜍	
Tamas,	⊖	

Col. LXXIX., Line 13—

Add (3321) שדברשהמעת שרתתן, the Spirit of the Spirits of the Moon. The final ן is counted as 700, as are the final ם's in Col. LXXVIII., line 13.

Col. LXXXV.—

Line 6.—Or חשמאל:

Line 9.—Or זפניאל.

Col. LXXXIX.—Add Daath, היהא.

Col. XCIII., Line 10.—Contains the Earth.

Col. XCVI.—Add Daath, היוה.

Col. XCIX.—Add among Archangels:—

Azrael, Angel of Death (נ).
Israfel, of Last Trump (ש).

Col. C.—Our order of Angelic Choirs is from R. Mosheh ben Maimon. R. Ishmael and the book Pliah prefer:—

1. Cherubim.
2. Chasmalim.
3. Chaioth.
4. Aralim.
5. Seraphim.
6. Tarshishim.
7. Auphanim. }
8. Auphanim. }
9. Aishim.
10. Taphsarim.

And there are many other schemes.

Col. CII.—Add Daath, אנרי.

Col. CIII.—Add Daath, Cerebrum medium, cujus locus est in parte capitis postica.

But these have many other attributions, and each is itself divisible: thus, Chesed and Geburah of Tiphareth are the breasts; Tiphareth the heart; Netzach and Hod the testicles; Jesod the membrum virile; and Malkuth the anus. The signs of the Zodiac are variously given, and the Planets agree with the face: thus, ♄ and ♃, the ears; ♂ and ♀, the nostrils; ☉ and ☽, the eyes; and ☿, the mouth. The hand: thumb, ☸; 1st finger, 🜁; 2nd, ▽; 3rd, 🜃; 4th, △. These, however, vary somewhat.

Col. CVI.—These Abodes are enclosed in four circles: the Waters of Weeping, of Creation, of Oceanus, and the False Sea. Compare the classical four rivers of Hell.

Col. CVIII.—Incomplete and redundant owing to unconcentrated nature of Qliphoth.

Line 2.—Three Evil Forms before Samael are:—

קמטיאל
בליאל
עתיאל

The Thaumiel, also called Kerethiel.

Col. CIX.—☉ = King. ♀ = Duke.

King בלע of בעור, Dukes עלוה, חמנע, and יתת, are all referred to Daath.

Edomite Kings and Dukes are taken e libro Maggid. and Gen. 36.

Col. CXIV., Line 1.—*I.e.* simple breathing without articulation.

Col. CXV.—The furniture, &c., is attributed as told in the ritual, here duly *h-d*, *c-d*, and *n-r r-d*.

Col. CXXI.—Add the "Waiting" Grades of "Lord of the Paths in the Portal of the Vault of the Adepts" between the 1st and 2nd Orders; and "Babe of the Abyss" between the 2nd and 3rd.

Col. CXXV.—Burton gives these upside down. The true attribution is checked by the Fire-Worshippers (Guebres) in 5. Yet, of course, the Kether Hell may be considered as more awful than the Malkuth.

COL. CXXVII.—These and many other (rather far-fetched and irrelevant) attributions of various things are to be found in Burton's *Arabian Nights*, in the Tale of Abn al-Husn and his Slave-Girl Tawaddud.

COL. CXXXIII.—The symbolic forms and Divination meanings of these cards can be readily constructed from considerations of their natures as here indicated.

LINE 5.—This is the First Decan, and begins from Cor Leonis.

COL. CXXXVIII.—Astrological symbols are derived from the primary forms—Cross, Crescent, Circle.

COL. CLXXIII.—For meaning and special functions see original. They should, but do not, accurately refer to the divisions of each sign into 7 planetary parts.

Pietro di Abano gives.—

THE NAMES OF THE HOURS AND THE ANGELS RULING THEM.

The Names of the Hours.

Hours of the Day—

1. Yain. 7. Ourer.
2. Janor. 8. Thamic.
3. Nasmia. 9. Neron.
4. Salla. 10. Jayon.
5. Sadedalia. 11. Abai.
6. Thamur. 12. Natalon.

Hours of the Night—

1. Beron. 7. Netos.
2. Barol. 8. Infrac, or Tafrac
3. Thami. 9. Sassur.
4. Athar. 10. Aglo.
5. Methon. 11. Calerva.
6. Rana. 12. Salam.

TABLES OF THE ANGELS OF THE HOURS ACCORDING TO THE COURSE OF THE DAYS

Sunday.

Angels of the Hours of the Day—

1. Michael. 7. Samael.
2. Anael. 8. Michael.
3. Raphael. 9. Anael.
4. Gabriel. 10. Raphael.
5. Cassiel. 11. Gabriel.
6. Sachiel. 12. Cassiel.

COL. CLXXIII. (*continued*)—

Angels of the Hours of the Night—

1. Sachiel. 7. Cassiel.
2. Samael. 8. Sachiel.
3. Michael. 9. Samael.
4. Anael. 10. Michael.
5. Raphael. 11. Anael.
6. Gabriel. 12. Raphael.

Monday.

Angels of the Hours of the Day—

1. Gabriel. 7. Raphael.
2. Cassiel. 8. Gabriel.
3. Sachiel. 9. Cassiel.
4. Samael. 10. Sachiel.
5. Michael. 11. Samael.
6. Anael. 12. Michael.

Angels of the Hours of the Night—

1. Anael. 7. Michael.
2. Raphael. 8. Anael.
3. Gabriel. 9. Raphael.
4. Cassiel. 10. Gabriel.
5. Sachiel. 11. Cassiel.
6. Samael. 12. Sachiel.

Tuesday.

Angels of the Hours of the Day—

1. Samael. 7. Sachiel.
2. Michael. 8. Samael.
3. Anael. 9. Michael.
4. Raphael. 10. Anael.
5. Gabriel. 11. Raphael
6. Cassiel. 12. Gabriel.

Angels of the Hours of the Night—

1. Cassiel. 7. Gabriel.
2. Sachiel. 8. Cassiel.
3. Samael. 9. Sachiel.
4. Michael. 10. Samael.
5. Anael. 11. Michael.
6. Raphael. 12. Anael.

Wednesday.

Angels of the Hours of the Day—

1. Raphael 7. Anael.
2. Gabriel. 8. Raphael.
3. Cassiel. 9. Gabriel.
4. Sachiel. 10. Cassiel.
5. Samael. 11. Sachiel.
6. Michael. 12. Samael.

Angels of the Hours of the Night—

1. Michael. 7. Samael.
2. Anael. 8. Michael.
3. Raphael. 9. Anael.
4. Gabriel. 10. Raphael.
5. Cassiel. 11. Gabriel.
6. Sachiel. 12. Cassiel.

Col. CLXXIII. (*continued*)—

Thursday.

Angels of the Hours of the Day—

1. Sachiel.	7. Cassiel.
2. Samael.	8. Sachiel.
3. Michael.	9. Samael.
4. Anael.	10. Michael.
5. Raphael.	11. Anael.
6. Gabriel.	12. Raphael.

Angels of the Hours of the Night—

1. Gabriel.	7. Raphael.
2. Cassiel.	8. Gabriel.
3. Sachiel.	9. Cassiel.
4. Samael.	10. Sachiel.
5. Michael.	11. Samael.
6. Anael.	12. Michael.

Friday.

Angels of the Hours of the Day—

1. Anael.	7. Michael.
2. Raphael.	8. Anael.
3. Gabriel.	9. Raphael.
4. Cassiel.	10. Gabriel.
5. Sachiel.	11. Cassiel.
6. Samael.	12. Sachiel.

Angels of the Hours of the Night—

1. Samael.	7. Sachiel.
2. Michael.	8. Samael.
3. Anael.	9. Michael.
4. Raphael.	10. Anael.
5. Gabriel.	11. Raphael.
6. Cassiel.	12. Gabriel.

Saturday.

Angels of the Hours of the Day—

1. Cassiel.	7. Gabriel.
2. Sachiel.	8. Cassiel.
3. Samael.	9. Sachiel.
4. Michael.	10. Samael.
5. Anael.	11. Michael.
6. Raphael.	12. Anael.

Angels of the Hours of the Night—

1. Raphael.	7. Anael.
2. Gabriel.	8. Raphael.
3. Cassiel.	9. Gabriel.
4. Sachiel.	10. Cassiel.
5. Samael.	11. Sachiel.
6. Michael.	12. Samael.

Note.—The first hour of the day, of every country, and in every season whatsoever, is to be assigned to the sun-rising, when he first appeareth arising in the horizon. And the first hour of the night is to be the thirteenth hour, from the first hour of the day.

The Year.

The Spring: Taloi.
The Summer: Casmaran.
The Autumn: Adarael.
The Winter: Earlas.

Col. CLXXIII. (*continued*)—

The Angels of the Spring: Caracasa, Core, Amatiel, Commissoros.
The Head of the Sign of the Spring: Spugliguel.
The Name of the Earth in the Spring: Amadai.
The Names of the Sun and Moon in the Spring: The Sun, Abrayen; The Moon, Agusita.

The Angels of the Summer: Gargabel, Tariel, Gariel.
The Head of the Sign of the Summer: Tubiel.
The Name of the Earth in the Summer: Festativi.
The Names of the Sun and Moon in the Summer: The Sun, Athemay; The Moon, Armatus.

The Angels of the Autumn: Tarquam, Gnabarel.
The Head of the Sign of the Autumn: Torquaret.
The Name of the Earth in the Autumn: Rabianara.
The Names of the Sun and Moon in the Autumn: The Sun, Commutaff; The Moon, Affaterium.

(No Winter given.)

Col. CLXXVII. — Musulman attribution of Planets:—

ג	♄
ת	♃
פ	♂
ם	☉
ם and ב	♀
ד	☿
ר	☽

Note that ם and not כ is the 7th of the double letters.

The Jesuit Kircher gives—

♄	♃	♂	☉	♀	☿	☽
פ	ר	ת	ב	ג	ד	כ

The order of the Planets is that of their apparent rate of motion. By writing them in their order round a heptagon, and tracing the heptagram unicursally, the order of the days of the week is obtained.

Col. CLXXVIII.—These intelligences are angelic in nature, but possessing material and even earthy dominion. Hence they preside over the geomantic figures, whose nature indeed expresses their relation to man.

Col. CLXXXI.—

Line 11.—He laughs; bearing a sphere containing Illusion in his left hand, but over his right shoulder, and a staff 463 lines long in his right. A lion and a dragon are at his feet, but he seems unaware of their attacks or caresses.

Col. CLXXXI. *(continued)*—

Line 12.—His attitude suggests the shape of the Swastika or thunderbolt, the message of God.

Line 13.—She is reading intently in an open book.

Line 14.—She bears a sceptre and a shield, whereon is figured a dove as symbol of the male and female forces.

Line 15.—His attitude suggests 🜍, and he is seated upon the Cubical Stone, whose sides show the Green Lion and White Eagle.

Line 16.—He is crowned, sceptred, and blessing, all in a threefold manner. Four living creatures adore him, the whole suggesting a pentagram by its shape.

Line 17.—He is inspired by Apollo to prophesy concerning things sacred and profane: represented by a boy with his bow and two women, a priestess and an harlot.

Line 18.—He drives furiously a chariot drawn by two sphinxes. As Levi drew it.

Line 20.—Before him goeth upright the Royal Uræus Serpent.

Line 21.—[☿, 🜍, and ⊖, or Sattva, Rajas, and Tamas].

Line 23.—From a gallows shaped like the letter ד hangs by one foot a young fair man. His other leg forms a cross with the suspending one. His arms, clasped behind his head, form an upright △, and this radiates light. His mouth is resolutely closed.

Line 25.—A winged and crowned goddess, with flashing golden belt, stands, and pours from her right hand the flame of a torch upon an Eagle, while from her left hand she pours water from an horn upon a Lion. Between her feet a moon-shaped cauldron of silver smokes with perfume.

Col. CLXXXI. *(continued)*—

Line 26.—Levi's Baphomet is sound commentary on this Mystery, but should not be found in the text.

Line 27.—Human figures thrown thence suggest the letter ע by their attitude.

Line 28.—A woman, naked, and kneeling on her left knee, pours from a vase in her right hand silver waters into a river, by which grow roses, the haunts of coloured butterflies. With her left hand she pours golden waters over her head, which are lost in her long hair. Her attitude suggests the Swastika. Above flames a great star of seven rays.

Line 29.—Below, a path leads between two towers, guarded by jackals, from the sea, wherein a Scarabæus marcheth landwards.

Line 30.—Below is a wall, in front of which, in a fairy ring, two children wantonly and shamelessly embrace.

Line 31.—An angel blowing a trumpet, adorned with a golden banner bearing a white cross. Below a fair youth rises from a sarcophagus in the attitude of the god Shu supporting the Firmament. On his left a fair woman, her arms giving the sign of Water—an inverted ▽ on the breast. On his right a dark man giving the sign of Fire—an upright △ on the forehead.

Line 32.—An ellipse, composed of 400 lesser circles. At the corners of the card a Man, an Eagle, a Bull, and a Lion. Within the circle a naking shining figure with female breasts, with closed eyes in the sign of Earth —right foot advanced, right hand advanced and raised, left hand lowered and thrown back. The hands grip each a ray of dazzling light, spiral, the right hand being dextro- and the left hand lævo-rotary. A red scarf conceals the fact of male genital organs, and suggests by its shape the letter כ. Such is the conventional hieroglyph.

APPENDIX I

The Trigrams of the Yi King

Attribution to Quarters.	Planetary Attribution.	Hindu Attribution.	Yetziratic Attribution.	Figure.	Name.	Part of Body.	*Key Scale.*
S.	☉	Lingam.	+ י	☰	Khien.	Head.	2 [and 30].
S.E.	♀	Apas.	▽ מ	☱	Tui.	Mouth.	14 [and 23].
E.	♃	Mano (Prana).	☉ ר	☲	Li.	Eyes.	6 [21 and 30].
N.E.	♂	Tejas.	△ ש	☳	*K*ăn.	Feet.	27 and 31.
S.W.	☿	Vayu.	🜁 א	☴	Sun.	Thighs.	11 [and 12].
W.	♄	Akasa.	☽ ג	☵	Khân.	Ears.	10 [13 and 32].
N.W.	🜃	Prithivi.	🜃 ת	☶	Kăn.	Hands.	32 bis.
N.	☽	Yoni.	○ ת	☷	Khwăn.	Belly.	3 and 13.

The Trigrams should be considered as the symbols which combine these meanings, the Hexagrams as combinations of these, chosen according to circumstances. Thus ䷧ is Fire of ☽, or Energy of ♄, and might mean beginning to change, or force applied to obstruction, as it actually does.

The Hexagrams of the Yi King

	Figure.	Nature.	Name	Divination and Spiritual Meaning.
1	䷀	+ of +	*K'hien*	Heaven, &c. (+ for Lingam.)
2	䷁	○ of ○	Khwăn	Earth, &c. (○ for Yoni.)
3	䷂	◡ of △	*K'un*	Danger and obscurity—γένος.
4	䷃	🜃 of ◡	Măng	Youth and ignorance.
5	䷄	◡ of +	hsü	Waiting, sincerity
6	䷅	+ of ◡	Sung	Contention, opposition, strength in peril
7	䷆	○ of ◡	Sze.	Multitude, age and experience.
8	䷇	◡ of ○	Pi	Help

	Figure.	Nature.	Name.	Divination and Spiritual Meaning.
9		🜁 of +	hsiao *kh*ū	Small, restraint.
10		+ of ▽	lî	Pleased, satisfaction, treating, attached to, a shoe.
11		○ of +	thai	Spring, free course.
12		+ of ○	phî	Decay, patience, obedience, autumn, shutting up, restriction.
13		+ of ⊙	thung zăn	Union (of men).
14		⊙ of +	tă yû	Great havings
15		○ of 🜃	*k*hien	Humility
16		△ of ○	yû	Harmony and satisfaction

	Figure	Nature.	Name.	Divination and Spiritual Meaning.
17		▽ of △	Sui	Following.
18		🜃 of 🜁	Kû	Troublesome services, arrest of decay, hard work.
19		○ of ▽	Lin	Approach of authority, inspect, comfort.
20		🜁 of ○	Kwân.	Manifesting, contemplating.
21		⊙ of △	Shih Ho. . . .	Union by gnawing, legal constraint
22		▽ of ⊙	Pî	Ornament, freewill.
23		🜃 of ○	Po	Overthrow, couch.
24		○ of △	Fu	Returning, visit from friends.

	Figure.	Nature.	Name.	Divination and Spiritual Meaning.
25	䷘	+ of △	Wû wang . . .	Simplicity and sincerity, earnestness
26	䷙	🜃 of +	Ta *khu*	Great accumulation.
27	䷚	🜃 of △	Î	Nourishment, upper jaw.
28	䷛	▽ of 🜁	Ta Kwo	Great carefulness, weak beam.
29	䷜	◡ of ◡	Khan	Pit, defile, peril.
30	䷝	☉ of ☉	Lî	Inherent in, attached to, docility.
31	䷞	▽ of 🜃	hsien	Influencing to action, all, jointly.
32	䷟	△ of 🜁	hăng	Perseverance, keeping to the path.

	Figure.	Nature.	Name.	Divination and Spiritual Meaning.
33		+ of 🜃	Thun	Returning, avoiding, retirement.
34		△ of +	Tâ *K*wang . . .	Violence, the Great Ram.
35		⊙ of ○	Tzin	To advance (good).
36		○ of ⊙	Ming I	Intelligence, wounded.
37		🜁 of ⊙	*K*ia Zăn	Household, wifely duty.
38		⊙ of ▽	Khwei	Disunion, family discord.
39		◡ of 🜃	*K*ien	Lameness, immobility, difficulty.
40		△ of ⊙	*K*ieh	Unravelling (a knot, &c.).

	Figure.	Nature.	Name.	Divination and Spiritual Meaning.
41	䷨	🜃 of ▽	Sūn	Diminution.
42	䷩	🜁 of △	Yi	Addition, increase.
43	䷪	▽ of +	Kwâi	Displacing, strength, complacency, tact.
44	䷫	+ of 🜁	Kau	Unexpected event, a bold woman.
45	䷬	▽ of ○	Tzhui	Collected, docility.
46	䷭	○ of 🜁	Shăng.	Advance and ascent.
47	䷮	▽ of ◡	Khwăn	Straightened, distressed, ⁘ Carcer, growth restrained.
48	䷯	◡ of 🜁	Tzing	A well, self-cultivation.

	Figure.	Nature.	Name.	Divination and Spiritual Meaning.
49		▽ of ☉	Ko	Change
50		☉ of 🜁	Ting	A caldron, a concubine, flexibility, quick ear and eye.
51		△ of △	*K'*ăn	Ease, development, moving power, thunder.
52		🜃 of 🜃	Kăn	Peace, a mountain.
53		🜁 of 🜃	*K'*ien	Fortunate marriage, gradual advance, goose
54		△ of ▽	Kwei mei	Unfortunate marriage (of a younger sister before the elder)
55		△ of ☉	Făng	Large, abundant, progress.
56		☉ of 🜃	Lû	Strangers.

	Figure.	Nature.	Name.	Divination and Spiritual Meaning.
57	䷸	🜁 of 🜁	Sun	Flexibility, penetration, vacillation, wind, wood, &c.
58	䷹	▽ of ▽	Tui	Pleasure, help from friends, still water
59	䷺	🜁 of ◡	Hwăn	Dissipation, dispersion, turning to evil.
60	䷻	◡ of ▽	*K*ieh	Joints of body, regular division.
61	䷼	🜁 of ◡	*K*ung fû	Inmost sincerity.
62	䷽	△ of 🜃	Hsiao Kwo . . .	Non-essential, success of trifles, a wounded bird, small divergences.
63	䷾	◡ of ☉	*K*î tzi	Help attained, complete success.
64	䷿	☉ of ◡	Wei tzî	Incomplete success, foolish impulse, failure.

SEPHER SEPHIROTH

SVB FIGVRÂ

D

(ὁ ἀριθμός)

EDITORIAL NOTE

THIS dictionary was begun by Allan Bennett (Fra ∴ Iehi Aour, now Bhikkhu Ananda Metteya) in the last decade of the nineteenth century since ψ-J.C. It was bequeathed to the present Editor, with many other magical MSS., on I.A.'s departure for Ceylon in 1899.

Frater Perdurabo used it, and largely added to it, in the course of his Qabalistic workings. With George Cecil Jones (Fra ∴ Volo Noscere) he further added to it by making it a complete cross-correspondence to the Book DCCLXXVII.

It was further revised and checked, re-copied by a Jewish scribe, and again checked through, in the year V of the present Era.

The mathematical additions were continued by Fra ∴ P. and Fra ∴ Lampada Tradam; and the MS. finally copied on a specially constructed typewriter by Gerald Rae Fraser (Fra ∴ ψ) who added yet further mathematical data.

This copy has again been checked by Fra ∴ P. and Soror ∴ N.N. and the proofs further by three separate scholars.

The method of employing the dictionary has been fully indicated in The Temple of Solomon the King [Equinox V].

None of the editors claim to possess even the smallest degree of scholarship. The method of compilation has been to include all words given in Von Rosenroth's Qabalistic Dictionary, those specially commented on in S.D., I.R.Q., and I.Z.Q., those given in 777, and those found by Fratres I.A. and P. Some of them are found in texts of the Hebrew Scriptures which appeared to those adepts to be of magical importance. Owing to their carelessness, the meaning of some few words has been lost, and cannot now be traced.

ABBREVIATIONS, SIGNS, AND FIGURES

K.D. L.C.K. p.— = KABBALA DENUDATA cuius Pars Prima continet Locos Communes Kabbalisticos.

Dec. = Decan.
S.P.M. = Sphere of the Primum Mobile.
S.S.F. = Sphere of the Fixed Stars.
L.T.N. = Lesser Angel governing Triplicity by Night.
L.T.D. = Lesser Angel governing Triplicity by Day.
K.Ch.B. = Kether—Chokmah—Binah.
(Ch.) = Chaldee.
S.D. = Siphra Dtzenioutha.
I.R.Q. = Idra Rabba Qadisha.
Tet. = Tetragrammaton.
L.A. Angel = Lesser Assistant Angel.
I.Z.Q. = Idra Zuta Qadisha.
M.T. = Magister Templi.
ש = Shemhamphorasch.
W. = Wands.
C. = Cups.
S. = Swords.
P. = Pentacles.
K. of S. = Key of Solomon.
O.P.A.A. = Oriens—Paimon—Ariton—Amaimon.

♈	=	Aries.	♄	=	Saturn.
♉	=	Taurus.	☉	=	Sun.
♊	=	Gemini.	☽	=	Moon.
♋	=	Cancer.	♂	=	Mars.
♌	=	Leo.	☿	=	Mercury.
♍	=	Virgo.	♃	=	Jupiter.
♎	=	Libra.	♀	=	Venus.
♏	=	Scorpio.			
♐	=	Sagittarius.			
♑	=	Capricornus.			
♒	=	Aquarius.			
♓	=	Pisces.			

⌴	enclosing a number shows that the number is a perfect square.				
$\sqrt[4]{}$	before	,,	,,	,,	a squared square.
⁀	above	,,	,,	,,	a perfect number.
⌊	about	,,	,,	,,	a factorial.*
‖⌊	about	,,	,,	,,	a sub-factorial.
R(n)	before	,,	,,	,,	a reciprocal (or 'amicable') number.

Σ (1—k) is an abbreviation for "the sum of the first k natural numbers."

* See special table following.

TABLE OF FACTORS

ODD NUMBERS FROM 1 TO 3321 (5'S EXCLUDED); SHOWING LOWEST FACTORS, AND PRIMES (P.). "—" INDICATES THAT THE NUMBER IS DIVISIBLE BY 3.

1	P.	83	P.	171	—	259	7	347	P.
2	P.	87	—	173	P.	261	—	349	P.
3	P.	89	P.	177	—	263	P.	351	—
5	P.	91	7	179	P.	267	—	353	P.
7	P.	93	—	181	P.	269	P.	357	—
9	3^2	97	P.	183	—	271	P.	359	P.
11	P.	99	—	187	11	273	—	361	19^2
13	P.	101	P.	189	—	277	P.	363	—
17	P.	103	P.	191	P.	279	—	367	P.
19	P.	107	P.	193	P.	281	P.	369	—
21	—	109	P.	197	P.	283	P.	371	7
23	P.	111	—	199	P.	287	7	373	P.
27	3^3	113	P.	201	—	289	17^2	377	13
29	P.	117	—	203	7	291	—	379	P.
31	P.	119	7	207	—	293	P.	381	—
33	—	121	11^2	209	11	297	—	383	P.
37	P.	123	—	211	P.	299	13	387	—
39	—	127	P.	213	—	301	7	389	P.
41	P.	129	—	217	7	303	—	391	17
43	P.	131	P.	219	—	307	P.	393	—
47	P.	133	7	221	13	309	—	397	P.
49	7^2	137	P.	223	P.	311	P.	399	—
51	—	139	P.	227	P.	313	P.	401	P.
53	P.	141	—	229	P.	317	P.	403	13
57	—	143	11	231	—	319	11	407	11
59	P.	147	—	233	P.	321	—	409	P.
61	P.	149	P.	237	—	323	17	411	—
63	—	151	P.	239	P.	327	—	413	7
67	P.	153	—	241	P.	329	7	417	—
69	—	157	P.	243	3^5	331	P.	419	P.
71	P.	159	—	247	13	333	—	421	P.
73	P.	161	7	249	—	337	P.	423	—
77	7	163	P.	251	P.	339	—	427	7
79	P.	167	P.	253	11	341	11	429	—
81	$3^4 = 9^2$	169	13^2	257	P.	343	7	431	P.

433	P.	529	23^2	623	7	719	P.	813	—
437	19	531	—	627	—	721	7	817	19
439	P.	533	13	629	17	723	—	819	—
441	-21^2	537	—	631	P.	727	P.	821	P.
443	P.	539	7	633	—	729	$3^6=9^3=27^2$	823	P.
447	—	541	P.	637	7	731	17	827	P.
449	P.	543	—	639	—	733	P.	829	P.
451	11	547	P.	641	P.	737	11	831	—
453	—	549	—	643	P.	739	P.	833	7
457	P.	551	19	647	P.	741	—	837	—
459	—	553	7	649	11	743	P.	839	P.
461	P.	557	—	651	—	747	—	841	29^2
463	P.	559	13	653	P.	749	7	843	—
467	P.	561	—	657	—	751	P.	847	7
469	7	563	P.	659	P.	753	—	849	—
471	—	567	—	661	P.	757	P.	851	23
473	11	569	P.	663	—	759	—	853	P.
477	—	571	P.	667	23	761	P.	857	P.
479	P.	573	—	669	—	763	7	859	P.
481	13	577	P.	671	11	767	13	861	—
483	—	579	—	673	P.	769	P.	863	P.
487	P.	581	7	677	P.	771	—	867	—
489	—	583	11	679	7	773	P.	869	11
491	P.	587	P.	681	—	777	—	871	13
493	17	589	17	683	P.	779	19	873	—
497	7	591	—	687	—	781	11	877	P.
499	P.	593	P.	689	13	783	—	879	—
501	—	597	—	691	P.	787	P.	881	P.
503	P.	599	P.	693	—	789	—	883	P.
507	—	601	P.	697	17	791	7	887	P.
509	P.	603	—	699	—	793	13	889	7
511	7	607	P.	701	P.	797	P.	891	—
513	—	609	—	703	19	799	17	893	19
517	11	611	13	707	7	801	—	897	—
519	—	613	P.	709	P.	803	11	899	29
521	P.	617	P.	711	—	807	—	901	17
523	P.	619	P.	713	23	809	9	903	—
527	17	621	—	717	—	811	P.	907	P.

909	—	1003	17	1099	7	1193	P.	1289	P.
911	P.	1007	19	1101	—	1197	—	1291	P.
913	11	1009	P.	1103	P.	1199	11	1293	—
917	7	1011	—	1107	—	1201	P.	1297	P.
919	P.	1013	P.	1109	P.	1203	—	1299	—
921	—	1017	—	1111	11	1207	17	1301	P.
923	13	1019	P.	1113	—	1209	—	1303	P.
927	—	1021	P.	1117	P.	1211	7	1307	P.
929	P.	1023	—	1119	—	1213	P.	1309	7
931	7	1027	13	1121	19	1217	P.	1311	—
933	—	1029	—	1123	P.	1219	23	1313	13
937	P.	1031	P.	1127	7	1221	—	1317	—
939	—	1033	P.	1129	P.	1223	P.	1319	P.
941	P.	1037	17	1131	—	1227	—	1321	P.
943	23	1039	P.	1133	11	1229	P.	1323	—
947	P.	1041	—	1137	—	1231	P.	1327	P.
949	13	1043	7	1139	17	1233	—	1329	—
951	—	1047	—	1141	7	1237	P.	1331	11
953	P.	1049	P.	1143	—	1239	—	1333	31
957	—	1051	P.	1147	31	1241	17	1337	7
959	7	1053	—	1149	—	1243	11	1339	13
961	31^2	1057	7	1151	P.	1247	29	1341	—
963	—	1059	—	1153	P.	1249	P.	1343	17
967	P.	1061	P.	1157	13	1251	—	1347	—
969	—	1063	P.	1159	19	1253	7	1349	19
971	P.	1067	11	1161	—	1257	—	1351	7
973	7	1069	P.	1163	P.	1259	P.	1353	—
977	P.	1071	—	1167	—	1261	13	1357	23
979	11	1073	29	1169	7	1263	—	1359	—
981	—	1077	—	1171	P.	1267	7	1361	P.
983	P.	1079	13	1173	—	1269	—	1363	29
987	—	1081	23	1177	11	1271	31	1367	P.
989	23	1083	—	1179	—	1273	19	1369	37^2
991	P.	1087	P.	1181	P.	1277	P.	1371	—
993	—	1089	– 33^2	1183	7	1279	P.	1373	P.
997	P.	1091	P.	1187	P.	1281	—	1377	—
999	—	1093	P.	1189	29	1283	P.	1379	7
1001	7	1097	P.	1191	—	1287	—	1381	P.

1383	—	1479	—	1573	11	1669	P.	1763	41
1387	19	1481	P.	1577	19	1671	—	1767	—
1389	—	1483	P.	1579	P.	1673	7	1769	29
1391	13	1487	P.	1581	—	1677	—	1771	7
1393	7	1489	P.	1583	P.	1679	23	1773	—
1397	11	1491	—	1587	—	1681	41^2	1777	P.
1399	P.	1493	P.	1589	7	1683	—	1779	—
1401	—	1497	—	1591	37	1687	7	1781	13
1403	23	1499	P.	1593	—	1689	—	1783	P.
1407	—	1501	19	1597	P.	1691	19	1787	P.
1409	P.	1503	—	1599	—	1693	P.	1789	P.
1411	17	1507	11	1601	P.	1697	P.	1791	—
1413	—	1509	—	1603	7	1699	P.	1793	11
1417	13	1511	P.	1607	P.	1701	—	1797	—
1419	—	1513	17	1609	P.	1703	13	1799	7
1421	7	1517	37	1611	—	1707	—	1801	P.
1423	P.	1519	7	1613	P.	1709	P.	1803	—
1427	P.	1521	-39^2	1617	—	1711	29	1807	13
1429	P.	1523	P.	1619	P.	1713	—	1809	—
1431	—	1527	—	1621	P.	1717	17	1811	P.
1433	P.	1529	11	1623	—	1719	—	1813	7
1437	—	1531	P.	1627	P.	1721	P.	1817	23
1439	P.	1533	—	1629	—	1723	P.	1819	17
1441	11	1537	29	1631	7	1727	11	1821	—
1443	—	1539	—	1633	23	1729	7	1823	P.
1447	P.	1541	23	1637	P.	1731	—	1827	—
1449	—	1543	P.	1639	11	1733	P.	1829	31
1451	P.	1547	7	1641	—	1737	—	1831	P.
1453	P.	1549	P.	1643	31	1739	37	1833	—
1457	31	1551	—	1647	—	1741	P.	1837	11
1459	P.	1553	P.	1649	17	1743	—	1839	—
1461	—	1557	—	1651	13	1747	P.	1841	7
1463	7	1559	P.	1653	—	1749	—	1843	19
1467	—	1561	7	1657	P.	1751	17	1847	P.
1469	13	1563	—	1659	—	1753	P.	1849	43^2
1471	P.	1567	P.	1661	11	1757	7	1851	—
1473	—	1569	—	1663	P.	1759	P.	1853	17
1477	7	1571	P.	1667	P.	1761	—	1857	—

1859	11	1953	—	2049	—	2143	P.	2239	P.
1861	P.	1957	19	2051	7	2147	19	2241	—
1863	—	1959	—	2053	P.	2149	7	2243	P.
1867	P.	1961	37	2057	11	2151	—	2247	—
1869	—	1963	13	2059	29	2153	P.	2249	13
1871	P.	1967	7	2061	—	2157	—	2251	P.
1873	P.	1969	11	2063	P.	2159	17	2253	—
1877	P.	1971	—	2067	—	2161	P.	2257	37
1879	P.	1973	P.	2069	P.	2163	—	2259	—
1881	—	1977	—	2071	19	2167	11	2261	7
1883	7	1979	P.	2073	—	2169	—	2263	31
1887	—	1981	7	2077	31	2171	13	2267	P.
1889	P.	1983	—	2079	—	2173	41	2269	P.
1891	31	1987	P.	2081	P.	2177	7	2271	—
1893	—	1989	—	2083	P.	2179	P.	2273	P.
1897	7	1991	11	2087	P.	2181	—	2277	—
1899	—	1993	P.	2089	P.	2183	37	2279	43
1901	P.	1997	P.	2091	—	2187	3^7	2281	P.
1903	11	1999	P.	2093	7	2189	11	2283	—
1907	P.	2001	—	2097	—	2191	7	2287	P.
1909	23	2003	P.	2099	P.	2193	—	2289	—
1911	—	2007	—	2101	11	2197	13	2291	29
1913	P.	2009	7	2103	—	2199	—	2293	P.
1917	—	2011	P.	2107	7	2201	31	2297	P.
1919	19	2013	—	2109	—	2203	P.	2299	11
1921	17	2017	P.	2111	P.	2207	P.	2301	—
1923	—	2019	—	2113	P.	2209	47^2	2303	7
1927	41	2021	43	2117	29	2211	—	2307	—
1929	—	2023	7	2119	13	2213	P.	2309	P.
1931	P.	2027	P.	2121	—	2217	—	2311	P.
1933	P.	2029	P.	2123	11	2219	7	2313	—
1937	13	2031	—	2127	—	2221	P.	2317	7
1939	7	2033	19	2129	P.	2223	—	2319	—
1941	—	2037	—	2131	P.	2227	17	2321	11
1943	29	2039	P.	2133	—	2229	—	2323	23
1947	—	2041	13	2137	P.	2231	23	2327	13
1949	P.	2043	—	2139	—	2233	11	2329	17
1951	P.	2047	23	2141	P.	2237	P.	2331	—

2333	P.	2429	7	2523	—	2619	—	2713	P.
2337	—	2431	11	2527	7	2621	P.	2717	11
2339	P.	2433	—	2529	—	2623	43	2719	P.
2341	P.	2437	P.	2531	P.	2627	37	2721	—
2343	—	2439	—	2533	17	2629	11	2723	7
2347	P.	2441	P.	2537	43	2631	—	2727	—
2349	—	2443	7	2539	P.	2633	P.	2729	P.
2351	P.	2447	P.	2541	—	2637	—	2731	P.
2353	13	2449	31	2543	P.	2639	7	2733	—
2357	P.	2451	—	2547	—	2641	19	2737	7
2359	7	2453	11	2549	P.	2643	—	2739	—
2361	—	2457	—	2551	P.	2647	P.	2741	P.
2363	17	2459	P.	2553	—	2649	—	2743	13
2367	—	2461	23	2557	P.	2651	11	2747	41
2369	23	2463	—	2559	—	2653	7	2749	P.
2371	P.	2467	P.	2561	13	2657	P.	2751	—
2373	—	2469	—	2563	11	2659	P.	2753	P.
2377	P.	2471	7	2567	17	2661	—	2757	—
2379	—	2473	P.	2569	7	2663	P.	2759	31
2381	P.	2477	P.	2571	—	2667	—	2761	11
2383	P.	2479	37	2573	31	2669	17	2763	—
2387	7	2481	—	2577	—	2671	P.	2767	P.
2389	P.	2483	13	2579	P.	2673	—	2769	—
2391	—	2487	—	2581	29	2677	P.	2771	17
2393	P.	2489	19	2583	—	2679	—	2773	47
2397	—	2491	47	2587	13	2681	7	2777	P.
2399	P.	2493	—	2589	—	2683	P.	2779	7
2401	$7^4 = 49^2$	2497	11	2591	P.	2687	P.	2781	—
2403	—	2499	—	2593	P.	2689	P.	2783	11
2407	29	2501	41	2597	7	2691	—	2787	—
2409	—	2503	P.	2599	23	2693	P.	2789	P.
2411	P.	2507	23	2601	-51^2	2697	—	2791	P.
2413	19	2509	13	2603	19	2699	P.	2793	—
2417	P.	2511	—	2607	—	2701	37	2797	P.
2419	41	2513	7	2609	P.	2703	—	2799	—
2421	—	2517	—	2611	7	2707	P.	2801	P.
2423	P.	2519	11	2613	—	2709	—	2803	P.
2427	—	2521	P.	2617	P.	2711	P.	2807	7

2809	53^2	2903	P.	2999	P.	3093	—	3189	—
2811	—	2907	—	3001	P.	3097	19	3191	P.
2813	29	2909	P.	3003	—	3099	—	3193	31
2817	—	2911	41	3007	31	3101	7	3197	23
2819	P.	2913	—	3009	—	3103	29	3199	7
2821	7	2917	P.	3011	P.	3107	13	3201	—
2823	—	2919	—	3013	23	3109	P.	3203	P.
2827	11	2921	23	3017	7	3111	—	3207	—
2829	—	2923	37	3019	P.	3113	11	3209	P.
2831	19	2927	P.	3021	—	3117	—	3211	13
2833	P.	2929	29	3023	P.	3119	P.	3213	—
2837	P.	2931	—	3027	—	3121	P.	3217	P.
2839	17	2933	7	3029	13	3123	—	3219	—
2841	—	2937	—	3031	7	3127	53	3221	P.
2843	P.	2939	P.	3033	—	3129	—	3223	11
2847	—	2941	17	3037	P.	3131	31	3227	7
2849	7	2943	—	3039	—	3133	13	3229	P.
2851	P.	2947	7	3041	P.	3137	P.	3231	—
2853	—	2949	—	3043	17	3139	43	3233	53
2857	P.	2951	13	3047	11	3141	—	3237	—
2859	—	2953	P.	3049	P.	3143	7	3239	41
2861	P.	2957	P.	3051	—	3147	—	3241	7
2863	7	2959	11	3053	43	3149	47	3243	—
2867	47	2961	—	3057	—	3151	23	3247	17
2869	19	2963	P.	3059	7	3153	—	3249	- 57^2
2871	—	2967	—	3061	P.	3157	7	3251	P.
2873	13	2969	P.	3063	—	3159	—	3253	P.
2877	—	2971	P.	3067	P.	3161	29	3257	P.
2879	P.	2973	—	3069	—	3163	P.	3259	P.
2881	43	2977	13	3071	37	3167	P.	3261	—
2883	—	2979	—	3073	7	3169	P.	3263	13
2887	P.	2981	11	3077	17	3171	—	3267	—
2889	—	2983	19	3079	P.	3173	19	3269	7
2891	7	2987	29	3081	—	3177	—	3271	P.
2893	11	2989	7	3083	P.	3179	11	3273	—
2897	P.	2991	—	3087	—	3181	P.	3277	29
2899	13	2993	41	3089	P.	3183	—	3279	—
2901	—	2997	—	3091	11	3187	P.	3281	17

3283	7	3293	37	3301	P.	3309	—	3317	31
3287	19	3297	—	3303	—	3311	7	3319	P.
3289	11	3299	P.	3307	P.	3313	P.	3321	—
3291	—								

The first dozen factorials, and sub-factorials; and the ratios they bear to one another; note that $\underline{|n} / \underline{||n} = e$

N	$\underline{\lvert N}$	$\underline{\lvert\lvert N}$	$\underline{\lvert N} \div \underline{\lvert\lvert N}$	$\underline{\lvert\lvert N} \div \underline{\lvert N}$
1	1	0	∞	0·000000
2	2	1	2·000000	0·500000
3	6	2	3·000000	0·333333
4	24	9	2·666666	0·375000
5	120	44	2·727272	0·366666
6	720	265	2·716981	0·368055
7	5040	1854	2·718446	0·367857
8	40320	14833	2·718262	0·367881
9	362880	133496	2·718283	0·367879
10	3628800	1334961	2·718281	0·367879
11	39916800	14684570	2·718281	0·367879
12	479001600	176214841	2·718281	0·367879

Factorial n, or $\underline{|n}$, is the continued product of all the whole numbers from 1 to n inclusive and is the number of ways in which n different things can be arranged.

Sub-factorial n, or $\underline{||n}$, is the nearest whole number to $\underline{|n} : e$, and is the number of ways in which a row of n elements may be so deranged, that no element may have its original position.

Thus $$\underline{|n} = 1 \times 2 \times 3 \times \ldots \times n,$$

and $$\underline{||n} = \frac{1 \times 2 \times 3 \times \ldots \times n}{2·71828188\ldots} \pm h,$$

where h is the smaller decimal fraction less than unity by which the fraction $\frac{1 \times 2 \times \ldots \times n}{2·718281\ldots}$ differs from a whole number, and is to be added or subtracted as the case may be.—The most useful expression for $\underline{||n}$ is:

$$\underline{||n} \equiv \underline{|n} - \frac{n}{1}\,\underline{|n-1} + \frac{n(n-1)}{1.2}\,\underline{|n-2} - \frac{n(n-1)(n-2)}{1.2.3}\,\underline{|n-3} + \text{etc.}$$

to $(n+1)$ terms.

$$e \equiv 1 + \frac{1}{\underline{|1}} + \frac{1}{\underline{|2}} + \frac{1}{\underline{|3}} + \ldots \text{ to } \infty$$

$$\equiv 2·71828188\ldots.$$

SEPHER SEPHIROTH

Names of the letters	Figures of the letters	Value of the letters	English equivalents of the letters
(M) Aleph	א	1	A
(D) Beth	ב	2	B
(D) Gimel	ג	3	G
(D) Daleth	ד	4	D
(S) Heh	ה	5	H (E)
(S) Vau	ו	6	V (U)
(S) Zayin	ז	7	Z
(S) Kheth (Cheth)	ח	8	Ch
(S) Teth	ט	9	T
(S) Yodh	י	10	Y (I or J)
(D) Kaph	כ ך	20 500	K
(S) Lamed	ל	30	L
(M) Mem	מ ם	40 600	M
(S) Nun	נ ן	50 700	N
(S) Samekh	ס	60	S
(S) Ayin	ע	70	O (A'a or Ng)
(D) Peh	פ ף	80 800	P
(S) Tzaddi	צ ץ	90 900	Tz
(S) Qoph	ק	100	Q
(D) Resh	ר	200	R
(M) Shin	ש	300	S Sh
(D) Tau	ת	400	T Th

When written large, the Value of a Hebrew letter is increased to one thousand times its ordinary value. A large Aleph is counted 1000: a large Beth, 2000: and so on.

Note that A, I, O, U, H, are really consonants, mere bases for the vowels. These vowels are not here given, as they have no importance in Gematria.

M, D, and S before the names of the letters shews their division into Mothers, Double and Single letters, referred respectively to active Elements, Air, Water, Fire, Planets, and Signs. But ש and ת also serve to signify the Elements of Spirit and of Earth. See Liber 777.

|1. ‖2. The Mystic Number of Kether. S. P. M. $\pi\sqrt{\ }$1

|2. ‖3. S. S. F. π 2

[Abbreviation for 422, אריך אנפין, q.v.] א:א:

Σ(1—2). ♄. The Mystic Number of Chokmah π 3

Father אב

To come, go בא

The Number of Abra-Melin Princes. ♃. 2^2 $\sqrt{\ }$4

Father אבא

Hollow; a vein בב

Proud גא

♂ π 5

Mist, vapour אד

Back בג

Σ(1—3). |3. ☉. The Mystic Number of Binah 6

To gather, collect גבא

Gog, the giant whose partner is Magog גג

A bear דב

A window הא

♀ π 7

Lost, ruined אבד

A name of GOD attributed to Venus. Initials of Adonai ha-Aretz אהא

Desire; either, or או

Gad, a Tribe of Israel; good fortune גד

Was weary דאב

Riches, power דבא

Fish דג

2^3. The Number of Abra-Melin Sub-Princes, and of the Servitors of Oriens. ☿ $\sqrt[3]{\ }$8

To will, intend אבה

Desired, beloved אהב

אוא

Then אז

The entrance, threshold באה

To be anxious, grieve דאג

Love; beloved, breast; pleasures of love דד

Nqn. Zauir Anpin 478 q.v. זא

‖4. 3^2. ♄. ☽ $\sqrt{\ }$9

Ventriloquus: the special 'fire' of black magic, whence Obi, Obeah. Cf. 11 and 207 אוב

He kindled אזא

Brother אח

A garment בגד

Became powerful, grew high גאה

Middle גו

Splendour; cf. 15 הד

Σ(1—4). The Mystic Number of Chesed. Elementorum Sphaera. The Number of Abra-Melin Servitors of Amaimon and Ariton 10

Enchanter אט

[Vide K.D. L.C.K. p. 185] בגה

Elevated, exalted, high — גבה
Flew, soared — דאה
Two — דו
Window — הה
A wolf — זאב
A hidden place; bosom — חב

π 11

Ahah — אהה
Firebrand, volcanic fire: the special 'fire' or 'light' of the Sacred Magic of Light, Life, and Love; hence "Odic Force" &c. Cf. 9 and 207 — אוד
Where — אי
When — בבוא
To tear, cut, attack — גדד
Gold (Ch.) — דהב
Proud, haughty — זד
To conceal — חבא
A circularity of form or motion; a feast — חג

12

He longed for, missed — אוה
He departed, went forth — אזד
A little book, pamphlet, letter; tools — גט
To multiply — דגה
A city of Edom — הבה
HE. [ה is referred to Mater, ו to Pater, א to Corona] — הוא
Vau; hook, nail, pin — וו
This, that — זה
To penetrate, be sharp; (Ch.) one — חד

π 13

A small bundle, bunch — אגדה
Beloved; Love — אהבה
Unity — אחד
Hated — איב
Emptiness — בהו
Raised up — גהה
Chokmah, 42-fold Name in Yetzirah. (See 777) — גי
Anxiety — דאגה
A fisher — דוג
Thunder; to meditate; he removed — הגה
A city of Edom — הדד
Here; this — זו
A locust — חגב
He shall come — יבא

14

Rhamnus; a thorn, spine — אטד
Rising ground; Earth of Geburah. (See 777) — גיא
Sacrifice v. & s. (Ch.). (?) — דבח
Love, beloved; David — דוד
Give, give! [Vide no. 17, יהב] — הב הב
To grind, direct, stretch out — הדה
Gold — זהב
Hand — יד

$\Sigma(1-5)$. $\Sigma\{1-(3\times 3)\}\div 3$. The Mystic Number of Geburah. The Number of Abra-Melin Servitors of Asmodee and Magot, and of Paimon — 15

Angel of 3rd Dec. ♐ — אבוהא
The month of Exodus and Passover — אביב
Steam, vapour — איד
Pride; a carrying out; exaltation — גאוה

Splendour, the Eighth Sephira הוד
Overflowing, abounding זוב
He who impels; to force זח
To hide חבה
The Monogram of the Eternal יה

The Number of Abra-Melin Servitors of Asmodee $\sqrt{\ }$ $\sqrt[4]{\ }$ 16

Hyssopus אזוב
He seized, cleaved to אחז
Elevated, exalted, high גבוה
(Verb. subst.) Injury, war, lust; fell הוה
She היא
Alas!—Woe וי
Like, equal to זוג

π 17

Nuts אגוז
Ah!—Alas! אוי
Capricornus גדי
Nerve, sinew. [Gen. xxxii. 25 & 32] גיד
Narrative, subtle discourse הגדה
K.D. L.C.K. p. 267 ההוא
To dream, rave הזה
A fly זבוב
Sacrificed זבח
To seethe, boil זוד
To brighten, make joyful חדה
A circle, orbit חוג
Good טוב
To give, place יהב

18

My favourite, my beloved אהבי
Hatred איבה
The antique Serpent חטא
Living חי
Notariqon of Yehi Aur, etc. יאוא

π 19

Angel L.T.D. of ♐ אהוח
An enemy אויב
Job איוב
Was black דיה
Chavvah; to manifest, shew forth; Eve חוה

The Number of Abra-Melin Servitors of Amaimon 20

Fraternity אחוה
Black liquid דיו
It was היה
The breast; a vision; a prophet; to gaze חזה
Jobab, an Edomite King יובב
The hand יוד

Σ (1—6). The Mystic Number of Tiphareth 21

Existence, Being, the Kether-name of GOD אהיה
But, yet, certainly אך
Deep meditation הגיג
Ah!—Alas! הוי
Purity, innocence זהו
Vide Sepher Yetzirah יהו

The Number of Abra-Melin Servitors of Ariton 22

With his hand; Night Demon of 1st Dec. ♒ בידו
By Yodh ביוד
Hearer in secret; Angel of 8 W. האאיה
The state of puberty זווג
A magical vision (Ch.) חזוא

Wheat חטה
Good טובה
Notariqon of "Tet. Elohim Tet. Achad." יא״א
Unity יחד

π 23

Parted, removed, separated זחח
Joy חדוה
A thread חוט
Life חיה

4. The Number of the 'Elders' in the Apocalypse 24

He whom I love אהובי
He who loves me אוהבי
A Mercurial GOD. His essence is אז, 8 אזבוגה
Substance; a body גויה
A pauper דך
Angel of 2 C. הבביה
Abundance זיז
A water-pot, a large earthenware vessel כד

5^2 √ 25

To break דכא
The Beast חיוא
Jehewid, GOD of Geburah of Binah יהוד
Let there be יהי
Will be separated יזח
Thus כה

The Numbers of the Sephiroth of the Middle Pillar; 1 + 6 + 9 + 10 26

[Vide K.D. L.C.K. p. 273] הויה
Seeing, looking at חווה
Sight, vision חזוה
TETRAGRAMMATON, "Jehovah," the Unutterable Name, the Lost Word יהוה
Kebad, husband of the impure Lilith. [K.D. L.C.K. 464] כבד

3^3 ∛ 27

Wept, mourned בכה
Purity זך
A parable, enigma, riddle חידה

Σ (1—7). The Mystic Number of Netzach 28

Clay טיט
Union, unity יחוד
Power כח

π 29

Is broken. [Ps. x. 10] דכה
To break down, overturn הדך

30

A party to an action at law; defendant, plaintiff. [Note ל = 30 = ♎ = 'Justice'] חייב
Judah יהודה
It will be יהיה

π 31

How? איך
GOD of Chesed, and of Kether of Briah אל
To go הוך
A beating, striking, collision הכאה
And there was. [Vide S.D.I. par. 31] ויהי
K. of S. Fig. 31 ייאי
Not לא

SEPHER SEPHIROTH

2^5. The Number of Abramelin Servitors of Astarot $\sqrt[5]{32}$ **32**

Coalescence of אהיה and יהוה Macroprosopus and Microprosopus. This is symbolized by the Hexagram. Suppose the 3 ה's conceal the 3 Mothers א, מ & ש and we get 358 q.v. — אהיהוה

Lord — בל

Angel of 5 W. — והויה

Copula Maritalis — זיווג

Was pure — זכה

Zig-zag, fork-lightning — חזיז

Unity K.D. L.C.K. p. 432 — יחיד

Glory — כבוד

Mind, heart — לב

33

Sorrow; wept, mourned — אבל

Day Demon of 1st Dec. ♈ — באל

To destroy (Ch.); (?) a King of Edom — בלא

Spring, fountain — גל

$\Sigma\{1-(4\times4)\}\div4$. ♃ **34**

"GOD the Father," divine name attributed to Jupiter — אל אב

To ransom, avenge, pollute — גאל

To reveal — גלא

A pauper — דל

A common person; uneducated, ignorant — הדיוט

Angel of 7 C. — חהויה

35

Agla, a name of GOD; notariqon of Ateh Gibor le-Olahm Adonai — אגלא

Boundary, limit — גבל

He will go — יהך

$6^2 = \Sigma(1-8)$. ☉. The Mystic Number of Hod $\sqrt{36}$ **36**

Tabernaculum — אהל

How? (Vide Lamentations) — איכה

Duke of Geburah in Edom; to curse; name of GOD attributed to ☿ — אלה

To remove, cast away — הלא

Confession — וידוי

Leah — לאה

Perhaps, possibly; would that! — לו

π **37**

Angel of 8 P. — אכאיה

GOD (Ch.) — אלהא

Behold! — אלו

Perished, grew old — בלה

To grow great — גדל

Banner — דגל

Tenuity, breath, vanity; in vain; Abel. [I.Z.Q., "the Supernal Breathers."] — הבל

Night Demon of 2nd Dec. ♐ — ואל

Profession — זל

Jechidah, the Atma of Hindu philosophy — יחידה

Flame — להב

(?) Devotion of force — לז

38

Night Demon of 2nd Dec. ♋	אואל
He departed	אזל
Gehazi, servant of Elisha	גיחזי
A City in the Mountains of Judah	גלה
Innocent	זכאי
The palate	חיך
To make a hole, hollow; to violate	חל
Green	לח

39

To abide, dwell	זבל
Dew	טל
The Eternal is One	יהוה אחד
Angel of 3 P.	יחויה
Metathesis of יהוה	כוזו
He cursed	לט

40

Bildad	בלדד
Liberator; a title of Jesod	גואל
To cut off	גזל
A rope; ruin; to bind	חבל
Milk	חלב
The Hand of the Eternal	יד יהוה
To me, to mine	לי

π 41

Fecundity	אחלב
Ram; force; hence = a hero	איל
Night Demon of 1st Dec. ♍	אלוד
My GOD	אלי
Mother	אם
To fail, cease	בטל
Divine Majesty	גאואל
Terminus	גבול
To burn	גחל
Terror	הול
To go round in a circle	חגל
[Vide Ps. cxviii. & I.R.Q. 778]	יה יהוה

The Number of the letters of a great name of GOD terrible and strong, and of the Assessors of the Dead 42

Angel of ♈	איאל
Eloah, a name of GOD	אלוה
The Supernal Mother, unfertilized; see 52	אמא
Terror, calamity	בלהה
Loss, destruction	בלי
To cease	חדל
The World, Earth of Malkuth	חלד
My glory	כבודי

π 43

Great	גדול
To rejoice	גיל
Challah; to make faint. [Vide K.D. L.C.K. p. 346]	חלה
[Vide K.D. L.C.K. p. 151; see no. 340]	לביא
Hazel, almond	לוז

|5. 220 ÷ 5 44

Drops	אגלי
A pool, pond; sorrow	אגם
Captive, captivity	גולה
Angel ruling ♊	גיאל

Aquarius דלי

Blood דם

Sand: also horror. See Scorpion Pantacle in K. of S. and 10th Aethyr חול

A ram; ♈ טלה

Tet. in ? World. יוד הא וו הא [Vide K.D. L.C.K. p. 251]

Flame להט

Σ(1—9). The Mystic Number of Jesod 45

Intelligence of ♄ אגיאל

Adam אדם

The Fool אמד

Redemption, liberation גאולה

To grow warm הם

Heaven of Tiphareth זבול

Hesitated. [Vide no. 405] זחל

Spirit of ♄ זזאל

She who ruins חבלה

Tet. in Yetzirah יוד הא ואו הא

Greatly, strongly מאד

Yetzirah's 'Secret Nature' [Vide I.R.Q. xxxiv.] מה

46

A name of GOD אלהי

A female slave; cubitus אמה

Tin, the metal of ♃ בדיל

A dividing, sundering, separation הבדלה

Angel of 7 S. ההחאל

A ruiner חובל

Angel ruling ♉ טואל

Levi, Levite לוי

π 47

Foolish, silly. (Stultus) אויל

A weeping בכייה

Cloud; high place; waves; fortress במה

Angel ruling ♍ יואל

To clutch, hold חלט

48

Mercy גדולה

Angel of 2 W. והואל

A woman [vide K.D. L.C.K. p. 320]; strength; an army חיל

To grow warm; heat, fire; black; Ham, the son of Noah חם

Jubilee יובל

A star, planet; Sphere of ☿ כוכב

[Vide Ps. xciii. & Prov. viii. 22] מאז

The Number of Abra-Melin Servitors of Beelzebub. 7^2. ♀ √‾49

The Living GOD אל חי

Qliphoth of Geburah גולחב

Resembled; meditated; silent דמה

Intelligence of ♀ הגיאל

Drooping, being sick חולה

Strength חילא

Heat, fury (Ch.) חמא

A bringing forth, birth, nativity לידה

A measuring, measure מדה

Solve. [Vide no. 103] מוג

The Rod of Aaron מט

50

Red earth, the soil; Earth of Chesed אדמה

Closed, shut up אטם

Angel of 9 P. אלדיה

Jonah's Whale דג גדול

To ferment המה

Pains, sorrows חבלי

Unclean, impure טמא

58th ש ייל

2nd ש ילי

The sea ים

All, every כל

To thee לך

What?—Which? מי

51

Edom אדום

Terrible; Day Demon of 2nd Dec. ♏ אים

Ate; devoured אכל

Pain אן

Tumultuously (vide no. 451); to harass, perturb הום

Angel of 8 S. [Vide K. of S., fig. 52] יההאל

Failure נא

52

Father and Mother אבא ואמא

Supernal Mother אימא

Elihu = Eli Hua, "He is my GOD," who is the Holy Guardian Angel of Job in the Allegory אליהו

[Vide K.D. L.C.K. p. 134] אנא

A mare; brute animal, beast בהמה

Day Demon of 2nd Dec. ♐ בים

From all, among all בכל

The Son: Assiah's "Secret Nature" בן

Meditation, imagination, sin זמה

A desirable one; to desire חמד

A husband's brother יבם

Angel of Kether of Binah, and of Jesod of Binah יהואל

Tet. in Assiah יוד הה וו הה

A dog כלב

Angel of 4 C., and of 10 P. לאויה

53

The Number of Abra-Melin Servitors of Astarot and Asmodee

The stone that slew Goliath; a stone, rock אבן

Elihu. (Vide 52) אליהוא

The garden גן

Angel of 9 P. הזיאל

To defend, hide; a wall; the sun; fury חמה

The spleen טחול

A lover מאהבה

54

A basin, bowl, vessel. [Ex. xxiv. 6] אגן

Rest דמי

A Tribe of Israel; to judge, rule. [Vide K.D. L.C.K. p. 37] דן

Pertaining to summer חום

My flame; enchantments להטי
A bed; stick, rod מטה
To remove נד

Σ (1 – 10). The Mystic Number of Malkuth 55
Thief; stole גנב
Robbery, pillage גזילה
Silence. [For name of Angels, see Sohar Sch. V. Cap. 18] דומה
A footstool הדום
To swell, heave. [Vide no. 51] הים
To walk הלך
Knuckle; member, limb חוליא
The bride כלה
Noon; midday נגב
Ornament נה

56

Dread, terror אימה
He suffered אנה
Angel of 4 C. הייאל
Day יום
Beautiful נאה

57

Rim אבדן
Consuming אוכל
Wealth, an age, Time; Night Demon of 1st Dec. ♏ און
Formidable, terrible איום
We אנו
A breaking down, subversion, destruction ביטול
Built בנה
♓. [Fish (pl.); vide 7] דגים
Angel of 8 C. ווליה
Angel of 5 C. לוויה
Altar מזבח
The laying-by, making secret מחבוא

58

[Vide no. 499] אהבים
[Vide K.D. L.C.K. p. 69.] An ear אזן
Night Demon of 1st Dec. ♐ דאגן
My strength, power, might חילי
Love, kindness, grace; notariqon of Chokmah Nesethrah, the Secret Wisdom חן
Ruler of Water טליהד
Angel of 6 S. ייזאל
Angel of 3 P. לההיה
[Vide K.D. L.C.K. p. 69] נח

π 59

Brethren. [Referred to Lilith & Samael—K.D. L.C.K. p. 54] אחים
Heathen גוים
A wall חומה
Menstruata נדה

60

Tried by fire; a watch-tower בחן
Excellence, sublimity, glory, pride גאון
Constitution, tradition הלכה
To behold הנה
A basket טנא
Angel of 8 C. ילהיה

Vision מחזה

The Southern district נגבה

π 61

Master, Lord, Adon אדון

The Negative, non-existent; not אין

Towards, to thee אליך

I, myself אני

The belly בטן

Angel of 10 S. דמביה

Wealth הון

Angel of 6 C. יייאל

Habitaculum נוה

62

Healing אסא

Angel of 2nd Dec. ♈ בההמי

The sons בני

To commit; healing זנה

63

Abaddon, the Hell of Chesed אבדון

Dregs, roll; faeces (globular); dung גלל

Fed זון

The nose חוטם

Fervour חימה

Tet. in Briah יוד הי ואו הי

Briah's "Secret Nature" סג

$8^2 = 4^3 = 2^6$. ☿ $\sqrt{\ }\ \sqrt[3]{\ }\ \sqrt[6]{\ }$ 64

A sigh, groan, deep breath אנחה

Justice דין

(Din and Doni are twin Mercurial Intelligences in Gemini) דני

The golden waters מי זהב

[I.R.Q. xl. 996] מיזהב

Prophecy נבואה

Sphere of ♀ נוגה

Noach נוח

$\Sigma\{1 - (5 \times 5)\} \div 5$. The Number of Abra-Melin Servitors of Magot and Kore 65

Adonai אדני

Weasels and other terrible animals אוחים

The Palace היכל

Shone, gloried, praised הלל

To keep silence הס

Defective. [Vide K.D. L.C.K. p. 339] חזן

6th ש ללה

A door post מזוזה

A beating, striking מכה

[Vide K.D. L.C.K. p. 563] נהי

The Mystic Number of the Qliphoth, and of the Great Work. 66
$\Sigma(1—11)$

Food, victuals אכילה

The Lord thy GOD (is a consuming Fire). [Deut. iv. 24] אלהיך

A ship אניה

A trial, an experiment בחון

A wheel. [Called "Cognomen Schechinae"] גלגל

A City of Edom דנהבה

π 67

[Vide K.D. L.C.K. p. 57] אוני

The Understanding בינה

Night Demon of 3rd Dec. ♊ וינא

Zayin זין

Debased זלל

To embalm חנט

Angel of 3 C. יבמיה

68

Wise.—Intelliget ista? ויבן

To be wise חכם

Emptiness חלל

To pity חם

Ramus Tabernacularis לולב

69

A manger, stable; an enclosure אבום

Myrtle הדם

L.A. Angel of ♓ וכביאל

70

(A proper name) אדניה

Hush, be silent הסה

Wine יין

Night ליל

[Vide Ps. xxv. 14.] The Secret סוד

π 71

Thy terror אימך

Nothing; an apparition, image אליל

Silence; silent אלם

Night Demon of 1st Dec. ♒ אמדוך

Lead, the metal of Saturn; a plummet-line, level, water-level אנך

Vision חזון

A dove, pigeon יונה

A dove ינוה

Plenitude, fullness מלא

[72 × 3 = 216, אריה; vide K.D. L.C.K. p. 151.] There are 72 quinaries (spaces of 5°) in the Zodiac. The Shemhamphorasch or 'divided name' of GOD consists of 72 triliteral names, which by adding יה or אל give 72 angels. Vide Lib. DCCLXXVII 72

Adonai, transliterated as by Lemegeton, etc. אדונאי

Geomantic Intelligence of ♐ אדוכיאל

In, so, thus, then בכן

In the secret בסוד

And they are excellent, finished ויכלו

Kindness, mercy חסד

Tet. in Atziluth יוד הי ויו הי

Maccabee מכבי

Atziluth's "Secret Nature"—thickness, cloud; Aub עב

π 73

Demon-King of Hod, and Night Demon of 2nd Dec. ♒ בליאל

Gimel גמל

The Wise One חכמה

To trust in, shelter in חסה

A day of feast יום טוב

74

A leader, chief, judge דיין

Worn-out (? shameless) Beggars דכים
Ox-goad למד
A circuit; roundabout סביב
All the way, constantly עד

75

Hues, colours, complexions גווני
Lucifer, the Herald Star הילל
[Vide K. of S., fig. 53] יכדיאל
A lamenting, wailing יללה
The Pleiades כימה
Night; by night לילה
NUIT, THE STAR GODDESS נוית

76

Secret, put away; a hiding-place חביון
Rest, peace ניחח
Slave, servant עבד

77

Prayed בעה
The river Gihon. [Gen. ii. 13] גיחון
Overflowing. [Ps. cxxiv. 5] זידון
Towers, citadels מגדל
The Influence from Kether מזל
Strength; a he-goat עז

There are 78 cards in the Tarot. $\Sigma(1-12)$. The Mystic Number of Kether as Hua. The sum of the Key-Numbers of the Supernal Beard 78

Angel of 10 W. אומאל
Angel of Ra Hoor Khuit איואס
Briatic Palace of Chesed היכל אהבה
Angel of ♂ זמאל

The breaker, dream חלם
To pity חמל
To initiate חנך
Angel of 2 S. יזלאל
Angel of 1st Dec. ♉ כרמדי
Bread (Ps. lxxviii. 25) = חלם, by metathesis. [K.D. L.C.K. p. 500] לחם
Angel of 2 S. מבהאל
The Influence from Kether מזלא
Salt מלח
The name of a Giant עזא

π 79

Boaz, one of the Pillars of the Temple of Solomon בעז
Die גוע
Angel of 8 S. ומבאל
Jachin, one of the Pillars of the Temple of Solomon יאחין
3rd ש סיט
Conjunction, meeting, union עדה

80

Union; an assembling ועד
GOD of Jesod-Malkuth of Briah יה אדני
Foundation יסוד
Universal, general כלל
Throne. [Exod. xvii. 16] כס
מם

$9^2 = 3^4$. ☽ $\sqrt{}$ $\sqrt[4]{}$ 81

GODS אלים
I. [Ex. xxiii. 20] אנכי
Anger, wrath; also nose אף

Hearer of Cries; Angel of 6 P., and of 5 W. — יילאל

Night Demon of 2nd Dec. ♍ — כאין

Throne — כסא

Here, hither — פא

82

Angel of ♀ — אנאל

A prayer (Ch.) — בעי

Briatic Palace of Hod — היכל נוגה

Kindly, righteous, holy — חסיד

Laban; white — לבן

The beloved thing; res grata — ניחוח

π 83

Abbreviatura quatuor systematum — אביע

The drops of dew. [Job xxxviii. 28] — אגלי טל

Benajahu, son of Jehoiada — בנייהו

See 73 — גימל

A flowing, wave — גלים

Person, self; (Ch.) wing — גף

Consecration; dedicated — חנכה

Angel of 2 P. — לכבאל

To flee, put one's things in safety. [Jerem. vi. 1] — זוע

84

7×12; or $(2^2 + 3)(2^2 \times 3)$—hence esteemed by some

A wing (army), squadron; a chosen troop — אגף

[I.Z.Q. 699] — אההע

[Vide K.D. L.C.K. p. 71] — אחהע

Was silent — דמם

A dream — חלום

Enoch — חנוך

Knew — ידע

85

Boaz (is referred to Hod) — בועז

A flower, cup — גביע

Put in motion, routed — המם

Circumcision — מילה

The mouth; the letter פ — פה

86

A name of GOD, asserting the identity of Kether and Malkuth — אהיה אדני

Elohim. [Note masc. pl. of fem. sing.] — אלהים

Hallelu-Jah — הללויה

A rustling of wings — המולה

Geomantic Intelligence of ♑ — הנאל

[Vide I.R.Q. 778] — יה יהוה אדם

A cup: hence Pudendum Muliebre — כום

A blemish, spot, stain — מום

Angel of 10 C. — מיהאל

Plenitude — מלוי

87

[Vide K.D. L.C.K. p. 114] — אלון

A cup — אסוך

Angel of 1st Dec. ♓ — בהלמי

Blasphemed — גדף

Standards, military ensigns — דגלים

Determined — זמם

White Storks חסידה

Whiteness; frankincense; Sphere of ☽ לבנה

88

Redness; sparkling חכלל

To be hot חמם

Darkness חסך

A duke of Edom מגדיאל

Roaring, seething; burning נחל

π 89

Shut up גוף

Body גוף

Silence דממה

Angel of 9 S. מחיאל

90

Very silent דוממ

The Pillar, Jachin יכין

Water מים

Kings מלך

Wicker-basket סל

Night Demon of 2nd Dec. ♌ פוד

91

Σ(1—13). The Mystic Number of Kether as Achad. The Number of Paths in the Supernal Beard; according to the number of the Letters, כ = 11, etc.

A tree אילן

Amen. [Cf. 741] אמן

The Ephod אפוד

The "יהוה ארני", interlaced יאהדונהי

Angel of 4 S. כליאל

Archangel of Geburah כמאל

Food, fare מאכל

Angel מלאך

Daughter, virgin, bride, Kore מלכא

Manna מנא

A hut, tent סוכה

Pekht, 'extension' פאהה

92

Angel of 5 S. אניאל

Mud בץ

(Deut. xxviii. 58.) [Vide no. 572] יהוה אלהיך

Terror, a name of Geburah פחד

93

A duke of Edom. [Vide also Ezekiel xxiii.] אהליבמה

The sons of (the merciful) GOD בני אל

Incense לבונה

A disc, round shield מגן

Possession נחלה

Arduous, busy; an army צבא

94

Corpse גופה

The valley of vision גיחזיון

To extinguish דעך

Destruction. [Ps. l. 20] דפי

A shore חוף

A window חלון

A drop טפה

Children ילדים

95

The great Stone אבן גדלה

Angel of 2 W.—Daniel דניאל

Angel of 10 P. ההעיה

The waters המים

Multitude, abundance; Haman המן

Zabulon זבלון

Angel of 2nd Dec. ♌ זחעי

♂ מאדים

Journey מהלך

Queen מלכה

Selah. [Ps. xxxii. 5, 6, etc.] סלה

96

A name of GOD אל אדני

Chaldee form of אלהים אלהין

By day יומם

Praiseworthy; Angel of 7 W. ללהאל

Work מלאכה

The secret (counsel) of the Lord. [Ps. xxv. 14] סוד יהוה

π 97

Breeder, rearer; Day Demon of 1st Dec. ♊ אומן

Changeless, constant; the GOD Amon אמון

The Son of Man בן אדם

Archangel of Netzach האניאל

The appointed time זמן

To seize suddenly (rapere) חטף

A hand-breadth, palm. [1 Kings vii. 26—Ex. xxv. 25] טפח

A brick, tile לבינה

A building; an architect מבנה

Aquae EL Boni. ["Quicksilver," K.D. L.C.K. p. 442] מי אל הטב

98

A name of GOD הוא אלהים

Temporary dwelling. [Ex. xxxiii. 11] זמנא

Image; hid, concealed—pertains to Sol and the Lingam-Yoni חמן

To consume, eat חסל

White צח

99

The pangs of childbirth חבלי לידה

The Vault of Heaven; an inner chamber; wedlock, nuptial חופה

Clay of Death, Infernal Abode of Geburah טיטהיון

Cognition, knowledge ידיעה

10^2 $\sqrt{100}$

A day; the seas; the times. [Vide no. 1100] ימים

Vases, vessels כלים

The palm; the letter Kaph כף

An effort, exertion. [I.R.Q. 995] מדון

Mitigation of the one by the other מחי טבאל

π 101

Swallowed, destroyed אלע

A storehouse אסם

[Vide K.D. L.C.K. p. 147] אך

Angel of 4 C. מומיה

Archangel of ⊙ and △; Angel of 7 S.; Angel of Malkuth of Briah, etc. מיכאל

Kingdom; a virgin princess; esp. THE Virgin Princess, i.e. Ecclesia מלוכה

Gut; gut-string נימא

102

A white goose אווז לבן

Trust, truth, faith אמונה

Bela, a King of Edom; to possess; lands, government בעל

Concupiscibilis נחמד

Grace, pride, fame, glory; a wild goat צבי

π 103

Dust אבק

To guard, protect גנן

Loathed געל

Food, meat (Ch.) מזון

Oblation מנחה

Prophets נבאים

A calf עגל

104

Father of the mob, or of the multitude אב המון

Quarrel, dispute מדין

Personal (belongings), small private property סגולה

Sodom סדם

Giving up, presenting, remitting סולח

Trade; a fish-hook צדי

Σ(1—14) 105

To subvert, ruin, change הפך

Desert land: Earth of Netzach ציה

106

Attained דבק

Angel of 7 C. מלהאל

Fish; the letter Nun נון

Angel of 9 C. סאליה

Stibium פוך

Line, string, linen thread קו

π 107

An egg ביצה

Angel of Netzach of Briah וסיאל

Angel ruling ♌ עואל

$2^2 \times 3^3$: hence used as the number of beads on a rosary by some sects 108

The ears אזנים

The fruit of a deep valley באבי הנחל

Hell of Jesod-Malkuth גיהנם

A wall חייץ

To force, do wrong to חמס

To love very much חנן

To shut up, obstruct חסם

The middle חצי

To measure out; a decree; tall. (Masc. gender.) Cf. 113 חק

Angel L.T.D. of ♌ סגהם

A Giant: "the lust of GOD" עזאל

π 109

Day-demon of 2nd Dec. ♒ אסכוזדאי

Lightning בכוז

Quiet מנוחה

Music נגון

Angel of ♃ סחיאל

Circle, sphere עגול

צדירא

110

Father of Faith אב האמונה

Tectum coeli fabrilis sub quo desponsationes coniugum fiunt גג החופה

Resemblance, likeness דמיון

Cherubic Signs—♏ replaced by ♈ וטהץ

To embrace חבק

At the end of the days; the right hand ימין

A sign, flag, standard נס

Angel of 6 W. סיטאל

Kinsman עם

The Number of Abra-Melin Servitors of O.P.A.A. $\Sigma\{1—(6 \times 6)\} \div 6$. ☉ 111

Red. [Vide Gen. xxv. 25] אדמונא

A name of GOD אחד הוא אלהים

A thousand; Aleph אלף

Ruin, destruction, sudden death אסן

AUM אעם

Thick darkness אפל

Passwords of ...... יוד יהוה אדני

Mad מהולל

Angel of ☉ נכיאל

Common holocaust; an ascent עולה

A Duke of Edom עלוה

Title of Kether. (Mirum occultum) פלא

112

Angel of 2 C. איעאל

A structure; mode of building בנין

Was angry בנס

Sharpness חדק

Jabok. [Gen. xxxii. 22.] Note $112 = 4 \times 28$ יבק

The Lord GOD יהוה אלהים

Ebal עיבל

π 113

Likewise; the same. (Fem. gender.) Cf. 108 חקה

A giving away, remitting סליחה

A stream, brook פלג

114

Qliphoth of Jesod גמליאל

Tear (weeping) דמע

Gracious, obliging, indulgent חנון

Science מדע

Brains מוחון

115

Geomantic Intelligence of ♍ דמליאל

Here am I הנני

The heat of the day חום היום

To make strong; vehement, eager חזק

116

Doves יונים

Heaven of Chesed מכון

The munificent ones נדיבים

Primordial עילאה

117

Fog, darkness אופל
Guide; Duke אלוף

118

To pass, renew, change חלף
To ferment חמע
Strength; Chassan, Ruler of Air חסן
The High Priest כהן גדול

119

Lydian-stone אבן בוחן
Beelzebub, the Fly-GOD בעלזבוב
Weeping (subst.) דמעה
Night Demon of 2nd Dec. ♈ חאלף
Abominable פגול

$\underline{|15} = \Sigma(1-15)$:—ה being the 5th Path 120

Master בעל
Foundation, basis מוסדי
The time of the decree מועד
Strengthening מכין
Prophetic sayings, or decrees: "His days shall be";—hence Abra-Melin מלים
Velum מסך
Prop; the letter Samekh סמך
A name of GOD ען

11^2 $\sqrt{\ }121$

Vain idols אלילים
?Termination of Abr-amelim? אמילם
An end, extremity אפס

Emanated from אצל
Of whirling motions הגלגלים
Nocturnal vision חזוה די ליליא
Angel ruling ♒ כעאל
It is filled נמלא
Angel L.T.N. of ♒ עכאל

122

Vi compressa אנוסה
Revolutiones (Animarum) גלגולים

123

A name of GOD, אהה יהוה אלהים implying Kether—Chokmah—Binah, 3, 4, & 5 letters
War מלחמה
A blow, plague נגע
Pleasure, delight ענג
Laesio aliqualis, violatio פגם

124

An oak; hardness חוסן
Pleasure, delight; Eden עדן
Qliphoth of Chokmah עגיאל

5^3 $\sqrt[3]{\ }$ 125

Night Demon of 2nd Dec. ♓ דנמאל
[Vide S.D. v. 16] כפכה
Angel of 4 P. מנדאל

126

A widow אלמנה
Darkness אפילה
Day Demon of 1st Dec. ♉ גימיגין
A name of GOD יהוה אדני אגלא
Hospitality מלון

Horse סוס

On, a name of GOD [see 120], penalty of iniquity; "being taken away" עון

π 127

Material מוטבע

Angel of 5 P. פויאל

2^7 $\sqrt[7]{\ }$ 128

Eliphaz אליפז

Angel ruling ♒ אנמואל

To deliver, loose חלץ

Robustus gratia. [Vide K.D. L.C.K. p. 399] חסין

GOD, the Eternal One יהוה אלהינו

129

Pleasure [Gen. xviii. 12] עדנה

Delight, pleasure עונג

130

Deliverance הצלה

The Angel of redemption מלאך הגאל

Decrees, prophetic sayings מלין

Eye; the letter Ayin עין

The Pillars עמודי

Destitute עני

A staircase, ladder סלם

Angel of 5 C. פהליה

π 131

He was angry אנף

Nose אפים

Turn, roll אפן

Title of Kether מכוסה

Angel of 6 C. נלכאל

Samael; Qliphoth of Hod סמאל

Angel L.T.N. of ♍ססיא

Humility ענוה

132

To make waste בלק

Angel of 4 W. ננאאל

To receive קבל

133

[Vide I.Z.Q. 699] גיכק

Vine גפן

Angel of 5 S. חעמיה

The salt sea ים המלח

134

Burning דלק

135

Day Demon of 2nd Dec. ♋ גוסיון

Geomantic Intelligence of ♈ מלכדיאל

A destitute female עניה

The congregation. [Vide no. 161] קהל

[Vide K.D. L.C.K. p. 673] קלה

Σ (1—16). ♃ 136

Spirit of ♃ הסמאל

Intelligence of ♃ יהפיאל

The Avenging Angel מלאך הגואל

Fines, penalties ממון

A voice קול

π 137

A wheel אופן

The belly, gullet. [? Hebrew: vide K.D. L.C.K. p. 138] אסטומכא

An image, a statue. [Gen. xxviii. 22] מצבה

A receiving; the Qabalah קבלה

138

The Son of GOD בן אלהים

To smoothe, divide חלק

To leaven, ferment חמץ

To pollute חנף

Libanon. [Cant. iv. 11, 15] לבנון

He shall smite מחץ

Forehead מצח

π 139

Hiddekel, the eastern river of Eden הדקל

140

Kings; Angels of Tiphareth of Assiah, and of Netzach of Briah מלכים

141

Robust; oaken אמיץ

Gathered, collected אסף

Angel of 4 P. כוקיה

Precept מצוה

Trusty, steady נאמן

L.A. Angel of ♋ פכיאל

Prima קמא

142

Geomantic Intelligence of ♉ אסמודאל

Wickedness, destruction בליעל

A stranger; Balaam בלעם

Night Demon of 3rd Dec. ♌ בעלם

Delights (△ & ▽) מחמדים

143

The unshoeing חליצה

Running waters. [Cant. iv. 15] נוזלים

12^2 $\sqrt{\ }$ 144

A sandal סנדל

Anterius; the East; days first of the first קדם

The numerical value of the 13 Paths of the Beard of Microprosopus 145

The Staff of GOD. [Ex. xvii. 9] מטה האלהים

Inscrutable מעלה

Angel of 6 P. נממיה

A feast סעודה

146

The First Gate. [Vide K.D. L.C.K. p. 184] בבא קמא

Limit, end; boundless סוף

The world; an adult עולם

The Four Names in the Lesser Ritual of the Pentagram; 147

viz.: יהוה אדני אהיה אגלא

148

A name of GOD אהיה יה יהוה אלהים

Angels of Hod in Assiah and Briah בני אלהים

Glutton and drunkard. [Deut. xxi. 20] זולל וסובא

To withdraw, retire חמק

Scales; ♎ — מאזנים
Victory — נצח
Flour, meal — קמח

π 149

The living GODS. [Cf. 154] — אלים חיים
A beating of the breast; a noisy striking — הספד

150

Ariolus. [K.D. L.C.K. p. 53] — ידעוני
A walking shoe — נעל
Thine eye. [Vide I.R.Q. 652] — עינך
Nest — קן

π 151

אהיה spelt in full — אלף הה יוד הה
"TETRAGRAMMATON of the GODS is One TETRAGRAMMATON" — יהוה אלהים יהוה אחד
Night Demon of 3rd Dec. ♈ — מאלף
The Fountain of Living Waters. [Jer. xvii. 13] — מקוה
A standing upright, stature — קומה
Jealous — קנא

152

Benjamin — בנימן
The Bringing-forth One — המוציא
Residence, station — נציב

153

Σ (1—17)

L.A. Angel of ♎ — חדקיאל

154

Elohim of Lives. [Cf. 149] — אלהים חיים

155

Adonai the King — אדני מלך
The faithful friend — דוד נאמן
The beard (correct). [S.D. ii. 1, et seq.] — דקנא
Letters of the Cherubic signs — ו:ט:נ:צ
Angel of 2nd Dec. ♑ — יסיסיה
"The Concealed and Saving"; Angel of 6 W. — עלמיה
A seed — קנה

156

12 × 13, the number of letters in each 'tablet of Enoch'

The Tabernacle of the congregation. [Lev. i. 1] — אהל מועד
A viper — אפעה
BABALON, THE VICTORIOUS QUEEN. [Vide XXX Aethyrs: Liber CDXVIII] — באבאלען
Angel of Hod of Briah — הסניאל
Joseph [referred to Jesod] — יוסף
Angel of 1st Dec. ♏ — כמוץ
נעול
A bird — עוף
"Crying aloud"; the name of a King of Edom — פעו
Zion — ציון
Limpid blood — צלול

π 157

The setting of the Sun — דמדומי חמה
Was angry, enraged; anger — זעף

Lingam זקן
The beard. [Vide S.D. ii. 467, and no. 22] זקן
Occult מופלא
Female; Yoni נקבה
Angel of 9 S. ענואל
A Duke of Edom קנז

158

Arrows חיצים
To suffocate חנק
Balances. [Ch.] מאזנין

159

Surpassing Whiteness. [Vide 934] בוצינא
Point נקדה

[Vide I.R.Q. 652] 160

Angel of 3 S. הקמיה
Silver כסף
Fell down. Decidit נפל
A rock, stone סלע
A tree עץ
A Duke of Edom פיכן
Lay, fell. [Ez. iii. 8] פניך
Image צלם
Cain קין

161

The heavenly man; lit. the 'primordial' or 'exalted' man אדם עילאה
The Congregation of the Eternal קהל יהוה
קינא

Nine Paths of the Inferior Beard; 14 + 15 + ... + 22 = 162

Son of the Right Hand; pr. n. of Benjamin בנימין
Day Demon of 1st Dec. ♐ גלאסלבול
Angel ruling ♏ סוסול

π 163

[Vide no. 361, a numerical Temurah of 163] הוא אלהים אדני
Woman, wife נוקבה

164

רצע
Ye shall cleave חדבקים
Outer; civil, as opposed to sacred. [Vide K.D. L.C.K. p. 342] חיצון
The Pillars עמדים

165

Strength. [Ez. iii. 8] חזקים
"To make them know." [Ps. xxv. 14] להודיעם
Nehema נעמה
NEMO. [Name of M.T.] Angel of 3 W. עממיה
An assembly עצה

166

A King of Edom בעלחנו
Reus mulctae. [Vide K.D. L.C.K. p. 498] חייב ממון
Heaven of Geburah מעון
Night Demon of 3rd Dec. ♏ נפול
Native land of Job עוץ
The Most High עליון

π 167
The Unnameable One (a demon) אסימון
Fetters. [Job xxxvi. 8] זיקים

168
Parentes Superni אבא ואמא עילאה

13^2 $\sqrt{\ }$ 169
The accentuator טעמים

170
The Wand; (David's) Staff מקל
Cloud ענן

Σ (1—18) 171
Principium emittens מאציל
Emanating from נאצל
Angel L.T.N. of ♒ פלאין
"The Face of God"; name of an angel פניאל

172
Cut, divided בקע
He affected. [Not written] יעצב
Clusters; grapes ענבים
The heel, the end. [Mic. vii. 20] Jacob עקב

π 173
Lighten mine eyes גל עיני
Day Demon of 3rd Dec. ♒ גצף

174
Torches לפידים
Splendor ei per circuitum נוגה לו סביב

$\Sigma\{1-(7\times 7)\}\div 7.$ ♀ 175
Suction יניקה
Duplicity מכפלה
A slipping, falling נפילה

Spirit of ♀ קדמאל

176
An advisor, counselling יועץ
To eternity לעולם
Illegitimate פסול

177
Dominus Dominorum ארון האדונים
The Garden of Eden גן עדן
To cry out for help זעק
Angel L.T.D. of ♑ סגדלעי
Plenitude of plenitudes מלוי המלוי

178
The lower part, the loins חלצים
Good pleasure, choice, decision, will חפץ
Quicksilver כסף חי

π 179
Ligatio עקדה

180
A spring, fountain. [Cant. iv. 15] מעיין
The front part פנים

π 181
Vicious, faulty פסולה

182
Deus Zelotes אל קנא
Outcry, clamour זעקה
Layer of snares, supplanter; Jacob יעקב
King of the Gods מלאך האלהים
Passive [as opposed to מחקבל = active] מקביל

183

184

Ancient time; eastward נקדל

185

186

A stone of stumbling; a rock to fall over. [Is. viii. 14] אבן נגף

An increase מוסף

Praefecti ממונים

A place מקום

Back of the Head; an ape; the letter Qoph קוף

187

Angels of Chokmah, and of Chokmah of Briah אופנים

Lifted up זקף

[K. of S., Fig. 52] סופיאל

188

Jaacob. [Vide K.D. L.C.K. p. 443] יעקוב

The Master of the Nose בעל החוטם

189

Fons obseratus. [Cant. iv. 11] גל נעול

The Ancient among the ancient סבא דסבין

Σ (1—19) 190

Ubi perrexit Angelus ויסע ויבא ויט

Internal פנימי

Corona florida prominens צי״ץ

The side or flank; rib צלע

First devil. V. Porta Coelorum Fig. XVI קמטיאל

The end, appointed time. [Dan. xii. 13.] [Vide no. 305] קץ

π 191

Countenance אנפין

[Vide K.D. L.C.K. p. 143] אפסים

Night Demon of 1st Dec. ♈ פאכין

A box, chest; a repository קופה

192

Poisonous wind, Simoon זלעפה

Ye shall cleave in TETRAGRAMMATON. [Vide no. 220] חדבקים ביהוה

π 193

194

Righteousness, equity, justice: the Sphere of ♃. [Vide K.D. L.C.K. p. 656] צדק

195

A flock מקנה

Visitation פקודה

14^2 $\sqrt{}$ 196

Mare Soph. [Vide K.D. L.C.K. p. 435] ים סוף

The crown, summit, point קוץ

π 197

El Supernus אל עליון

[Vide K.D. L.C.K. p. 71] אנא חטא עם הזה

198

Victories נצחים

π 199

A giving freely; Ἐλεημοσύνη צדקה

200

Alae. [Vide K.D. L.C.K. p. 483] כנפים

A branch ענף

A bone עצם

Archetypal קדמון

Belonging to the Spring קיץ

A sling; a casting-net קלע

Divination קסם

201

Light (Ch.) אר

202

To make empty בקק

Pure; a field; son בר

Elevatio זקיפה

Apertures נקבים

L.A. Angel of ♏ סאיציאל

Many, much רב

203

Initials of the Trinity: אבר
אב:בן:רוח

Passed away, perished; feather, wing; (it. membrum et quid. genitale) אבר

To lie in wait ארב

A well, spring באר

Created ברא

Exotic, foreign גר

204

Commencement of the name Abra-Melin אברא

Foreign resident; race S.; an age (Ch.) דר

The righteous צדיק

205

Day Demon of 2nd Dec. ♈ אגאר

Splendrous אדר

Mighty; hero גבר

Mountain הר

206

Assembly; area אדרא

Hail ברד

Spake; word; cloud דבר

They of the World ימי עולם

207

♏, a scorpion אגראב

Lord of the Universe אדון עולם

Light. Cf. 9 and 11. Aur is the balanced Light of open day אור

Limitless אין סוף

Ate ברה

Walled, fenced גדר

That which cuts. [Vide no. 607] הבר

The Elders. [Deut. xxi. 19] זקנים

Melt, fuse זקק

The Crown of the Ark זר

Grow great רבה

208

Feather אברה

A cistern בור

Bowed גהר

To make strife, contend גרה

Hagar הגר

To kill הרג

Abominable זרא

Jitzchak. [Vide K.D. L.C.K. p. 266] יצחק

Multitude רוב

209

Chief Seer or Prophet (hence Abra-Melin)	אבראה
Reward, profit, prize	אגרה
To delay, tarry; behind (prep.)	אחר
Way	ארח
10th Spirit of Goetia.	בואר
Dispersed	בזר
Sojourned, dwelt	גור
Honour; a King of Edom; the Supernal Benignity	הדר
Oppressed	זרב

Σ(1—20) **210**

Adam Primus. [Vide no. 607]	אדהר
Day Demon of 1st Dec. ♋	בזאר
Choice	בחר
Pass on, fly	ברח
To decide, determine	גזר
To dwell; circle, cycle; generation	דור
To conceive	הרה
A joining of words; incantations; to conjoin; a brother	חבר
A sword	חרב
Angel of 1st Dec. ♑	מסנין
Naaman	נעמן
[Vide ΘΕΛΗΜΑ]	נ:ע:ץ
Punctata	נקודים

π **211**

[Worthy]	אבחר
A lion	ארי
Strong	גבור
A flash; lightning	הארה
A girdle	חגר
A flood; Jeor	יאר
"Fear," the fear of the יהוה (i.e. wonderment)	ירא

212

Great Voice	דבור
Night Demon of 1st Dec. ♑	האור
Splendour; to enlighten	זהר
To spread out; harlot; golden	זרה
To enclose; secret chamber	חדר

213

Strong, powerful, mighty	אביר
Calx	גיר
[I.R.Q. 234 (?)]	הדדר
Slaughter	הרגה
Loaded	וזר
To be strange; a stranger	זור
The Supernal Mercy of GOD	חסד עלאה דאל
Nubes Magna	ענן גדול

214

A girdle	אזור
Angel of 1st Dec. ♈	זזר
Whiteness	חור
Came down	ירד
Air; Spirit; wind; Mind	רוח

215

Eminent; a Prince. [Ps. viii. 1]	אדיר
A path, narrow way	אורח
Posterior; the reversed part	אחור
A rising; to rise "as the Sun," give light	זרח

To encompass. [Vide K.D. L.C.K. p. 340] חזר

6^3 $\sqrt[3]{\ }$ 216

Night Demon of 1st Dec. ♎ אוראוב

Lion אריה

The middle Gate. [Vide K.D. L.C.K. p. 184] בבא מציעא

Courage גבורה

Oracle דביר

Blood of grapes דם ענבים

Dread, fear יראה

Profound. [Ps. xcii. 6] עומק

Anger, wrath רוגז

Latitude רוחב

217

The air אויר

Temple, palace בירה

Food בריה

A bee דבורה

The navel טבור

Angel ruling ♐ מויעסאל

Angel L.T.N. of ♏ סהקנב

Controversia Domini ריבה

218

Ether. [Vide K.D. L.C.K. p. 55] אוירא

The Creative World בריאה

The benignity of Time חסד עולם

The Moon ירח

Multitude רבוי

Arcana רזיא

Odour, a smell ריח

219

Mundatio, mundities טהרה

The Number of Verses in Liber Legis R 220

The Elect בחיר

Heroina; Augusta; Domina גבירה

Ye shall cleave unto TETRAGRAMMATON. [*Not* written] חדבקים ליהוה

Clean, elegant טהור

Giants. [Fully written only in Num. xiii. 33] נפילים

Left-handed Svastika, drawn on the square of ♂ given by Agrippa. Cf. 231 221

Long ארך

Angel of 10 S. מנקאל

222

Urias אוריה

"Unto the Place." [Ex. xxiii. 20] אל המקום

Whiteness הוורה

Goodly mountain. [Ex. iii. 25] הר טוב

Now, already; K'bar, "the river Khebar"; Day Demon of 3rd Dec. כבר

I will chase ראויה

π 223

224

Male (Ch.) דכר

Walk, journey; The PATH דרך

Principia emanandi חוקקי

Effigurata חקוקי

Union יחור

15^2 √ 225

[Vide K.D. L.C.K. p. 234] גזרדיא

226

Profound, hidden; the North. [Vide K.D. L.C.K. p. 666] צפון

π 227

Long, tall ארוך

A piscine, pond; [Blessing, Prov. x. 22] ברכה

Remember; male (sacred Phallus—Vide S.D. ii. p. 467) זכר

Damna. [Vide K.D. L.C.K. p. 569] נזיקין

228

First-born בכור

Blessed! ברוך

Ruler of Earth כרוב

The Tree of Life עץ חיים

π 229

230

Astonishment הכרה

[Vide K.D. L.C.K. p. 153] מקיף

Fasciata עקודים

Angel of 2nd Dec. ♍ ראידיה

Hod, 42-fold Name in Yetzirah. [Vide Liber 777, Col. xc. p. 18] יגלפזק

Σ (1—21). Right-handed Svastika, drawn on Sq. of ♂ 231

Prolonged; grew long אריך

Male דכורא

Sum of the Four Ways of spelling TETRAGRAMMATON in the Four Worlds 232

Geomantic Intelligence of ♓ אמניציאל

Ruler of Fire אראל

Equivalent to יהי אור, Fiat Lux. [Vide K.D. L.C.K. p. 55] יה אויר

Let there be Light! The Mystic Name of Allan Bennett, a Brother of the Cross and Rose, who began this Dictionary. יהי אור

π 233

Memento זכור

The Tree of Life. [Vide no. 228] עץ החיים

234

Night Demon of 3rd Dec. ♒ דכאוראב

235

Archangel of Chesed, and Angel of Chesed of Briah צדקיאל

236

Angel L.T.N. of ♈ ספעטאוי

A handful קומץ

237

Angel of 3 C. ראהאל

238

Dominus Mirabilium אדון הנפלאוה

Rachel רחל

π 239

Azrael, the Angel of Death אזראל

Iron ברזל

The lot גורל

Angel of 3rd Dec. ♉ יכסגנוץ

240

Myrrh מר

Plagae Filiorum Hominum. [I.e. Succubae, K.D. L.C.K. p. 562] נגעי בני אדם

Prima Germina נצנים

Angel of 1st Dec. ♒ סספם

Cash; counted out, paid down פקודים

High, lofty רם

π 241

L.A. Angel of ♑ סמקיאל

242

Ariel, Angel of Air אריאל

Recollection זכירה

243

Abram. [Vide 248] אברם

Created (he them). [Gen. v. 2] בראם

Learned, complete. To finish, bring to pass (Ch.) גמר

A bone; to destroy גרם

244

Angel of 7 P. הרחאל

To be insensible; in deep sleep, in trance. [Vide no. 649] רדם

245

Adam Qadmon אדם קדמון

Gall, bile מרה

Spirit of God רוח אל

246

Angel of 3 S. הריאל

Myrrh מור

Vision, aspect מראה

מרגג

Angel L.T.D. of ♉ ראידאל

Height, altitude רום

247

Angel L.T.N. of ♑ אלויר

To overwhelm (Ps. lxxvii. 18); a flood זרם

A light מאור

Night Demon of 1st Dec. ♉ ראום

Sensus symbolicus רמז

248

Abraham. [Vide 243 and 505, 510. Discussed at length in Zohar] אברהם

The Three that bear witness, above and beneath, respectively. אדם the Spirit, the Water, and the Blood; א being Air (Spiritus), ד standing for דם Blood, and מ being both Water and the initial of מים, water. For ברא see 203 אדם + ברא

Uriel or Auriel, archangel of Earth, and angel of Netzach; = "The light of God" אוריאל

In vision. [Vide K.D. L.C.K. p. 553] במראה

Gematria גמרה

Wine; bitumen; an ass (from "to disturb") חמר

Mercy; womb רחם

A lance רמח

249

L.A. Angel of ♉ ארזיאל

Night Demon of 2nd Dec. ♎ גמור

Fear, terror מגור

250

The living GOD of the Worlds; or, of the Ages אלחי העולמים

[The South.] Midday דרום

Habit, action (Ch.) מדור

π 251

Fir, cedar ארן

The angel Uriel: "Vrihl," i.e. Magical Force. [Vide Lytton's "Coming Race," andAbra-Melin—forehead Lamen] וריהל

Angel of 10 W. רייאל

252

Serpent's den מאורה

253

Σ (1—22)

Proselytes גרים

Matred; who symbolizes the Elaborations on the side of Severity מטרד

254

Angel of 3rd Dec. ♒ גרודיאל

Geomantic Intelligence of ♎ זוריאל

An ass חמור

A mark, aim מטרה

A solemn promise, vow נדר

Spikenard. [Cant. iv. 14] נרד

A spear רומח

Merciful רחום

255

Night Demon of 3rd Dec. ♐ אנדר

Burdensome; with difficulty חומרא

The East מזרח

A river, stream. [Gen. ii. 10] נהר

Cantatio elata רנה

256

$16^2 = 4^4 = 2^8 = 256$ $\sqrt{\ }$ $\sqrt[4]{\ }$ $\sqrt[8]{\ }$

Aaron אהרן

Tidings (Ps. lxviii. 12); a saying, speech. [Vide K.D. L.C.K. p. 128] אמירה

The Sons of the Righteous בני צדק

[See no. 705] [Vide K.D. L.C.K. p. 20] מפולמין

The Spirit of the Mother רוח אמא

Aromatarius רוכל

π 257

The Ark ארון

A Magician חרטם

"To His fearers." [Ps. xxv. 14] ליראיו

The White Wand מקל לבנה

Terribilis Ipsa נורא

258

The red light אור אדום

Hiram (King of Tyre) חירם

Mercy רחמי

259

Throat גרון

Nitre נטר

Reuben ראובן

$\Sigma\{1-(8\times 8)\}\div 8.$ ☿ 260

Intelligence of ☿ טיריאל

The Concealed טמירא

I.N.R. [Vide 270] י:נ:ר:

Exaltabitur ירים

A vineyard כרם

Ineptos et profanos לפסילים

[Ps. viii. 1] מה אדיר

Declined סר

To gather, draw together צמצם

261

He bound; an obligation, a prohibition אסר

Abhorrence, abomination. [Is. lxvi. 24] דראון

262

Lofty; Aaron אהרון

Severities גבוראן

Terrible הנורא

Conclavia חדרים

Eye to eye. [I.R.Q. 645] עין בעין

π 263

Angel of 2nd Dec. ♒ אבדרון

Angel of 2nd Dec. ♓ אורון

Geomantic Intelligence of ♏ ברכיאל

Gematria גמטריא

Pained גרם

264

Emanantia. [Vide K.D. L.C.K. p 338] חקוקים

Jarden. [Vide K.D. L.C.K. p. 455] ירדן

Footprints (foot's breadth). [Deut. ii. 5] מדרך

A straight row. [Vide K.D. L.C.K. p. 455] סדר

Channels, pipes רהטים

||6 265

Architect אדריכל

Broke down הרם

A cry of the heart; anguish, anxiety צעקה

266

Chebron חברון

Termination of Qliphoth of 12 Signs ירון

Contraction צמצום

267

Illicit, forbidden אסור

Geomantic Intelligence of ♌ ורכיאל

Currus; Vehiculum; Thronus מרכבה

Nasiraeus נזיר

268

Stones of the sling אבני הקלע

π 269

By-ways ארחין

Father—Spirit—Son בן רוח אב

Angel of Binah of Briah כרוביאל

270

Levers, bars בריחים

I.N.R.I. Initials of: Jesus Nazaraeus Rex Judaeorum; Igni Natura Renovata Integra; Intra Nobis Regnum deI; Isis Naturae Regina י:נ:ר:י:

Ineffabilis; and many other sentences. Vide Crowley Coll. Works Vol. I. Appendix

π 271

Earth (Ch.); whence = low, mean — ארע

Angel of 2nd Dec. ♐ — והרין

[Vide no. 256, אמירה] — לאמר

272

Earth — ארעא

To consume, injure; brutish — בער

Percussione magna — מכה רבה

The evening: an 'Arab,' i.e. a person living in the West — ערב

Day Demon of 3rd Dec. ♐ — רינוו

273

The stone which the builders rejected [Ps. cxviii. 22] — אבן מאסו הבונים

The Hidden Light — אור גנוז

Four — ארבע

Rebuked — גער

Took away — גרע

274

Paths — דרכים

275

[Vide K.D. L.C.K. p. 72] — אחוריים

Domicilium pulchrum. [Vide K.D. L.C.K. p. 395] — דירה נאה

Fluvius Iudicii. [Vide K.D. L.C.K. p. 117] — יאר דין

Qy. Sruti "scripture" — סרטו

Σ (1—23) 276

Angel L.T.N. of ♎. [Vide Liber 777, p. 29] — אחובראין

A Cithara — כנור

Night Demon of 1st Dec. ♌ — כרוכל

The Moon — סיהרא

π 277

To sow, propagate; seed, semen — זרע

[For multiplying.] [*Not* written. Vide K.D. L.C.K. pp. 157 and 837] — למרבה

Angel of 3rd Dec. ♌ — סהיבר

Gratia, benevolentia — רעוא

278

Angels of Jesod, and of Binah of Briah—Cherubim — כרובים

Passing over — עובר

The Material World — עולם המוטבע

279

Leprosy. [Vide K.D. L.C.K. p. 495] — סגירו

[7 × 40, the Squares on the walls of the Vault. See Equinox I. 3. p. 222] 280

Qliphoth of ♑ — דגדגירון

A record (Ch.) — דכרון

Angel of the Wood of the World of Assiah — יער

The Letters of Judgment: the 5 letters having a final form — כ:מ:נ:פ:צ:

Archangel of Malkuth — סנדלפון

Citizenship — עיר

[Vide S.D. 528] פר

Terror רף

π 281

A crown—Ashes אפר

Attire; adorned פאר

282

Angels of Briah, and of Malkuth of Briah אראלים

Spirit of Lives רוח חיים

π 283

Aurum inclusum זהב סגור

Memoriale. [Vide no. 964] זכרון

That goes on foot רגלים

284

Geomantic Intelligence of ♊ אמבריאל

The small area of an enclosed garden ערוגה

285

286

High, lofty מרום

287

Pars Azymorum אפיקומן

Night Demon of 3rd Dec. ♉ ופאר

Little זעיר

Geomantic Intelligence of ♋ מוריאל

288

Vindication ביעור

Day Demon of 1st Dec. ♍ זאפר

Breeding, bearing; offspring. [Vide K.D. L.C.K. p. 313] עִיבור

[Vide K.D. L.C.K. p. 571] רפח

17^2 √289

Apertio. [Vide no. 537] פטר

Particulare פרט

290

Thine enemy ערך

291

Torrentes Aquarum אפיקי מים

(He) treasured אצר

Earth: in particular, the Earth of Malkuth ארץ

Qy. spotted? נמרא

Adhaesio; adhaerens; princeps סירכא

L.A. Angel of ♒ צכמקיאל

292

A young bird. [Deut. xxii. 6] אפרוח

Gold בצר

A medicine, drug רפואה

π 293

Day Demon of 2nd Dec. ♉ צארב

294

Purple ארגמן

Pertaining to Autumn חורפ

Melchizedec. [Gen. xiv. 18] מלכיצדק

295

Curtain, canopy; vault. [Ps. civ. 2] יריעה

Eyelids כנפי העין

[Vide K.D. L.C.K. p. 498] פטור

296

Of the Earth. [Vide no. 992] הארץ

Incurvens se כורע

Rigorose procedere; fumarie; rock. [Vide K.D. L.C.K. pp. 459, 663] צור

297

Thesaurus; gazophylacium; conservatorium אוצר

A name of GOD attributed to Geburah אלהים גבור

A secured house; a fortified castle ארמון

A City of Edom בצרה

The Throne; a Name of Briah כורסיא

Nuriel נוריאל

The neck צואר

298

Amen, our Light אמן אור

Son of the GODS בר אלהין

White צחר

Pathetic appeals; commiserations רחמים

299

Angel of 2nd Dec. ♋ רהדץ

Σ (1—24) 300

Khabs am Pekht אור בפאהה

Vide Beth Elohim. Dissert. II. Cap. 1. A spelling of אלהים in full. אלף למד הי יוד מם

Formation יצר

Profundities מעמקים

God of Chesed, and of Hod of Briah; *Temura* of יהוה מצפצ

Incircumcisus ערל

Separation פירוד

The Spirit of GOD. [Vide Gen. i. 3] רוח אלהים

301

"My Lord, the faithful King"; a name of GOD אדני המלך נאמן

Fire אש

A candlestick מנורה

302

Earth of Hod ארקא

To cut open, inquire into; Dawn בקר

L.A. Angel of ♊ סראיאל

Hath protected קבר

To putrefy רקב

303

Did evil; putrefaction באש

304

A species of gold חרוץ

Green דש

Geomantic Intelligence of ♒ כאמבריאל

White קדר

305

Dazzling white light אור צח

Tender herb. [Gen. i. 11] דשא

Netzach, 42-fold Name in Yetzirah. [Vide Liber 777, col. xc.] הקממנע

Yetzirah: "formation" יצרה

A curving, bending כריעה

The end of days, appointed time. [Dan. xii. 13] קץ הימין

A lamb שה

השׁ

306

Father of Mercy אב הרחמים

Merciful Father אב הרחמן

A woman, wife; virago אשה

Honey דבש

Domina. [Vide K.D. L.C.K. p. 528] מטרונא

[Vide K.D. L.C.K. p. 571] ניצוצין

Coldness; pertaining to Winter קור

Angel of 6 S. רהעאל

Malo-Granatum רימון

π 307

Night Demon of 2nd Dec. ♏ וריאץ

Ribkah רבקה

308

Daybreak בוקר

Sparsor זרקא

Investigation חקר

A harsh, grating sound חרק

Approaching, near קרוב

Ice קרח

309

A leper. [Vide K.D. L.C.K. p. 495] מוסגר

Angel of 2nd Dec. ♉ מנחראי

Strepitus cordis, mussitatio, susurratio, rugitus שאגה

Field, soil, land שדה

310

To trample on, conquer דוש

To govern, bind חבש

Formed. [I.R.Q. 227] ייצר

The Initials of Idra Rabba Qadisha. [Each Letter is half of each Letter of כחר, Kether] י:ר:ק:

Is, are; essence, being יש

Leo iuvenis כפיר

Habitations מדורין

π 311

Man: but vide K.D. L.C.K. p. 83 איש

Angel of 9 C. עריאל

Archangel of Binah צפקיאל

Archangel of Air; Angel of ☿, and of Chokmah of Briah, etc. רפאל

Rod. [Ps. xxiii. 4] שבט

26 × 12, the Twelve Banners 312

Night Demon of 3rd Dec. ♎ וישו

To renew; hence = a new moon, a month חדש

West. [Cf. 272] מערב

π 313

Angel of 1st Dec. ♍ אננאורה

314

[Vide K.D. L.C.K. p. 275] הלל נמור

Metatron, Archangel of Kether, and Angel of Tiphareth of Briah. [When spelt with י after מ it denotes Shekinah] מטטרון

Out of the way, remote — רחוק

Shaddai: "The Almighty"; a name of GOD — שדי

315

Ice; crystal — גביש

Gullet — ושט

Formation — יצירה

Visio Splendoris — מראה הנוגה

Gomorrah — עמרה

The Number of Servitors of Abra-Melin Sub-Princes — 316

Day Demon of 3rd Dec. ♈ — ושאגו

Ligatus — חבוש

Green — ירוק

JESU — ישו

A bundle, handful — עומר

Visitans iniquitatem — פוקד עון

Aporrhea — קוטרא

[Vide K.D. L.C.K. p. 54] — שאיה

To worship, bow down — שחח

π 317

Day Demon of 3rd Dec. ♉ — ואלפר

[Vide Ps. xcvii. 11] — זרעם

Arida — יבשה

Iron (Ch.) — פרזל

Hoariness — שיבה

318

Labrum lavacri, et basio eius — כיור וכנו

A copse, bush — שיח

319

320

"Boy," Name of Enoch, and of Metatron — נער

A Duke of Edom. [Vide Liber 777, p. 22] — עירם

The friends — רעים

L.A. Angel of ♐ — סריטיאל

321

Angel of 3rd Dec. ♋ — אלינכיר

Angel L.T.D. of ♍ — לסלרא

Angel of 9 W. — שאהיה

Qliphoth of ♉ — אדימירון

322

Lamb — כבש

Angel L.T.N. of ♐ — לברמים

Linea media — קו האמצעי

323

Long-absent brother — אח רחוק

Qliphoth of ♒ — בהיסירון

Angel of 3rd Dec. ♈ — סטנדר

18^2 $\sqrt{\ }$324

See no. 314; it denotes Shekinah — מיטטרון

Σ (1—25). ♂ 325

Spirit of ♂ — ברצבאל

Intelligence of ♂ — גראפיאל

Angel of 2nd Dec. ♏ — נינדוהר

Need, indigence — צריכה

326

Jesus. [Note the letters of TETRAGRAMMATON completed by ש 300 q.v. the Spirit of GOD] — יהשוה

Vision שאייה

327

Day Demon of 2nd Dec. ♍ בוטיש

[Vide K.D. L.C.K. p. 461] ישיבה

Night Demon of 3rd Dec. ♑ כיצאור

328

4 Princes + 8 Sub-Princes + 316 servient to Spirits

Angel of 3 W. החשיה

To steam; darkness. [Vide K.D. L.C.K. p. 280] חשך

329

Angel of 1st Dec. ♎ טרסני

330

Boundary, terminus; crosspath מצר

Revolution; hurricane, tempest סער

Error: fault של

π 331

Ephraim אפרים

Arbor magna. [Gen. xxi. 33] אשל

Archangel of Chokmah רציאל

332

Lux Ardoris אור היקוד

Night Demon of 3rd Dec. ♓ אנדרומאל

A Duke of Edom. [Vide Liber 777, p. 22] מבצר

Locus vacuus. [Vide K.D. L.C.K. p. 551] מקום פנוי

333

Qabalah of the Nine Chambers איק בכר

Choronzon. [Vide Dr Dee, & Lib. 418, 10th Aire] חורונזון

Snow שלג

334

A still, small Voice. קול דממה דקה [1 Kings, xix. 12]

335

Dies Mali ימי רעה

The KING above the King of Kings. [Vide K.D. L.C.K. p. 537] מלך מלכי המלכים

Ordering, disposition מערכה

336

An attack; a request, petition שאלה

Night Demon of 1st Dec. ♊ שבכיר

π 337

Ruler of Earth פורלאך

Hell of Supernals; a City of Edom; the Place of Askings. [Vide Liber 777, p. 23] שאול

338

To cast down חלש

He hath pardoned (or, subjected) יכבוש

A garment; clothing לבוש

To send forth שלח

339

340

Angel of 3rd Dec. ♐ יסגדיברודיאל

"Ferocious" lion ליש

Uncus focarius—fire-shovel מגרופיא

Book ספר

Pares; a word written on the wall at Belshazzar's feast. [Vide Dan. v. 28] פרס

There; The Name שם

The sum of the 3 Mother letters; א, מ, and ש 341

Yesterday	אמש
Guilty, damned	אשם
A red cow	פרה אדומה
Expansum; sepimentum; diaphragma	פרסא
The Name (Ch.)	שמא

342

Coctio	בישל
Perfume	בשם
Night Demon of 2nd Dec. ♉	פוכלור
A blaze, flame	שלהבה

7^3 $\sqrt[3]{343}$ 343

"And GOD said." [Gen. i. 3]	ויאמר אלהים
A sweet smell	זפרון

344

A plantation, garden. [Cant. iv. 13]	פרדם

345

Di Alieni	אלהים אחרים
GOD Almighty	אל שדי
"In that also"—referred to Daath	בשגם
The NAME	השם
Lioness. [Vide K.D. L.C.K. p. 501]	לישה
5th ש	מהש
Moses. [See 543, numerical Temurah of 345]	משה
Dominator	שולט
Shiloh	שילה
He was appeased. [Esther, vii. 10]	שככה

346

A spring; spring water	מקור
A water-pipe; channel	צנור
Good pleasure; the Will-power	רצון

π 347

Palanquin (Cant. iii. 9); Bridal bed; nuptial chariot. ["thalamus seu coelum fabrile sub quo copulantur nubentes"]	אפריון

348

Five; to set in array	חמש
Third King of Edom	חשם

π 349

350

Day Demon of 3rd Dec. ♌	אליגוש
A sapphire (Ex. xxviii. 18). [Vide K.D. L.C.K. p. 19]	ספיר
Ophir; a young mule; dust of the Earth	עפר
The Horn; head	קרן
Vacuum	ריקם
Intellectus	שכל

Σ (1—26) 351

Man	אנש
Angels of Malkuth; burnt or incense offering; "The flames"	אשים
Hiram-Abif, a cunning artificer at the Temple of Solomon; the hero	חירם אביף

of a famous allegory prophetical of FRATER PERDURABO

♄ in ♌. Angel ruling 1st Dec. ♌, that was rising at the birth of FRATER PERDURABO — לוסנהר

Moses the Initiator — מושה

Elevatus — נשא

352

The Exalted Light — אור מעלה

Long of Nose; i.e. Merciful; a title of the supreme GOD — ארך אפים

Lightning — ברקים

An approach — קרבן

π 353

Goshen — גשן

The fifth — חמשה

The Secret of TETRAGRAMMATON is to His fearers. [Ps. xxv. 14] — סוד יהוה ליראיו

Delight, joy — שמחה

354

Grew fat; anointed — דשן

Heptaeteris intermissoria — שמטה

355

Thought; idea — מחשבה

Year — שנה

356

The Cedars of Lebanon — ארזי לבנון

Expiationes. [Vide K.D. L.C.K. p. 612] — כפורים

A young mule — עופר

Ophra, mother of Goliath — עורף

Spirits of the living — רוחין דחיין

357

42-fold Name, Geburah in Yetzirah — כגד יכש

Iniquity — נושא

358

Shame — גשנה

Shiloh shall come — יבא שילה

Messiach, the Messiah — משיח

Nechesh, the Serpent that initiated Eve — נחש

(Taking the three ה's in אהיהוה as concealing the Mothers, we get I. A. Ω. &) — אשיאום

π 359

Angel of 3rd Dec. ♓ — סטריף

The Sacred Wind — שטים

Satan. [Vide K.D. L.C.K. p. 235] — שטן

360

The Messiah — המשיח

[Vide K.D. L.C.K. p. 235] — הנשה

[Vide K.D. L.C.K. p. 235] — השנה

Angels of Jesod of Binah — ישים

Seeking safety; Angel of 7 W. — מהשיה

Tonitrus — רעמים

Shin; a tooth — שין

Two — שני

19^2. 3 6 1		$\sqrt{\ }$361
God of Malkuth	אדני הארץ	
"Men"; "impurities"	אנשי	
Foundations. [Ch.]	אשין	
The Mountain Zion	הר ציון	
Ruler of ♄	כשיאל	
Angel of 7 P.	מצראל	
		362
		363
The Almighty and Ever-living GOD	שדי אל חי	
		364
Lux Occulta	אור מופלא	
Satan	השטן	
Demons	שדין	
Opposition; resistance	שטנה	
		365
Earth of Tiphareth	נשיה	
An uncovering, exposing	פריעה	
		366
Night Demon of 2nd Dec. ♑	אנדראלף	
		π 367
Black [scil. of eye-pupil]: middle: homunculus	אישון	
Day Demon of 3rd Dec. ♊	פאיכורן	
		368
The Spirit of the GODS of the Living	רוח אלהים חיים	
$\Sigma\{1-(9\times 9)\}\div 9$. ☾		369
Spirit of ☽. [Vide Liber 777, p. 19]	חשמודאי	
The World of Briah	עולם הבריאה	
Angel of 2nd Dec. ♊	שהדני	
		370
A foundation, basis	עקר	
Creation	עש	
Salices rivi. [Lev. xxiii. 40]	ערבי נחל	
Zopher	צפר	
White lead, tin	קסטרא	
To rend, cut, blame, curse	קרע	
Green. [Vide S.D. p. 104]	רענן	
Salem	שלם	
		371
Sinistrum	שמאל	
		372
Aqua spherica	אספירכא	
Agni	כבשים	
An oven, furnace	כבשן	
♏	עקרב	
Herbage, grass	עשב	
Seven	שבע	
		π 373
		374
		375
Generally and specially	כלל ופרט	
Solomon	שלמה	
A City of Edom	שמלה	
		376
Dominator	מושל	

Esau, father of the men of Edom. עשו (Ad-om, Adlantes*)

A bird צפור

Peace. [Refers to Kether] שלום

377

Nervus luxatus; Vena Ischiatica. [Gen. xxxii. 32] גיד הנשה

Seven שבעה

Σ (1—27) 378

'In peace' בשלום

Pruna ignita; Chaschmal חשמל

Iuramentum. [K.D. L.C.K. p. 695] שבוע

π 379

Abschalom אבשלום

[The sum of the letters of TETRA-GRAMMATON multiplied severally by those of Adonai; (י × ה)+(נ × ו)+(ד × ה)+(א × י)] = :ן:ש:כ:י 380

Difficulty, narrowness מצרים

Pain, trouble, misery עצב עצבון

Thick darkness, fog ערפל

[Vide no. 370] קסטירא

Heaven of Hod רקיע

381

Clamour, prayer שועה

382

Day Demon of 3rd Dec. ≏ צאראץ

π 383

Iuramentum. [Vide K.D. L.C.K. pp. 67, 695] שבועה

384

385

Angel of 2nd Dec. ≏ מהרנץ

Assiah, the World of Matter עשיה

Gloria cohabitans [vide K.D. L.C.K. p. 711]; the Glory of God שכינה

Lip שפה

386

Jesus ישוע

Tongues לשון

Tziruph, a table of Temurah צירוף

387

388

The hardest rock. [Ps. cxiv. 8] חלמיש

To search out diligently חפש

Table; bread שלחן

π 389

390

Gen. v. 2 זכר ונקבה

Retrorsum מפרע

Alens, pascens פרנס

Heaven שמים

Oil שמן

Night Demon of 2nd Dec. ♊ שיץ

---

* Refers to a theory that the 'Kings of Edom' who perished before the creation of Adam were a previous race inhabiting 'Atlantis.'

391

Salvation, help ישועה

The Inscrutable Height. [Kether] רום מעלה

392

Aromata בשמים

Habitaculum משכן

393

394

Table. [Vide no. 388] שולחן

395

Robustus (virilitas) Iacob אביר יעקב

The Heavens השמים

Oil השמן

Manasseh מנשה

Second משנה

Judge שופט

396

Day Demon of 1st Dec. ♏ יפוש

π 397

Lux Interna. (Title of Kether) אור פנימי

398

Fifty חמשים

Book חפשי

Angel L.T.D. of ♈ סטרעטן

Pride; esp. of gait שחץ

399

שגופי

20^2 $\sqrt{}$400

To use Magic, witchcraft כשף

Erudiens, a title of Yesod משכיל

Sensus literalis. [Vide K.D. L.C.K. p. 12] פשוטה

(He had) Karnaim (in his hand) קרנים

Angels of Chesed of Briah שיככים

Sack שק

π 401

Cursing ארר

Essence; "the" את

402

Sought into, or after בקש

Tested, purified ברר

Filia בת

A spider עכביש

Paths שבילין

403

The Stone; Sapphire אבן ספיר

404

Law, edict דת

Almond; to watch, be awake; to hasten שקד

405

Fearful things, serpents of the dust. [Job] זחלי עפר

[Cf. no. 227, זכר.] Phallus; urethra. [Vide Deut. xxiii. 2] שפכה

Σ (1—28) 406

THOU: a name of GOD אתה

Vulgar, common; plebeian עם הארץ

Leg שוק

Alterations שנוים

The letter Tau תו

407

Signum אות

The Precious Oil שמן טוב

408

Lapis sapphirinus אבן הספיר

Haec זאת

[Vide Deut. x. 10, 15] חשק

π 409

Patriarchs אבהתא

Fathers אבות

One (fem.) אחת

Ha-Qadesh ; Holy Ones הקדש

410

Liberty ; a swallow דרור

Visions, imaginations. [Dan. iv. 2] הרהר

Metzareph מצרף

The Tabernacle משכן

Sacred ; Saint קדוש

Holy קודש

He heareth שמע

Hod, 42-fold Name in Yetzirah שקי

411

Elisha אלישע

Briatic Palace of Tiphareth היכל רצון

Fundamenta Terrae מוסדי ארץ

Habitaculum משכנא

Ordo temporum סדר זמנים

Desolation, emptiness. (Expresses first root of all good) תהו

412

The letter Beth בית

New. (Ch.) חדת

Jesus GOD יהשוה אלהים

White whorl צמר לבן

Celsitudo superna רום עליון

A longing for תאוה

413

414

Azoth, *the* fluid. A + Z (Lat.) + Ω (Grk.) + ת (Heb.). Initial and final in 3 tongues אזות

The Limitless Light אין סוף אור

Meditation. [Ps. xlv. 4] הגות

Going forth. [Vide no. 770] משוטטים

415

The Voice of the Chief Seer אבראה דבר

Sister אחות

The Holy One ; Sodomite הקדוש

Work מעשה

Angel of 10 C. עשליה

416

Thought, meditation הרהור

A pledge משכון

417

Olive זית

Arca. (Noah's Ark) תיבה

(Note 4 + 1 + 8 = 13)

418

Boleskine בולשכין

Peccatum. (Est femina Lilith impia) חטאת

Kheth, a fence חית

Servans misericordiam נוצר חסד

"The Word of the Aeon." [Vide Liber 418] מאכאשאנה

אבראהאדאברא

418=בית הא=חית, the House of Hé: because of I.Z.Q. 694; for ה formeth כ, but ח formeth יוד: each = 20. Thus is Abrahadabra a Key of the Pentagram.

Also, by Aiq Bkr, it = 22: and 418 = 19 × 22. 19 = Manifestation; it therefore manifests the 22 Keys of R.O.T.A.

The first meaning is ABRAH DBR, = The Voice of the Chief Seer.

It resolves into Pentagram and Hexagram as follows:

1st *method.*

R A B / A / A☆A / DH / B A R — forms 12 and 406, הוא

and אתה [406 = תו], where AThH = Microprosopus, and HVA = Macroprosopus. The Arcanum is therefore that of the Great Work.

2nd *method.*

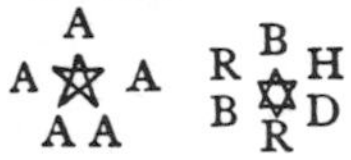

A / A☆A / A A — R B H / B✡D / R — Here BHR = 207 = אין סוף אור, etc., and DBR = Voice ("The Vision and the Voice"); thus showing, by Yetziratic attribution, the Three Wands—Caduceus: Phoenix: Lotus. Note always אבר are the three Supernals.

3rd *method.*

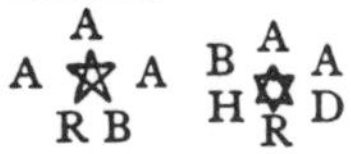

A / A☆A / R B — B A A / H✡D / R — give 205 + 213; both mean "Mighty," whence Abrahadabra is "The Word of Double Power." AAB show AB : AIMA : BN, viz., Amoun : Thoth : Mout. By Yetziratic Method, H:D:R: are Isis : Horus : Osiris. (Also, for H:D:R:, vide I.R.Q. 992.)

Dividing as 3 and 8, we get △ of Horus dominating the Stooping Dragon, ארר יאו; also—

from R A B (triangle) we get A—B / A—D and A—H / R—A

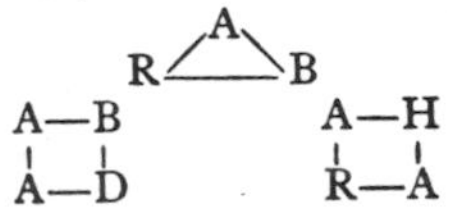

8 = דד, Love, and 207 = אור, Light; 8 × 207 = 18, which is equivalent to חי, Living; further, 297 = 23 × 9 = חיה, Life: hence, Licht : Liebe : Leben.

Again, 418 = את + יאו, = 21 + 397, q.v. דבר and 678 = 6 + 7 + 8 = 21. 2 × ב + 2 × ר + ד = 32. The Five different letters represent Amoun : Thoth : Isis : Horus : Osiris. They (A + B + R + H + D) add to 212 (q.v.).

Finally, א is the Crown, ב the Wand, ד the Cup, ה the Sword, ר the R.C.

See Equinox, V and VII, for further details.

π 419

Serpent: the letter Teth טית

Sodom and Gomorrah סדם + עמרה

420

It was היתה

Dolium, vas חבית

Vapour, smoke עשן

Pacifica שלמים

רצפים

π 421

Angel ruling ♑ כשויעיה

Angel ruling ♓ פשיאל

422
The Vast Countenance אריך אנפין
Linea Flava (quae circumdat Mundum) קו ירוק

423
[Ex. xxvii. 10, 11.] לווי העמורים [Vide K.D. L.C.K. p. 420]

424
Angel L.T.N. of ♉ טוטת

425
[Vide no. 1175] הגזית
[Vide K.D. L.C.K. p. 208] נעשה
Auditus שמיעה

426
Servator; salvator מושיע
Medium תוך

427

428
The Breakers-in-pieces; the Qliphoth of Chesed געשכלה
The Brilliant Ones; Angels of Chesed, and of Tiphareth of Briah חשמלים
Iuraverunt נשבעו

429
A lion's whelp. [Gen. xl. 9] זור אריה
Judgment, equity משפט
שגעון

430
Nephesch, the animal soul of Man נפש
Covered with mist; darkness, twilight נשף
Membra פרקים
Full Title of Ninth Sephirah. "The Righteous is the Foundation of the world" צדיק יסוד עולם
Concealed שפן
Tohu v-Bohu; see Gen. i. תהו ובהו
Dew תל

π 431
Notariqon נוטריקון

432
Eventide shadows צללי ערב
Earth of Jesod תבל

π 433
Day Demon of 1st Dec. ♌ בלאת
Merit זכות

434
The Lord of War. [Ex. xv. 3] איש מלחמה
The letter Daleth; door דלת

435 Σ (1—29)
Deceived התל
[Vide K.D. L.C.K. p. 156] משפטו

436
Tutor, curator; praefectus; administrator אפטרופס
Angel L.T.D. of ♏ ביתחוי
Hoschanah הושענה
"Σαταvâς." [Vide K.D. L.C.K. p. 505] שטן עז
[Vide K.D. L.C.K. p. 505; 723 & 701, nos. 9, 10; also at שבירה] שעטנז

437

Balm; the balsam tree אפרסמון

438

The whole (perfect) stone. [Deut. xxvii. 6] אבן שלימה

π 439

Exilium גלות

Angel L.T.N. of ♊ עוגרמען

440

Collaudatio. [Vide K.D. L.C.K. pp. 90, 729] תהלה

The Great Dragon; means "curls." [I.R.Q. 834; vide 510] תלי

Irreproachable; perfect תם

21^2 $\sqrt{\ }441$

Cerva אילת

Truth; Temurah of אדם, by Aiq Bekar אמת

A live coal גחלת

Day Demon of 2nd Dec. ♌ לריאר

Angel L.T.D. of ♓ רמרא

442

Termini Terrae אפסי ארץ

π 443

A virgin; a city. ♍ בתולה

Goliath גלית

444

The Sanctuary מקדש

Damascus דמשק

The total value of the Single Letters; ה, ו, ז, ח, ט, י, ל, נ, ס, ע, צ, and ק 445

Number of Stars in the Northern hemisphere 446

Destruction; death מות

Pison פישון

Tali pedum קרסולים

447

Initials of the Three Above and the Three Beneath. [Vide 248] דמר רבא

448

Excelsa במות

π 449

Lux fulgentissima אור מצוחצח

Cloak טלית

450

Tabulae לוחות

[Vide K.D. L.C.K. p. 508] מדות

The Fruit of the Tree פרי עץ

Transgression פשע

Beneplacitum termino carens; Arbitrum illimitatum רצון באין גבול

Inhabitans Aeternitatem שוכן עד

Craftiness, cunning שעלים

The Dragon תן

451

The Essence of Man את האדם

Mortis מיתא

Angels of Tiphareth שנאנים

The Abyss תהום

452

[Vide no. 552] חמדת

The crop; the maw קרקבן

453

Behemoth בהמות

The Animal Soul, in its fullness; i.e. including the Creative Entity or Ego, Chiah — נפש חיה

454

Sigillum — חותם

The "Holy Ones"; Consecrated catamites kept by the Priesthood — קדשים

455

456

Formido maxima — אימתה

The Mountain of Myrrh. [Cant. iv. 6] — הר המור

Paries — כותל

Crura — שוקים

The Fig-tree and fruit — תאנה

π 457

Olives — זתים

458

A covenant; an engagement; a betrothed — חתן

Contusores; cloudy heavens; Heaven of Netzach — שחקים

459

460

[Vide K.D. L.C.K. p. 371] — טנתא

Qliphoth of ♊ — צללד מירון

"Holy unto TETRAGRAMMATON." [Ex. xxxix. 30] — קדש ליהוה

π 461

[Vide K.D. L.C.K. p. 539] — אדנות

Robustus, validus, asper, horridus, rigidus — איתן

462

Terra Superna (est Binah) — ארץ עליונה

A path — ניתב

Profundum Celsitudinis — עומק רום

π 463

Day Demon of 3rd Dec. ♍ — באתין

Pillar of Mildness—paths, ג, ס, and ת — גסת

Crystal, glass — זכוכית

A rod of almond — מטה השקד

The Special Intelligence. [I.Z.Q. 264, et seq.] — תבונה

Caps, crowns, diadems — תגין

Precatio — תחנה

464

465

Σ (1—30)

A kiss; a little (or, sweet) mouth — נשיקה

466

Skull — גלגלת

Renes — כליות

The World of Formation — עולם היצירה

Simeon — שמעון

π 467

[Vide S.D. 33] — גלגלתא

468

Angel of 3rd Dec. ♊ — ביתון

469

Trabeationes ligaturae illarum — חשוקיהם

470

Eternity. (Literally, a cycle of cycles) דור דורים

Angel of 8 S. נתהיה

Pure Wool עמר נקי

Period of time; Time עת

Solum; fundus קרקע

471

Palatia היכלות

Mount Moriah. [2 Chron. iii. 1] המוריה הר

472

Was terrified בעת

473

The Three Persons. [ATH: HVA: ANI coalesced] אתהואני

Skull גולגלתא

Molitrices טחנות

474

Knowledge. [Vide K.D. L.C.K. p. 252, et seq.] דעת

(Plural)—Wisdom חכמות

The Testimony within the Ark עדת

A ram, he-goat; a prepared sacrifice עתד

Angel L.T.D. of ♋ רעדר

475

[Vide no. 473.] In Golgotha בגולגלתא

476

Domus Iudicii; Curia; Consistorium iudiciale בית דין

477

478

Cranium, calvaria גולגולת

The Lesser Countenance, Microprosopus זעיר אנפין

Hagiographa כתובים

π 479

Molentes טוחנות

480

Lapides inanitatis אבני תוהו

[Vide K.D. L.C.K. p. 252] דעות

Lilith, Qliphoth of Malkuth לילית

[Vide K.D. L.C.K. p. 252] עדות

Malkuth, 42-fold Name in Yetzirah עית

481

בעונת

Hills גבעות

Reus mortis חייב מיתא

Annulus טבעת.

482

A looking-glass, mirror אספקלריא

483

Ferens iniquitatem נושא עון

22^2 $\sqrt{\ }$484

485

Filia scaturiginum. [Is. x. 30, "Daughter of Gallim"] בת גלים

Mockeries [Job xvii. 2. Vide 435] התלים

486

A name of GOD יהוה בחכפה ימד ארץ

Foundations יסודות
Azymum fractum מצה פרוסה
A King of Edom עוית
Angel of 8 P. נהתאל

π 487

488

Ianua, ostium פתח
Qliphoth of Kether תאומיאל
Ye shall worship תעבודו

489

Retribuens; rependens retributionem משלם גמול

490

The giving. [Vide no. 1106] מתן
Fine flour, meal סלת
Perfect תמים
Binah, 42-fold Name in Yetzirah תץ

π 491

Nutrix אמנת
Angel of 4 W. ניתאל

492

493

The Name given in Deut. xxviii. 58; without את=92, q.v. את יהוה אלהיך

494

Galea salutis כובע הישועה
An apple תפוח

495

Similitudo hominis דמות אדם
Gift מתנה

496

Σ (1—31)

Leviathan לויתן
Malkuth מלכות
A small bundle צרור

497

Nutrix אומנת
Gemini; ♊ תאומים

498

Briatic Palace of Geburah היכל זכות

π 499

Cerva amorum. [Prov. v. 19, "a loving hind"] אילת אהבים
Busy, arduous; an army; 'hosts' צבאות

500

The humerus כתף
Kimelium aureum מכתם
Princeps שר
A Duke of Edom תימן

501

Asher; blessedness אשר
Fortis; fortia, robusta אתנים
The head ראש
Flesh; Night Demon of 1st Dec. ♓ שאר
Schechinah Superior שכינה עילאה
Likeness, similitude תמונה

502

To tell glad tidings; flesh, body בשר
To cut בתק

ג ר ש ☿ The Cup of the Stolistes π 503

Expelled, cast forth גרש

504

Sought for דרש

505

Sarah; Principissa. [Vide 510 & cf. 243 & 248] שרה

506

אבגיתץ

[Vide no. 1196] כפות

Bovis α′ sinistra; an ox; Taurus. [Vide K.D. L.C.K. p. 99.]—♉ שור

507

That which causes ferment; yeast שאור

508

Daybreak; black שחר

π 509

Bridge גשור

510

Sensus allegoricus. [Vide K.D. L.C.K. p. 12] דרוש

Rectitudo, aequitas recta; rectilineum ישר

The head ריש

Song שיר

Sarai. [Vide 505] שרי

Draco; see 440 תנין

511

עתיאל

The HEAD רישא

[Vide K.D. L.C.K. p. 463] שורה

$8^3 = 2^9$ $\sqrt[3]{\ }\ \sqrt[9]{\ }$ 512

Adhaesio, cohaesio דבקות

Angel of 3rd Dec. ♎ שחדר

513

514

[Vide K.D. L.C.K. p. 213] חקות

515

Possessio sine angustiis נחלה בלי מצרים

Minister iudicii שוטר

Phylacterium תפלה

516

Lucus. [Vide K.D. L.C.K. p. 168] אשירה

Personae פרצופין

517

Qliphoth of ♉. [Vide no. 321, & Liber 777] ארימירון

The good gift, i.e. Malkuth מתנה טובה

Occultae. [Vide 417] פלאות

Confractio. [Vide K.D. L.C.K. p. 698, et seq.] שבירה

518

519

Day Demon of 2nd Dec. ♊ ברבטוש

520

Tears דמעות

Legitium כשר

π 521

Ignis descendens אש יורד

Angel of 2 P. ושריה

Nudatio candoris מחשוף הלבן

522

π 523

524

525

The LORD of Hosts, a name of GOD referred to Netzach יהוה צבאות

526

Superliminare משקוף

527

528 $\Sigma(1-32)$

√ 529 23^2

Affatura ollaris cum iusculo dulci ציקי קדירה

Day Demon of 3rd Dec. ♋ שיטרי

530

The Rose חבצלת

Voices קלת

Tekel, a word of the 'writing on the wall' at Belshazzar's fabled feast תקל

531

532

533

Heaven of Jesod of Malkuth טבל וילון שמים

King of Terrors מלך בלהות

534

A certain Name of GOD קלדשק

535

536

A white cloak טלית לבנה

Sphere of the fixed stars מסלות

The World of Assiah, the 'material' world עולם העשיה

537

Emanatio; Atziluth, the Archetypal World אצילות

Medulla spinalis חוט השדרה

Apertio uteri פטר רחם

538

Daughter of the Voice.—Echo. [The Bath Qol is a particular and very sacred method of divination] בת קול

539

540

Lumbi; the upper part מתנים

π 541

Israel ישראל

542

543

"Existence is Existence," the NAME of the Highest GOD אהיה אשר אהיה

544

Apples. [Cant. ii. 5] תפוחים

545

Aper de Sylva חזיר מיער

546

Sweet מתוק

P's; a watchman שומר

Custodi שמור

L.A. Angel of ♈ שרהיאל

π 547

548

Qliphoth of ♈ בעירירון

Night Demon of 3rd Dec. ♋ הצגנת

A Name of GOD, יהוה אלוה ודעת referred to Tiphareth

Qliphoth of ♎ עבירירון

549

Moral מורגש

Ventus turbinis רוח סערה

550

Aquila; decidua. [Vide K.D. L.C.K. p. 600; connect with no. 496, Malkuth] נשר

A rod of iron. [Ps. ii.] שבט ברזל

L.A. Angel of ♌ שרטיאל

Principes שרים

Dragons. (Restricted.) [Ps. lxxiv. 13] תנינם

551

552

Desiderium dierum חמדת ימים

553

Draco magnus תנין גדול

554

Day Demon of 2nd Dec. ♓ מרחוש

555

Obscurity עפתה

556

Mark, vestige, footstep רשימו

Sharon. [Cant. ii. 1] שרון

π 557

The First ראשון

558

559

560

דרושים

Waters of quiet מי מנוחות

Puncta נקודת

A Duke of Edom תמנע

Dragons תנינים

Σ (1—33) 561

Cain אתקין

Concealed Mystery דצניותא

562

Primordial ראשונה

π 563

Lotio manuum נטילת ידים

Angel of 1st Dec. ♊ סגרש

564

Lapis capitalis אבן הראשה

[I.R.Q. 941.] ויהי האדם לנפש חיה "And the Adam was formed into a living Nephesh"

Sphere of Malkuth חלם יסודות

565

Parvitatio קטנות

Praetoriani שוטרים

566

A valley; a plain ישרון

Puncta נקודות

[SMK + VV + DLTh, SVD = a secret, spelt in full] ס:ו:ד:

The Shadow of Death; Hell of Netzach צלמות

Redintegratio, configuratio, depositio, conformatio, restoratio, restitutio — תיקון

567

Firstborn — ראשוני

568

π 569

Fingers — אצבעות

570

Naphtali — נפתלי

Lectus — ערש

Ten — עשר

Heads — רישין

Concussion, earthquake — רעש

[Vide K.D. L.C.K. p. 691] — רשע

Gate; the Door — שער

π 571

The mountains of Zion — הררי ציון

Balance — מתקלא

572

A chastening GOD. [Deut. xxviii. 58.] [ך counted as final] — יהוה אלהיך

Jeschurun — ישורון

He was touched. [I.R.Q. 1117] — יתעצב

Active — מתקבל

Day Demon of 1st Dec. ♓ — פורפור

573

574

Chaldee. [Hath a general meaning of movement. S.D. p. 87] — ירחשן

575

Beerschebha, Fons Septenarii. [2 Sam. xxiv. 7—Gen. xxi. 31.] [Vide K.D. L.C.K. p. 183] — באר שבע

"And the GODS said, Let there be LIGHT" — ויאמר אלהים יהי אור

24^2 √ 576

Wands — מקלות

The tenth — עשור

π 577

The Concealed of the Concealed; a name of GOD most High — טמירה דטמרין

578

579

Media nox — חצות לילה

Qliphoth of Netzach — ערב זרק

Sons of Adam — תענוגים

580

Rich — עשיר

Ancient — עתיק

"Le bouc émissaire"; shaggy, hairy. [Levit. xvi. 22] — שעיר

Angel of Fire — שרף

581

The Ancient One — עתיקא

Barley — שעורה

582

583

584

585

The GODS of Battle (lit. of Hosts); the Divine Name of Hod אלהים צבאות

[Vide K.D. L.C.K. p. 386] תקיעה

586

War-trumpet שופר

587

Day Demon of 1st Dec. ♒ פוראש

588

589

Viror. [Vide K.D. L.C.K. p. 15] אב לשון ענף

590

Rib. [Gen. ii. 22] צלעת

591

592

π 593

594

The Stone of Israel. [Gen. xlix. 24] אבן ישראל

Σ (1—34) 595

596

Jeruschalim ירושלים

597

598

Our iniquities עונותינו

π 599

600

Mirabilia, vel occulta sapientiae פליאות חכמה

Peniculamentum, fimbria peniculata ציצית

A knot, ligature קשר

Red שרק

Six; marble שש

π 601

602

Lux simplicissima אור פשוט

Brightness; splendores צחצחות

Extremitates קצוות

603

Qliphoth of ♌ שלהבירון

604

Congeries; epistola אגרת

Israel Senex ישראל סבא

605

Magnificentia אדרת

[Vide K.D. L.C.K. p. 226] גברת

606

Let them bring forth ישרצו

Ipseitas, seu ipsa essentia. [Vide K.D. L.C.K. pp. 571, 631] עצמות

Nexus, ligature קשור

Ruth רות

A turtle-dove תור

π 607

Adam Primus אדם הראשון

The mountains of spices. [Cant. viii. 14] הרי בשמים

A span, palm. [Lit. "the little finger"] זרת

608

The last Gate. [Vide K.D. L.C.K. p. 184] בבא בתרא

[Vide K.D. L.C.K. p. 640] חתר

609

610

Numulus argenteus אגורת

Citrus, malum citrum; (lust and desire). [Vide K.D. L.C.K. p. 178] אתרוג

Tenth מעשר

611

"The Fear" of the LORD. [Ps. cxi. 10] יראת

The Law. (Occasional spelling) תורה

612

(The covenant)—Day Demon of 1st Dec. ♑. [Ps. xxv. 14] ברית

The number of the Divine Precepts π 613

The Quintessence of Light את האור

Moses, our Rabbi משה רבינו

[Vide K.D. L.C.K. p. 179] תריג

614

615

616

Qliphoth of ♓ שימירון

The Five Books of Moses; the Law on Sinai. Cf. Tarot תירו

π 617

"Mighty acts." (Plur. of "Strength.") [Ps. cvi. 2] גבורות

Columnae Nubis et Ignis עמודי האש והענן

A King of Edom רהבית

618

Contentiones ריבות

π 619

Novissimum אחרית

620

Chokmah, Binah, Daath; the first descending triad חכמה בינה ודעת

The Crown: Kether כתר

Angel of 3rd Dec. ♍ משפר

[Vide Ps. xxxi. 20] צפנת

The Doors שערים

[Temurah of בבל] ששך

621

Mucro gladii אבחת חרב

By-paths. [Vide no. 1357] אורחות

[Vide I.R.Q. 234] 622

Blessings ברכת

Profunda Maris. [Samael et Uxor Eius] מצולות ים

Latitudines; Rechoboth רחובות

623

Barietha; Doctrina extranea; conclusio extra Jeruschalem facta ברייתא

624

His Covenant. [Ps. xxv. 14] ובריתו

Liberty חירות

Qliphoth of ♐ נחשירון

$25^2 = 5^4$ $\sqrt{\ }\ \sqrt[4]{\ }$ 625

The Mountain of Ararat הרי אררט

626

The tenth portion עשרון

627

628

Light. [Spelt in full, with ו as וא] א:ו:ר:

Blessings ברכות

629

The great trumpet שופר גדול

630

Angel L.T.D. of ♊ סעריש

The Holy Spirit רוחא קדישא

שליש

Angels of Geburah, and of Kether of Briah שרפים

π 631

Concealed Mystery דצניעותא

632

633

Light. [Spelt in full, when ו = וו] א:ו:ר:

[Gen. v. 2] זכר ונקבה בראם

634

635

636

Qliphoth of ♍ צפרירון

637

Day Demon of 3rd Dec. ♑ פורנאש

Day Demon of 1st Dec. ♎ שאלוש

638

639

The Tree of Knowledge עץ הדעת

640

The Cup of Consolations כוס תנחומים

Third. [Vide K.D. L.C.K. p. 719] שליש

Sun; Sphere of ☉ שמש

Palm of the hand; palm-tree תמר

π 641

Dema purpureum אמרת

Angel of 9 W. ירתאל

"Lights"; defective. [S.D. 142] מארת

642

Day Demon of 2nd Dec. ♏ פורשון

π 643

Light. [Spelt in full, when ו = ויו] א:ו:ר:

Severities of TETRAGRAMMATON גבורות יהוה

The Cup of Benedictions כוס של ברכה

$(12 \times 13 \times 4) + 20$ = number of letters in the five tablets of Enoch. [Vide Equinox VII] 644

645

A King of Edom משרקה

646

Elohim. [ם counted as Final] אלהים

Licitum מותר

Rejoicing משוש

π 647

Lights מארות

648

649

Trance, deep sleep. [Vide no. 244] תרדמה

650

Nitre נתר

651

Temurah תמורה

652

π 653

654

655

656

A rose, lily. [Vide no. 706] שושן

Delight, joy ששון

A furnace תנור

657

Angel of 3rd Dec. ♏ ותרודיאל

Zelbarachith; ♌ זלברחית

658

π 659

660

Scintillae ניציצית

Zones; members קשרין

תינר

π 661

Esther אסתר

Day Demon of 3rd Dec. ♓ ישטולוש

Crinorrhodon (vide K.D. L.C.K. p. 708); a rose שושנה

Angel L.T.D. of ♎ תרגבון

662

Corona Dei אכתריאל

663

Lapides marmoris. [Vide Zohar, pt. I. fol. 34. col. 134] אבני שש

Cantio זמירות

664

665

The womb בית הרחם

Σ(1—36). ⊙. The Number of THE BEAST 666[1]

Aleister E. Crowley אלהיסטהר ה כרעולהי

Aleister Crowley [Rabbi Battiscombe Gunn's v.l.] אליסטיר קרולי

The number 5, which is 6 (הא), on the Grand Scale הא × אלף

Qliphoth of ♓ נשימירון

Spirit of ⊙ סורת

Ommo Satan, the 'Evil Triad' of Satan-Typhon, Apophras, and Besz עממו סתן

The Name Jesus שם יהשוה

667

The oil for lighting שמן למאור

668

Negotiatrix סחרת

669

670

ערת

Deprecatus עתר

671

Ferens fructum עושה פרי

The Law תערא

The Gate תרעא

[1] See Equinox, V & VII, for further details.

Adonai. [Spelt in full] א:ד:נ:י:

672

π 673

674

[Vide K.D. L.C.K. p. 395] סוחרת

675

Briatic Palace of Netzach היכל עצסשמים

$\sqrt{\ }676$ 26^2

Artificial. [ם final] גלגלים

Angel L.T.D. of ♒ עתור

π 677

678

Planities coeli; Assiatic Heaven of 1st palace ערבות

679

The chrysolite stone. [Cant. v. 14] אבן מעולפת

680

Phrath, one of the four rivers of Eden פרת

681

Joyful noise; battle-cry; the sound (of a trumpet) תרועה

682

Of the evening; of the West ערבית

π 683

684

685

686

687

688

689

690

The candlestick מנרת

Palm-trees תמרים

π 691

692

The fourth portion רביעית

693

Sulphur גפרית

694

695

The Moral World עולם מורגש

696

697

Castella munita; domus munitae ארמנות

698

699

700

The Mercy Seat כפרת

The Veil of the Holy פרכת

Seth שת

π 701

[Deut. xxiii. 1] אשת

"And lo! three men." והנה שלשה [These be Michael, Gabriel and Raphael, —אלו־מיכאל־גבריאל־ורפאל]

Prolapsus in faciem נפילת אפים

702

Sabbathum quies שבת

703 $\Sigma(1—37)$

Taenia מסגרת

Qliphoth of Binah סאתאריאל

704

"Arbatel." [The *Arbatel* of Magic, by Pietro di Abano] ארבעתאל

Angel L.T.N. of ♓. נתדוריגאל

705

The stones of dampness. [Job xxviii. 3] אבנים מפולמות

706

Propitiatorium כפורת

"Lilies" (I.R.Q. 878), or "Roses" (von Rosenroth) שושנים

707

708

The Angel of the Covenant מלאך הברית

Perdition שחת

π 709

The Seven Double Letters
ב, ג, ד, כ, פ, ר, ת

710

Spelunca מערת

Six. (Ch.) שית

711

712

713

Sphere of ♄ שבתאי

Conversio תשובה

714

715

Secret נסתרה

Perfumed, fumigated קטורת

716

Vaschti. [Est. i. 9] ושתי

Matrona מטרוניתא

717

718

π 719

|6 720

חשבתי

Thy Navel. [Cant. vii. 3] שררך

721

The Primordial Point נקדה ראשונה

722

The voice of the trumpet קול שופר

723

724

The end of the days אחרית הימים

725

726

π 727

728

[Vide K.D. L.C.K. p. 506] תשכח

$27^2 = 9^3 = 3^6$ $\sqrt{\ }\ \sqrt[3]{\ }\ \sqrt[6]{\ }$ 729

[Vide K.D. L.C.K. p. 505] קרע שטן

730

731

732

π 733

The white head: a title of GOD most High רישא הוורה

734

To bring forth שתלד

735

Tiphareth, 42-fold Name in Yetzirah במרצתג

736

Tortuosae עקלקלות

737

(Live coal)—Blaze, flame שלהבת

שת הבל

738

π 739

740

Σ (1—38) 741

(ן counted as Final) Amen: see 91 אמן

The four letters of the elements; hence a concealed יהוה אמתש

742

The Ark of the Testimony. [Lit. "of tremblings," scil. "vibrations"] ארון העדות

π 743

744

745

746

The Names שמות

747

The voice of the turtle-dove. [Cant. ii. 12] קול התור

748

The oil of Anointment שמן המשחה

749

750

Conclave לשכת

Lead עפרת

π 751

Vir integer איש תם

752

Satan שאתאן

753

Abraham and Sarah. [Either spelling. Vide 243, 248, 505, & 510]

754

755

756

Emanations: numbers ספירות

Years שנות

π 757

Netzach and Hod אשכלות

758

Perdition משחית

Copper ore; bronze נחשת

759

Pulvis aromatarii אבקת רוכל

760

"Both Active and Passive"; said in the Qabalah concerning the Sephiroth מקביל ומתקבל

Confinement, detention עצרת

Yesod, 42-fold Name in Yetzirah קרעשמן

π 761

762

763

764

765

766

767

768

π 769

770

Going forth. [Said of the Eyes of TETRAGRAMMATON] משוטטות

Unfruitful, barren עקרת

771

L.A. Angel of ♍ שלתיאל

772

Septennium שבע שנים

π 773

Lapis, seu canalis lapideus Potationis אבן השתיה

774

Filia Septenarii בת שבע

775

[Vide no. 934] דקרדינותא

776

777

The Flaming Sword, if the path from Binah to Chesed be taken as = 3. For ג connects Arikh Anpin with Zauir Anpin

One is the Ruach of the Elohim of Lives אחת רוח אלהים חיים

The World of Shells עולם הקליפות

778

779

780

I dwell, have dwelt. (*Not* written.) [I.R.Q. 1122; Prov. viii. 12] שכנתי

Shore, bank שפת

781

782

783

$\sqrt{\ }$ 784 28^2

Qliphoth of ♋ שיחרירון

785

786

Smooth פשות

π 787

788

The Secret Wisdom: i.e., The Qabalah. [Vide 58] חכמה נסתרה

789

790

My presence. [I.R.Q. 1122; Prov. xii.] שיכנתי

791

792

[Vide K.D. L.C.K. p. 460, and Ps. xviii. 51] ישועות

793

794

795

796

Calix horroris כוס התרעלה

π 797

798

Mount Gaerisim and mount Ebal. [Deut. xi. 29] הר גריזים והר עיבל

Consisting of Seven שביעיות

799

800

A bow; ♐. The three Paths leading from Malkuth; hence much symbolism of the Rainbow of Promise — קשת

801

401 × 2 = The Reflection of 401, which is את, α and ω — 802

Consessus vel Schola vel Academia Superna. [Refers to A.·.A.·., the three grades which are above the Abyss. Vide K.D. L.C.K. p. 461] — ישיבה של מעלה

Vindicta foederis — נקם ברית

An ark, as of Noah or of Moses — תבת

803

804

805

806

807

808

"A piece of brass"—the Brazen Serpent — נחשתן

π 809

810

A Duke of Edom — יתת

Octava — שמינית

π 811

812

813

Signa — אותות

Ararita; a name of GOD which is a Notariqon of the sentence : אחד ראש אחדותו ראש ייחודותו : תמורתו אחד. "One is His Beginning; one is His Individuality; His Permutation One." — אראריתא

ויאמר אלהים יהי אור ויהי אור [Genesis i. 3]

814

815

Ahasuerus — אחשורש

816

817

818

819

Σ (1—40) — 820

π 821

822

π 823

Lapis effigiei seu figuratus. [Lev. xxvi. 1] — אבן משכית

Litterae — אותיות

824

825

826

π 827

828

π 829

830

Issachar — יששכר

Three (? third) — תלת

831

832

Albedo Crystalli — לבנת ספיר

833

Choir of Angels in Kether — חיות הקדש

Transiens super prevaricatione — עובה על רפשע

834

835

Brachia Mundi — זרועות עולם

836

837

The profuse giver. [Cf. the Egyptian word Tat.] — תת זל

[ם counted as Final. Vide 277. This *is* written] — לסרבה

838

π 839

840

$\sqrt{}$ 841

29^2

Laudes — תהלות

842

843

844

845

כב אותיות

Oleum influxus — שמן השפע

846

847

848

849

Exitus Sabbathi — סוצאי שבת

850

Blue; perfection — תכלת

My perfect one. (*Not* written.) [Cant. v. 2.] Vide 857 — תמתי

851

Souls. [I.R.Q. 1052 et seq.] — נשמתהון

852

Occellata Aurea; Netzach and Hod receiving influence from Geburah — משבצות זהב

π 853

An orchard — שדה תפוחים

854

855

856

Summitatis bifidae in Lulabh — תיומת

π 857

My twin-sister. [*Is* written] — תאומתי

858

"To Thee be Power unto the Ages, my Lord" [Vide 35 s.v. אגלא] — אתה גבור לעולם אדני

π 859

Iunctio, copula, phylacterium, ornamentumve manus. [Connect with נשר] — תפלה של יד

860

861 — $\Sigma(1—41)$

862

π 863

864

The Woman of Whoredom אשת זנונים

⊙ and ☽ שמש וירח

865

866

Latera aquilonis ירכתי צפון

867

868

Semitae נתיבות

869

Qliphoth of Tiphareth תגרירון

870

Twelve תריסר

871

872

Septiduum שבעת ימים

873

874

875

876

π 877

878

879

880

A King of Edom השסהתימני

π 881

Os cranii, cranium קרקפתא

882

Dilationes fleminis רחובות הנהר

π 883

Lux oriens אור מתנוצץ

884

Domination תועבות

885

886

π 887

888

889

890

Spelunca duplex מערת המכפלה

891

892

Defectus cogitationis אפיסת הרעיון

893

894

895

896

897

898

899

$\sqrt{}$900 30^2

901

902

Briatic Palace of Jesod—Malkuth היכל לבנת הספיר

903 $\Sigma(1-42)$

Secret name of Cagliostro אשאראת

904

905

906

Licentia. [Vide K.D. L.C.K. p. 693] רשות

Vermis תולעת

π 907

908

909

910

Beginning. [Vide I.Z.Q. 547, et seq.] רשית

π 911

Hell of Tiphareth בארשחת

Beginning ראשית

Remnant שארית

912

Pl. of 506 שור q.v. שורות

913

Berashith; "in the Beginning." [With *small* B.] [Vide A Note on Genesis, Equinox II 163–185, and 2911] בראשית

914

915

916

917

918

π 919

920

921

Nekudoth; intuitus aspectus. [Vide K.D. L.C.K. p. 547] הסתכלות

922

923

924

925

926

927

928

π 929

Gazophylacia Septentrionis אוצרות צפון

Briah, the Palace of the Supernals therein היכל קודש קדשים

930

931

932

The Tree of the Knowledge of Good and Evil עץ הדעת טוב ורע

933

Foedus nuditatis vel Sabbathi vel arcus ברית המעור

934

Coruscatio vehementissima; splendor exactissime dimeticus בוצינא דקרדינותא

935

The Cause of causes סבת הסבות

[Vide Eccles. ii. 8, & S.D. v. 79] תענוגות

936

Kether. [Spelt in full] כ:ת:ר:

π 937

938

939

940

π 941

Angel of 1st Dec. ♐ משראת

942

943

944

945 The small point: a title of GOD most High נקרה פשות

946 $\Sigma(1-43)$

π 947 Angel of 1st Dec. ♋ מתראוש

948

949

950 [Vide no. 1204] המתהפכת

951 The Book of the Law ספר תורה

952

π 953 Vigiliae אשמורות

954

955

956

957 Unguentum Magnificentiae משחא רבות

958

959

960 Tubae argenteae חצוצרות כסף

$\sqrt{961}$ 31^2

962

963 Achad; unity. [Spelt fully] א:ח:ד:

Garland, Crown; a little wreath. [Vide K.D. L.C.K. p. 614] עטרת עטרה

964 Memoriale iubilationis. זכרון תרועה [Note Root זכר, 227 q.v. showing phallic nature of this 'memorial']

965

966

π 967

968

969

970 Angel of Water תרשים

π 971 Shemhamphorasch, the 'Divided Name' of GOD שם המפורש

972

973

974

975

976

π 977

978

979

980

981

982

π 983 Urbs Quaternionis קרית ארבע

984 The Beginning of Wisdom (is The Wonderment at TETRAGRAMMATON. Psalms). ראשית חכמה

985

986

Vehementia; obiectio rigorosa התקפתא

987

988

Foedus pacis ברית שלום

989

Pascens inter Lilia רועה בשושנים

$\Sigma(1-44)$ 990

π 991

992

The joy of the whole Earth. [Vide no. 296] משוש כל הארץ

993

994

995

996

The Most Holy Ancient One עתיקא קדישא

π 997

998

Foedus linguae ברית לשון

999

10^3 $\sqrt[3]{\ }$ 1000

[Vide no. 1100] ששת

A Qabalistic Method of Exegesis; "spelling Qabalistically backward" תשרק

1001

1002

The bank of a stream שפת היאור

1003

1004

1005

1006

The law תרות

1007

TAROT. [But vide 671] תארות

1008

π 1009

1010

1011

1012

π 1013

1014

1015

1016

[Vide no. 1047] יותרת

1017

Vasa vitrea, lagenae, phiale אשישות

1018

π 1019

1020

π 1021

1022

1023

$32^2 = 4^5 = 2^{10}$ $\sqrt{\ }$ $\sqrt[5]{\ }$ $\sqrt[10]{\ }$ 1024

Qliphoth of ♍ נחשתירון

1025

Absconsiones sapientiae תעלומות חכמה

1026

1027

1032 Sphere of Primum Mobile ראשית הגלגלים

1047 Diaphragma supra hepar (vel hepatis) יותרת הכבד

1056 The lily שושנת

1060 The Tabernacle [N final] משכן

π 1061 אסתתר

[Vide I.R.Q. 939] ויפח באפיו נשמת חיים

$\Sigma(1—46)$ 1081 Tiphareth תפארת

π 1091 The Rose of Sharon חבצלת השרון

1100 Sextiduum ששת ימים

1106 The giving of the Law מתן התורה

1146 Jars, globular vessels צנתרות

1147 Byssus contorta שש משזר

1157 Specula turmarum מראות הצובאות

1173 [With ן counted as Final] את יהוה אלהין

1175 Conclave caesum לשכת הגזית

1196 Fasciculi; rami palmarum כפות תמרים

1204 Flamma gladii versatilis להט חרב המתהפכת

1206 The Holy Intelligence נשמתא קדישא

A water-trough שקתות

1210 Angel of Geburah of Briah תרשיש

1219 Formator eius quod in principiis יוצר בראשית

1220 Hell of Hod שערימרת

The beaten oil שמן כתית

$\Sigma(1—49) = 35^2$. ♀. $\sqrt{\ }$1225

The Ancient of the Ancient Ones עתיקא דעתיקין

1260 Angels of Netzach and of Geburah of Briah תרשישים

π 1279 Ignis sese reciprocans אש מתלקחת

1294 Chorda fili coccini תקות חוט השני

π 1307 Angel L.T.D. of 2nd Dec. ♑, and King-Demon of Geburah אשתרות

π 1321 The Lily of the Valleys

The numerical value of the 9 Paths of the Lesser Beard: viz. נ, ס, ע, פ, צ, ק, ר, ש, and ת 1350

1357 Crooked by-paths. [Jud. v. 6] אורחות עקלקלות

1380 The lip of the liar שפת שקר

1400 Chaos, or = את, 401 q.v. את

Tria Capita תלת רישין

1445
The remnant of his heritage לשאירית נחלתו

1460
Quies cessationis שבת שבתון

1480
Septem heptaeterides שבע שבתות

1482
Rotunditates, seu vasa rotunda capitellarum, seu capitella rotunda גולות הכותרות

The total numerical value of the Paths of the Tree; i.e. of the Beards conjoined; i.e. of the whole Hebrew Alphabet 1495

1542
The Oil of the Anointing שמן משחת קדש

1664
The pure olive oil beaten out שמן זית זך כתית

1755
קדוש קדוש קדוש יהוה צבאות
Holy, Holy, Holy, Lord GOD of Hosts!

Σ (1—64). ☿ 2080

Spirit of ☿ תפתרתרת

32 × 10² The paths of the Whole Tree in excelsis 3200

בראשית ברא אלהים

Σ (1—81). ☽. 3321

The Intelligence of the Intelligences of the Moon מלכא בתרשישים ועד ברוה שהרים

The Spirit of the Spirits of the Moon שדברשהמעת שרתתן